The Development of Anthroposophy
since Rudolf Steiner's Death

OTHER BOOKS BY T. H. MEYER

Representative Men
In the Light of Anthroposophy
With a chapter on the Twelve Worldviews

Rudolf Steiner's Core Mission
The Birth and Development of Spiritual-Scientific Karma Research

Reality, Truth, and Evil
Facts, Questions, and Perspectives on September 11, 2001

Clairvoyance and Consciousness
The Tao Impulse in Evolution

D. N. Dunlop
A Man of Our Time

Ludwig Polzer-Hoditz, a European
A Biography

The Development of Anthroposophy since Rudolf Steiner's Death

An Outline and Perspectives for the Future

T. H. Meyer

Compiled and edited by Paul V. O'Leary
Translated by Matthew Barton

SteinerBooks | 2014

2014
SteinerBooks
An imprint of Anthroposophic Press, Inc.
610 Main Street, Great Barrington, MA 01230
www.steinerbooks.org

Copyright © 2014 by Thomas H. Meyer.
Thomas Meyer's essay "The Development of Anthroposophy since Rudolf Steiner's Death" is the final chapter in his larger work entitled *Wegmarken* (Basel, 2013), whose English title is *Milestones*. There the reader will find a more complete description of certain actions and statements behind which stand named personalities only hinted at in this brief sketch. Translation by Matthew Barton.

All rights reserved. No part of this book may be reproduced, stored in a retrieval system, or transmitted in any form or by any means, electronic, mechanical, photocopying, recording, or otherwise, without the written permission of SteinerBooks.

The "Memorandum" was originally published in *Who Was Ita Wegman? Volume III, 1924–1935: Struggles and Conflicts* (Chestnut Ridge, NY: Mercury Press, 2005)

Book and cover design: William Jens Jensen
Cover image: Monument of Rudolf Steiner's tomb in the park of the Goetheanum at Dornach, Switzerland; photo © by AlMare (used by permission)

LIBRARY OF CONGRESS CONTROL NUMBER 9781621481164

ISBN: 978-1-62148-116-4 (paperback)
ISBN: 978-1-62148-117-1 (eBook)

Contents

Introduction *by Paul V. O'Leary* — vii

The Development of Anthroposophy since Rudolf Steiner's Death — 1

Appendices

1. A Chronology of Relevant Events — 47

2. The "Memorandum"
   Concerns in the Anthroposophical Society, 1925–1935 — 51

3. Address to the General Meeting in Dornach
   by Count Polzer-Hoditz, April 14, 1935 — 216

4. The Executive Board's Letter to Adolf Hitler
   English Translation and Original German — 228

Bibliography — 235

Introduction

Thomas Meyer's essay "The Development of Anthroposophy since Rudolf Steiner's Death" forms the closing section of a larger volume entitled *Milestones*, published as *Wegmarken* by Perseus Verlag (Basel) in June 2012.[1] Therefore, what is presented here has been taken out of its original context.

Milestones features in twenty-three chapters a symptomatic treatment of the whole of Steiner's life, progressing chronologically from event to significant event, both inner and outer. It reviews such salient turning points as: Steiner's occult experiences as a seven-year-old child in Pottschach; his first experience of happiness upon discovering geometry at age nine; his meeting with Friedrich Nietzsche in 1896; the decision to create a new, Western Christian esotericism in 1901; the laying of the Foundation Stone in September 1913; the burning of the First Goetheanum in 1922; the founding of the General Anthroposophical Society (the Society) and Michael School at the Christmas Foundation Conference of 1923; and the circumstances of his death in March 1925.

"The Development of Anthroposophy since Rudolf Steiner's Death" does not treat of milestones in Steiner's life but of the evolution of Anthroposophy since Steiner's death and its future prospects.

Milestones is not your typical biography that recounts, in greater or lesser detail, the arc of a life through its achievements, failures, crises,

---

1 A French edition of *Wegmarken* appeared in late 2013. An English translation of the entire book will be published by Temple Lodge in 2015.

and so forth, documenting them with historical references, eyewitness accounts, and first-person reflections from diary notes, correspondence, and internal memoranda. Other such biographies of Steiner exist, penned by authors[2] who knew him personally or were students of Anthroposophy. Meyer's symptomatic treatment reveals characteristic and karmic trends within discrete biographical episodes.

Five appendices supplement the present volume. Appendix 1 presents a *Chronology* that denotes, by year and day, significant episodes in Steiner's life and in the development of Anthroposophy.

The remaining appendices feature, for the first time in English in one volume, significant documents pertinent to the Anthroposophical Society's Easter 1935 Annual Meeting. Appendix 2 contains the "Memorandum" written by supporters of Marie Steiner, which sets forth a list of grievances in support of the expulsion motions adopted at the 1935 Annual Meeting. Appendix 3 records Ludwig Polzer-Hoditz's[3] address to the 1935 Annual Meeting counseling against the expulsion measures. Appendix 4 contains an English translation of a letter written by the Society's executive board on November 17, 1935, to Adolf Hitler, seeking to annul the banning of

---

2   Cf. A. P. Shepherd, *Rudolf Steiner: Scientist of the Invisible;* Johannes Hemleben, *Rudolf Steiner;* Rudi Lissau, *Rudolf Steiner;* Emil Bock's studies of Steiner's life; Christoph Lindenberg's *Rudolf Steiner: A Biography;* and several works by Peter Selg, including his 7-volume *Rudolf Steiner, Life and Work: 1861–1925* (SteinerBooks, 2014–).

3   Count Ludwig Polzer-Hoditz (Apr. 23, 1869–Oct. 13, 1945), the scion of a noble Austrian family with a military background, retired from the Austro-Hungarian army for health reasons at the rank of Captain in 1902. In 1908 he attended a lecture of Steiner's in Vienna. He later became a pupil and intimate of Steiner's, and a leading member of the (first) Anthroposophical Society. In 1917 he consulted with Steiner on ideas for the postwar reorganization of society, known as the Threefold Commonwealth. He was able to present these ideas to Charles I, Emperor of Austria-Hungary, through his brother Arthur, who was Charles I's Cabinet Secretary. Polzer joined the General Anthroposophical Society when it was created at the Christmas Conference of 1923 and was appointed by Steiner as a First Class reader. Having failed in his speech at the Society's 1935 Annual Meeting to prevent the rift in the Society from becoming a schism, he resigned his membership on May 30, 1935. He passed away ten years later in Vienna.

Introduction

the German Anthroposophical Society, and appendix 5 is a copy of the original letter to Hitler in German.

❦

"The Development of Anthroposophy since Rudolf Steiner's Death" is unique in that it offers in a single essay an overview of the eighty-seven years of the development of the anthroposophic movement and the Anthroposophical Society, the worldwide charitable organization headquartered in Dornach, Switzerland, since the death of its founder. The Society went through a very difficult and controversial period in the ten years immediately following Steiner's death which culminated at its Annual Meeting in 1935. The result was the expulsion from the Society of two members appointed by Rudolf Steiner to its executive board (*Vorstand*)—Ita Wegman and Elizabeth Vreede—the British and Dutch branches of the Society as well as such important anthroposophists as Zeylmans von Emmichoven, Daniel Dunlop, Karl König, George Adams, Eugen Kolisko, and others. Meyer adopts the position of Ludwig Polzer-Hoditz, who opposed the expulsions, that membership in the Society as such is not the crucial element in spiritual work, but that

> the Foundation Stones that rest in strong hearts are no longer tied to a particular location and a single building. They must become the Foundation Stones for the Mystery centers of the future at diverse locations. Those who will sow the seeds for these Mystery centers can only be called to do so by their destiny, directly by the world of spirit. This, however, requires esoteric courage above all, rather than paternalism and restrictiveness.

Approximately seven months later, on November 1, 1935, the German branch of the Society was banned by the Gestapo, the Third Reich's secret police. In retrospect this seems to have been a mere formality, since the Society had inflicted its own mortal wound at the 1935 Annual Meeting. Meyer reveals the extraordinary concordance of three November 17 dates highly significant in the development of Anthroposophy. On November 17, 1901, on the very anniversary of the founding of the Theosophical Society in 1875, Marie von Sivers asked Rudolf Steiner to create an esotericism suited to the Western mind, thereby setting Steiner on his mission. On November 17, 1923, Ita Wegman urged Steiner to found a new Society, with Steiner joining as member and President, which was the request he needed for anthroposophic renewal. Twelve years later, on November 17, 1935, the then three-person executive board wrote Adolf Hitler to reverse the Nazi's decision to ban the German branch of the Society. Profound connections underlie these events whose dates cannot be merely accidental.

※

All progress in spiritual work and moral improvement depends first and foremost upon self-knowledge. "Know Thyself" is a spiritual maxim as old as the ancient mystery wisdom itself. It is found in the inscriptions on the temples of ancient Greece and in the mantras and meditations of the world's profound religions. In Spiritual Science as developed by Rudolf Steiner, self-knowledge is more than simply a means of protecting us from the false paths of narcissism, power-seeking, and untruthfulness. Since the human being is the microcosm of the macrocosm, a fractal of the whole world, self-knowledge is a path to world knowledge and vice versa: world knowledge can become a path to self-knowledge.

Meyer's "The Development of Anthroposophy since Rudolf Steiner's Death" can be viewed as a candid and long overdue step in the progress which the General Anthroposophical Society must take in advancing a consciously-acknowledged awareness of its own past. The essay offers a kind of "institutional self-knowledge," as it were. Just as each one of us eventually comes to a point where we must acknowledge the truth about ourselves and our past—even requiring third-party "interventions"—so, too, does the Anthroposophical Society (the legally registered institution) require a mirror to be held up to itself. For to date, the Society has never fully "come clean" about its tragic past: the mistakes leading to the expulsions of 1935; the sundering of the karmic configuration of the first executive board; the shameful pandering to the Nazis; and the continuing irrelevance the Society maintains, sidelined as a creative focal point of Western culture. Meyer traces the development of the Society from 1925 through a current date by observing the evolutionary dynamic of "involution and evolution." This dynamic manifests in individuals, groups, in societies great and small, in cultural epochs, and in the conditions of consciousness of our very planet.[4] Erroneous involution—colored by internal conflicts, personality cults, distortions, personal ambition, the formation of cliques, narcissism, and other "human, all-too-human" qualities—leads inevitably to erroneous evolution. He reviews the postwar litigation over Steiner's literary estate, when the executive board ignored Marie Steiner's copyright and, after she won her lawsuit against them in 1952, refused to carry copies of Steiner's works in the Goetheanum bookshop until 1968. Fifty years later further litigation ensued over the "constitution debate," an internal wrangling which drained the Society's resources, both fiscal and spiritual, and was settled with an underwhelming result. This part of the tale is not pleasant. These matters require openness, honesty, and discussion from a variety of alternative perspectives. Thomas Meyer leaves no doubt as to his point of view.

More positive developments include the blossoming of the Waldorf School and other daughter movements after World War II and the development of a significant body of anthroposophic literature. Many of these salutary developments have little or nothing to do with the Society per se, and the issue of whether the "movement" and the Society are one and the same thing is not addressed. Meyer also offers sections about the German Folk Spirit, the German language, and Steiner's prophecies for the rise of new domed buildings in Europe by 2086.

However, in the arc of history the facts speak for themselves. From the perspective of September 20, 1913, when Rudolf Steiner laid into the Dornach earth the double-dodecahedral Foundation Stone, *the very worst things that could then have been imagined had already happened.*

---

4   An involutionary phase, which Rudolf Steiner termed a *pralaya,* separated the evolutionary stages of ancient Sun, ancient Moon, and our Earth condition of consciousness.

World War I happened, a tragedy so enormous that its after-effects are still being worked out one hundred years later. Eight and a half million died in a senseless slaughter which continued in acts of dumb repetition as if the European races had all gone insane and, in consequence, Germany was "cut down to size." Steiner, the Herald of the Second Coming, saw his great artistic achievements embodied in the first Goetheanum, the new Christian mystery temple, burned to the ground by an arsonist. He suffered an assassination attempt in Munich in 1922 by persons allied with National Socialism. On January 1, 1924, he escaped an attempt to poison him[5] at the close of the Christmas Foundation Conference, where he had joined the newly-formed General Anthroposophical Society as President of its executive board. He died prematurely at age 64, in his workshop, the ruins of the First Goetheanum next door.[6]

As a result of the harsh measures imposed by the Treaty of Versailles and the failure of spiritually-minded people to take an ethical stand against it, National Socialism came to power by lawful means in January 1933. Some anthroposophists (and not an insignificant number) welcomed the Nazis as part of the new revelation of the Michael Age; some actually became members of the Nazi Party. World War II followed with its sixty million (or more) dead, the shattering events of the Holocaust, Auschwitz, and the use of atomic bombs. Germany was further reduced in size and population and occupied by the four principle Allied Powers.[7] After nearly two thousand years of Christian culture what did

---

5 See an account by Sergei O. Prokofieff in supplement 5, "The Tragedy of 1 January 1924," *May Human Beings Hear It!*

6 Steiner himself saw the incineration of the First Goetheanum as symbolic of the failures of the (first) Anthroposophical Society, which he had never joined but acted as its advisor.

7 At the outset of World War I, Germany had a population of 67 million and a territory covering 208,826 square miles, including land that today exists as parts of France, Belgium, The Netherlands, Denmark, Poland, the Czech Republic, Lithuania, and Russia. The Treaty of Versailles stripped Germany of 25,000 square miles and seven million people. As result of the defeat of the Third Reich in World War II Germany lost an additional 46,000 square miles, bringing its size down to 137,846 square miles.

Introduction

Central Europe produce? A New Race of Anti-human, consciously bred through eugenic programs such as the Lebensborn movement, determined to extinguish the Abrahamic peoples (the Jews), all people of conscience, and other "life unworthy of life"—Gypsies, homosexuals, and the handicapped. World War II dramatically speeded up technological and cultural developments. The mechanization of death on an industrial scale and the wholesale slaughter of civilians by aerial bombing—especially the bombing of Hiroshima and Nagasaki—released asuric forces into the world prematurely, forces which have now become part of our everyday life. Our ethical standards continue to remain far behind our technological achievements.

Steiner forewarned his audiences about World War I and the high likelihood of a second, larger conflagration. He also warned that every new spiritual impulse which enters evolution faces the danger of being turned into its opposite.[8] The ultimate purpose of National Socialism, the polaric counter-inspiration to Anthroposophy, was the annihilation of the Abrahamic peoples, to wipe out the roots of Western Christian culture, of which Anthroposophy represented an esoteric part, and to thwart the revelation of the return of Christ in the etheric. Although the revelation and conceptual framework underlying the Second Coming was *initially* to be revealed through the Germanic peoples, it then ought to have spread throughout humanity. The two world wars can be better viewed as a single conflict waged against the Second Coming by the Sun Demon Sorat and the spiritual beings through whom he worked and continues to work: Lucifer, Ahriman, the Asuras, and their cadres. Thus, the twelve-year Reich was only part of a far broader phenomenon of evil attacking humanity throughout the

---

Today's Germany has been reduced to ⅔ of its size before World War I. See Wikipedia under "German Empire," "Weimar Republic," and "Territorial Changes to Germany after World War II."

8   Well-known examples of this phenomenon include the de-spiritualization of Aristotelian thought, the history of the Roman Catholic Church, and the idealistic eroding of the principles set forth in the United States' Founding Documents.

twentieth century and continuing to the present day. Karmic connections, already in disorder at the beginning of the century, were further confused, delayed, distorted, and prevented by the millions upon millions of dead and injured in these apocalyptic catastrophes. Has there been a wide-spread experience of the Etheric Christ? Did the end of the twentieth century produce a powerful wave of spirituality brought upon by the return of former Platonists uniting with reincarnating Aristotelians? From the perspective of Rudolf Steiner's time, the powers opposing the conscious experience of the Second Coming seem to have made great progress in their mission. Steiner warned us: "Evil will approach the people of the fifth post-Atlantean Age in all possible forms, doing it in such a way that people will have to resolve the nature, the essence, of evil in a scientific way..."[9] On the other hand, it is just through such experiences of loss, betrayal, imprisonment, powerlessness, and death that one's "I" will develop the spiritual capacities needed to courageously oppose and overcome these powers in the future.

⁂

The postwar period saw the rise and eventual triumph of the United States of America, outlasting and out-spending the Marxist Russian Bear and enabling the reunification of Europe under a Pax Americana. By the end of the century at least 186 million had died in war—perhaps 200 million, or more, if all the deaths caused by civil wars and famine are counted. However, evil has become more sophisticated and more subtle since World War II; it no longer arrives wearing a black uniform with a death's head on its cap. The third millennium began with continued acceleration into the Digital Age[10] and, after the 9/11 attacks on the World Trade Center in New York, the emergence of a global war on terror and the rise of the Surveillance State authorized by the Patriot Act in the USA

---

9 *Secret Brotherhoods and the Mystery of the Double*, CW 178, Nov. 18, 1917, quoted by Peter Selg in "The Encounter With Evil: Auschwitz Main Camp, Block 24," *Deepening Anthroposophy* (3.1), Jan. 5, 2014.

10 Moore's Law—that computing power doubles every two years—continues to hold true nearly 50 years after Gordon Moore postulated it in 1965.

and similar legislation elsewhere. The world economy, driven now by the manipulations of fiat capital traveling at the speed of light, increasingly concentrates wealth in society's top one percent, while workers become less important as the long-term trend for machines to replace people speeds up. Fear of the future pervades most societies...and rightly so. Dire predictions of devastating sea level rise, global warming, droughts, continued species extinctions, genetic modification of our food supplies which may have negative long-term health effects—these are all part of the same overall phenomena. Human beings are being forced to face the consequences of their actions or we will destroy ourselves and our precious planet. Scientific materialism offers us two contradictory pictures of human nature: we are either flawed machines that will be perfected by burgeoning discoveries in neuroscience, or we are the smartest animals, driven by our instincts, which new, complex pharmaceuticals will help us control. The third alternative, that we are finite images of the infinite, microcosms of the macrocosm, with a divine destiny important to the gods themselves, receives little attention and at best is dismissed either with ridicule or as an illusion.

Where has the General Anthroposophical Society[11] been during these apocalyptic times? The requirements for membership[12] laid down by Rudolf Steiner exhibit tolerance and open-mindedness. Has the Society allied with other individuals, groups, and movements seeking to stem the tide of spiritual decay? Has it become a focal point of Western

---

11 The reader should be reminded that the institution of the GAS, the legal entity listed in the Swiss Business Register according to Article 61 of the Swiss Civil Code, is under discussion and not individual anthroposophists, many of whose achievements are noteworthy, courageous, and even heroic.

12 "Anyone can become a member, without regard to nationality, social standing, religion, scientific or artistic conviction, who considers as justified the existence of an institution such as the Goetheanum in Dornach, in its capacity as a School of Spiritual Science. The Anthroposophical Society rejects any kind of sectarian activity." See the Society's website, http://www.goetheanum.org/Principles.255.0.html?&L=1. Nearly identical language exists under Article 4 in Rudolf Steiner's "Letter to the Members," dated January 13, 1924. See *The Life, Nature and Cultivation of Anthroposophy*, CW 260a.

culture—or even of European culture? Or has the Society devolved into a pedantic, self-important, centralized bureaucracy welcoming all things "Made in Dornach" and shunning the rest? Do some of its members actually think (it is worse than disturbing to have to write this) *that the Christ Impulse is confined to the Society as guided by its executive board in Dornach*? We believe so.

The Society had approximately 12,000 members worldwide in 1925; in 2014 its membership totaled 46,000. Its growth has been minimal, increasing in the interim at approximately the same rate as the world population[13]—about 350 percent. While its daughter movements experienced tremendous growth after World War II, especially Waldorf schools and, to a lesser degree, biodynamics, anthroposophically extended medicine, and the Camphill movement, many participants in those fields know little about Anthroposophy and rarely study Steiner's works. Although Steiner spent the decade of 1904 to 1914 elucidating the profound mysteries of the Bible, attendees of anthroposophic conferences rarely engage in biblical studies. Meyer's overall critique of the Society is not uncommon.[14] We believe, as do others,[15] that the Society faces a grave crisis and will atrophy and eventually die out if it does not receive an injection of new life and new purpose in the immediate future.

Meyer does not wish to destroy or dissolve the current Society; he would like to see it reformed, revitalized, remade. However, Meyer differs with the Dornach Executive on one major point. Whereas the latter believe that Rudolf Steiner's esoteric connection with the executive board created at the 1923 Christmas Conference is karmically linked forever with the Society and the Dornach site, Meyer believes that such a connection can arise in human hearts and be maintained independently of the executive board and the Goetheanum. In the words of Polzer-Hoditz:

---

13 World population was estimated as of 1925 at two billion. As of 2014, it was seven billion.

14 See Peter Selg, *Rudolf Steiner's Intentions for the Anthroposophical Society*.

15 See Peter Selg and Sergei O. Prokofieff, *Crisis in the Anthroposophical Society*.

Introduction

"The Goetheanum exists wherever esoteric work is undertaken as Rudolf Steiner intended."

An alternative course might be for something to come about as envisioned by Daniel Dunlop: the creation of a "society of societies" where the same qualifications for membership in the Anthroposophical Society would hold true, but a new umbrella organization would open itself up to the widest spiritual streams struggling against the tide of "super-materialism" that rises higher as each year goes by. Today, the forces of control, decay, and destruction are opposed more consciously and more vigorously than they were in the somnambulant Europe of 1914. Polarities collide at the present time; the battle of light with darkness continues to intensify. Yet, the number of people seeking freedom, justice, and goodness is on the increase. Humanity is waking up...gradually, it is true, but more so than in the past. The truth is, *the Christ Impulse is universal and cosmopolitan in scope and exists for all humanity. By no means has Sorat and allied forces succeeded! Michaelic people acting morally, heroically, with conscience and conviction, can be found in all walks of life throughout the world.* These are our allies with whom we should seek a connection. Otherwise, what is all this anthroposophic lecturing, conferencing, book writing, stage performances, branch meetings, and so forth about? What, in the end, is the Christ Impulse all about? The Foundation Stone meditation, the common "pole star" for Polzer-Hoditz, Marie Steiner, Ita Wegman, and the members and leadership of the General Anthroposophical Society, is also described as the "Stone of Love." What is human evolution all about? The fourth section of the Foundation Stone meditation offers an answer which echoes the words of Saint Paul written nearly two thousand years ago:

> If I speak in the tongues and of angels, but have not love, I am only a resounding gong or a clanging cymbal. If I have the gift of prophecy and can fathom all mysteries and all knowledge, and if I have a faith that can move mountains, but have not love, I am nothing. If I give all I possess to the poor and surrender my body to the flames and have not love, I gain nothing.

Love is patient, love is kind. It does not envy, it does not boast, it is not proud. It is not rude, it is not self-seeking, it is not easily angered, it keeps no record of wrongs.

Love does not delight in evil but rejoices with the truth. It always protects, always trusts, always hopes, always perseveres. Love never fails. But where there are prophecies, they will cease; where there are tongues, they will be stilled; where there is knowledge, it will pass away....

And now these three remain: faith, hope and love. But the greatest of these is love. (1 Corintians 13)

This part of Anthroposophy's mission remains to be accomplished.

The Development of Anthroposophy since Rudolf Steiner's Death

On one occasion I was prompted to ask him this: "Where, really, are the 'initiates' of humanity committed to furthering work such as yours?" And he replied, "The important thing now is for people to grasp higher truths through their thinking."

FRIEDRICH RITTELMEYER
Rudolf Steiner Enters My Life

From Steiner's death until 1935

After Rudolf Steiner's death, the first difficulty faced by many of his pupils was to determine how anthroposophic work within the General Anthroposophical Society (the Society) should continue and progress. As Ludwig Polzer-Hoditz made clear, Rudolf Steiner could obviously no longer be regarded as connected to an *earthly organization.* In Polzer's view, *certain individual* pupils will have to carry the anthroposophic movement safely through the impending disaster [the approaching Second World War World]. He (Steiner) can reach these individual human souls. He can help them and guide them if only they have good will toward him. Earthly communities can only develop slowly, with difficulty and in accordance with individual karma. His work upon earth will be maintained in many diverse groups, perhaps soon continuing, until powers arise that can once again reunite all these groups with one another.

Marie Steiner and others also thought in a similar fashion. However, this realistic view of things was opposed by the idea that Rudolf Steiner had appointed an "esoteric" executive board (*Vorstand*), and that he himself would continue as its leader. For a while, Ita Wegman wrote Leading Thoughts—essays whose title (being identical with that used by Steiner) inevitably gave the impression of a spiritual succession. Yet, Polzer was clear:

> Even ordinary common sense must see that direct continuation of what only he [Steiner] could keep united is impossible. Lamentations about the impossibility of this have been detrimental to the public reputation of Anthroposophy. It would have been necessary to come to terms with the fact of a great teacher's death, and draw the right consequences from it. This would have been less harmful to his life's work than frantically refusing to accept it and vainly hoping for miracles.

These consequences would have involved the Society becoming a quite ordinary administrative association. The esoteric Michael School (the First Class) had been founded by Rudolf Steiner some months after a specific request was made to him by Ita Wegman on November 17, 1923, during a conference in The Hague: that he should not leave the society, as he was then considering. This same evening Steiner made his landmark decision to reestablish the Society, this time with himself as a member and its leader. The previous esoteric school, which had existed since the early 1900s, consisted largely of private instructions given on an individual basis to members. It had fallen into disuse since the onset of World War I and was revived sporadically after the war ended. Wegman's second request was for a more formal esoteric school, incorporating the revelations of the Michael Age. The affairs of the Michael School and its meditative path, which Steiner handled very rigorously, could have been governed only by agreements based on trust and never by a central executive. This administrative executive body should have *elicited* trust and not demanded it. At most, people should have sought their own individual spiritual connection with Anthroposophy and its founder, and have born the *fruits* of this striving into the Society, rather than elevating the Society itself to some hallowed spiritual status, as became the norm over centuries in the Catholic Church.

The realities and consequences described by Polzer, and many people's difficulties in coming to terms with the first, and drawing the second, were at the root of many unproductive conflicts and disputes during the decade following Steiner's death. *Those conflicts culminated in 1935.* Here is not the place to detail the complex entanglements that led up to those events. Such accounts have often been given elsewhere, albeit usually without drawing conclusions relevant to the *subsequent period.* Here I propose only to elaborate the salient and sometimes tragic developments and fractures in the development of Anthroposophy after Steiner's death.

Two members of the executive board appointed by Steiner (Ita Wegman and Elisabeth Vreede), and a series of other prominent officials—including Eugen Kolisko, Willem Zeylmans, and D. N. Dunlop—were planned to be expelled from the General Anthroposophical Society at the April 1935 Annual Meeting, along with thousands of members of the Dutch and British branches of the Society.

Polzer, as a result of his meditative work with the mantras of the Michael School, was knowingly and repeatedly graced by spiritual experiences that maintained his connection with his deceased teacher. He had two nighttime experiences that called on him to intervene in the unfolding events. He heard his teacher ask him, "Do you know the Jesuit who seeks to introduce Jesuitical methods into the Society?" Yet, he did not search for a single "guilty party," but rather sought to expose the dogmatic, Jesuit Catholic outlook that had gradually spread through the Society, and that had led to the expulsion motions. He rejected these and drafted a speech he wished to give in Dornach at the Annual Meeting at Easter, to warn against the threatened step and, if possible, to avert it.

A few weeks before this decisive meeting, a fanatical "Memorandum" was published, whose repellent attacks focused, among other things, not least on certain karmic revelations relating to Ita Wegman. One can see this publication as one in a series of more-or-less ahrimanically inspired, or at least co-inspired, writings that had appeared since Nietzsche's *Anti-Christ.* This is scarcely surprising if we recall the comment by Steiner that "Ahriman most fears a forthright disclosure of karmic truths." Readers who regard this view of the "Memorandum" as incomprehensible or even unjustified should form their own judgment by studying it with an open mind. We can be grateful to Emanuel Zeylmans for reprinting it in the third volume of his multi-volume biography, *Who Was Ita Wegman*.[1]

A Michaelic Speech at the 1935 Easter Annual Meeting

In the mood primed in this way, Polzer gave his speech[2] in a hall largely filled with advocates for the expulsion motions. He warned against succumbing to the illusion that the expulsions might solve deeper social and spiritual problems. In his view, the only means of averting the impending catastrophe was to embrace wholeheartedly a decentralized mode of thinking for all spiritual concerns within the Society. Above all, Dornach should not seek to issue authorizations for reading the Class Lessons of the Michael School's meditative path, as Rudolf Steiner had done. "Issuing authorization [for reading the 'Class'] in recompense for diligent 'achievements' or for great erudition would be unacceptable to me," he said, "since we would then soon find ourselves in an entirely superficial, authoritarian mode." Moreover, in relation to the new Foundation Stone of the Christmas Foundation Meeting, which should be cultivated inwardly, he said:

> The Foundation Stones that rest in strong hearts are no longer tied to a particular location and a single building. They must become the Foundation Stones for the Mystery centers of the future at diverse locations. Those who will sow the seeds for these Mystery centers can be called to do so only by their destiny, directly by the spiritual world. However, above all, this requires esoteric courage rather than paternalism and restrictiveness.

Polzer's speech, which lasted nearly forty minutes, is infused with a true Michaelic spirit. In the same way that Steiner introduced an Urielic impetus into the Gabriel mood of his evening lectures at the Christmas Foundation Meeting, Polzer similarly introduced a *Michaelic dynamic*

---

[1] A copy of the "Memorandum," taken from volume 3, forms appendix 2 of this book.

[2] A copy of Polzer's speech at the 1935 Annual Meeting of the General Anthroposophical Society, translated by George Adams-Kaufmann (later George Adams), forms appendix 3 of this book.

into the Raphael mood of Easter. Yet, most of the 1,700 people present were left unmoved by his speech. Instead, after he sat down, a leading representative of the Society, Hans-Erhard Lauer, a former colleague in the Austrian Executive, revoked his right to continue working in the Michael School—a task that, as we have seen, Rudolf Steiner had personally conferred on him and others. Polzer spoke of a "wooden sword of Michael" wielded against him here.

He spent the following evening and night in a guest room at the clinic in Arlesheim, and there once again had a remarkable experience during the night. He woke up feeling "as if I had been consecrated."[3]

George Adams-Kaufmann translated Polzer's speech into English, so that D. N. Dunlop, General Secretary of the British Society, could read it. As with many others who were similarly affected, Dunlop decided to stay away from the Dornach Annual Meeting after the expulsion motions were announced. Polzer's speech, in full accord with Dunlop's own outlook, must surely have warmed his heart. He died unexpectedly soon after, on Ascension Day, May 30, 1935.

The Impact of the Dornach Catastrophe on Contemporary History

In Polzer's view, the most important aspect of the expulsion catastrophe was not that it revealed tremendous weaknesses in the internal state of the Society, but that it would inevitably give an impetus to the anti-spiritual powers that had been casting their ever-darkening shadow over Germany since the 1920s. Ita Wegman and Elisabeth Vreede felt and thought likewise. In a sense, the banning of the Anthroposophical Society by the Gestapo on November 1, 1935, provides symptomatic confirmation of this view.

The Society's three-member Executive's letter of November 17, 1935,[4] addressed to the "Führer and Reichskanzler Adolf Hitler," sought

---

3   The entire experience is described in Thomas Meyer, *Ludwig Polzer-Hoditz: Ein Europäer*, p. 418.

4   See appendices 4 and 5 of this book, which include the executive board's letter in English and a copy of the original letter in German.

annulment of the Gestapo's order dissolving the German branch of the Society. The letter's opening sentence displays a supplicating tone that offers a shameful subservience to its object: "The undersigned members of the executive board of the Anthroposophical Society, with its seat in Dornach, near Basel (Switzerland)...find themselves compelled to trouble Your Excellency with the urgent request for your kind-hearted help in the following matter."

With this letter, the executive board attempted to come to some form of compromise with the Nazis regarding the ban of the German Anthroposophical Society on the basis that the Society "is a society that stands up for German culture and civilization in a most valuable way." The letter projects a theme that the Society is no danger and presents no threat to the Third Reich. To quote further:

> The Anthroposophical Society, constituted and founded by Dr. Rudolf Steiner in 1923, has neither stood in relationship to, nor in contact with, Freemason, Pacifist, or Jewish circles. Furthermore the Aryan heredity of Rudolf Steiner has been decisively confirmed by the Race-Political Authority in Berlin.

The appeal offers more such sycophantic language, hoping to secure approval from a government and specific persons whom Rudolf Steiner had identified with "the beast from the Abyss" that would arise in 1933. In the early 1920s, Steiner had already warned the membership about the danger posed by Nazis, especially after their attempted assassination of him in 1922. Any thoughtful student of the spiritual history of the twentieth century knows that National Socialism and Anthroposophy were polar counter-movements that arose at the dawn of a New Age, the age of the Second Coming of Christ, and that the Nazi mission was to destroy Germany and its profound spiritual heritage and prevent individuals from experiencing the Etheric Christ, which Steiner prophesied would begin to take place precisely in 1933.

It is also highly significant to observe that the executive board's letter to Hitler was not only written twelve years to the day after

Wegman's decisive question to Dr. Steiner, but also on the very day when Marie Steiner—November 17, 1901—had asked the Parzival question about creating a Western Christian occultism within the Theosophical Society.[5]

The real significance of the Dornach tragedy of 1935 lies in this negative power shift, with its disastrous impact on the whole contemporary situation. Monica von Miltitz, someone deeply connected with the being and work of Novalis, felt similarly. In an unpublished essay entitled "Thirty-three Years after the Ban," she wrote:

> I must start with a report of the Annual Meeting of 1935, one of the most difficult experiences of my life. Two individuals, Frau Dr. Wegman and Frau Dr. Vreede, whom Dr. Steiner had appointed to be members of the Society's esoteric executive board, were expelled by the Annual Meeting, along with forty of Dr. Steiner's closest friends, the truest of the true.[6]

She continues, revealing a deeper glimpse of the real significance of these events:

> At the end of the meeting, an older member stood up and said, "What has occurred here will have grave consequences in the public domain." In the fall of that year, the Anthroposophical Society was banned. Superficially, this had nothing to do with the Annual Meeting, of course, but in terms of higher causality, perhaps it did after all.

On the other hand, we could no doubt also ask whether the antispirit of Nazism, first repulsing the voice of spirit, then descending on Central Europe like a dark cloud, may also have influenced the souls of numerous members of the Society and may have metamorphosed into all kinds of fanatic impulses of dismissal, expulsion, and eradication.

---

5 Adding further significance is the fact that the original Theosophical Society was founded in New York on November 17, 1875.

6 Miltitz did not include in her figures the members of the Dutch and British Societies, who were expelled *en bloc*.

This is not to minimize what happened, but is a question that might foster a deeper understanding of the Dornach catastrophe.

Monica von Miltitz was also one of the very few to consider the meaning of the events in Dornach from the perspective of the thirty-three-year cycle:

> I realized only later that this Annual Meeting took place thirty-three years after Dr. Steiner had begun his anthroposophic work. He, of course, pointed out that the thirty-three-year cycle is significant as the period during which an impulse can unfold. It can also, however, provide us with a verdict, as in a court of law, and here the verdict is this: "You have not taken up what I gave you."

Monica von Miltitz wrote these words thirty-three years after 1935, at a time when the aftereffects of the Dornach catastrophe could again be observed, as we shall consider below.

Polzer's Deeper Analysis: The Shadow Cast by the Council of 1869

Like Miltitz, Ludwig Polzer-Hoditz saw the Dornach tragedy against the backdrop of broad historical perspectives. Like her, he related it to the year 1902, when Steiner began his public spiritual-scientific work. Polzer went a step further, however. Pursuing a suggestion by a journalist friend, he began to study the origins and nature of the Vatican Council of 1869/70, which declared the Pope's *ex cathedra* utterances to be infallible. These explorations led him to the following conclusion:

> The way in which the majority view formed in Rome back then is strikingly similar to what was done in Dornach. At the time of the Council, Church dignitaries, with their large, peripheral ecclesiastical dioceses, were not considered, nor the deeper religious mood and disposition of the northern peoples. Instead, ascendancy was asserted by the imperialistically minded peoples of the Mediterranean, with their more outward form of Christianity. The majority vote was obtained by calling upon a great many ecclesiastical authorities who had no dioceses, along with a large number of bishops located close to the center of Rome, who were

primed beforehand by strictures both spiritual and material in nature. *What happened at the Annual Meeting at the Goetheanum was very similar.*[7]

Then, too, in a memorial written after Ita Wegman's death, he revealed his own destiny connection with the year 1869 in the following words: "Easter 1935! Twice thirty-three years since I was born and since the last Vatican Council in Rome."[8]

It would be possible to draw further parallels. When Polzer came to Dornach on March 11, 1935, to ask Albert Steffen, the President of the Society at the time, not to publish the exclusion motions that had so far been circulated only internally, Steffen described the motions as something for which he was not responsible, but that he must nevertheless heed. In all seriousness, he advised Polzer to speak to the authors of the "Memorandum." In a similar though far crasser fashion, when necessary, Pope Pius IX hid behind those who, while promoting his aims, seemingly expressed their independent views at the Council of 1869. Polzer stated:

> The warning Rudolf Steiner gave me during the night six weeks before the Annual Meeting was one I increasingly understood. This was indeed the spirit of Jesuitism at work! That is why I think that Rudolf Steiner, from then on, no longer regarded the Society as a suitable form for the anthroposophic movement. I feel certain that this is connected with its prohibition and potential destruction resulting from this.[9]

Did the Easter Annual Meeting at Dornach produce something comparable to the dogma of infallibility? It did indeed. The individuals working for expulsion sowed the seed of a conviction that reared its head once again in the last quarter of the century: that, despite everything, Rudolf Steiner was still connected with the earthly Society as

---

7   T. H. Meyer, *Polzer*, op. cit., p. 435. Author's emphasis.
8   Ibid., p. 748.
9   Ibid., p. 435.

such, and not only with the strivings of individual pupils. In this view, the Society was still identical with the "movement," in a unity presided over by an "esoteric" executive board, in organic, unbroken succession from the original executive board.

This conviction flies in the face of reality. From 1935 onward, there were suddenly thousands of anthroposophists who were no longer members of the Society, in addition to those who had never belonged to it. Rebuilding the Society ought to have fully recognized this fact. Ludwig Polzer-Hoditz himself felt it necessary to leave the Society to pursue, unhindered, his work on the meditative path of the Michael School, although his right to do so was revoked by the Dornach executive board. Ita Wegman had come to the same conclusion by 1934.

> In her notebook entries Wegman repeatedly emphasized the need to engage with the "karma of the Christmas Foundation Meeting": with its prehistory, its active form, but also with its final earthly destruction through the dissolution of the karmic configuration of the executive board in Dornach (*"First and foremost we must be clear that the Christmas Foundation Meeting is broken, has been destroyed"*).[10]

Polzer left the Society in full deliberation on the day Daniel Dunlop died, a man he greatly esteemed. Henceforth, as he expressed it, he considered the Goetheanum to be located wherever people were working as Rudolf Steiner intended.

A New Start after the War: The Waldorf School Movement

There is no doubt that World War II, with its traumatic experiences, led to a new spiritual deepening in many of the anthroposophists who survived it. The great catastrophe swept many petty sectarian concerns away with it. In other words, the war induced a great deal of healthy inner self-scrutiny, or spiritual *in*volution. After the war, a pioneering spirit of renewal prevailed among many spiritual pupils, some of whom had been

---

10   Peter Selg, *Spiritual Resistance: Ita Wegman, 1933–1935*, p. 86.

personally instructed by Rudolf Steiner. This wind of renewal was primarily apparent in the flourishing and expansion of the Waldorf School movement, starting in Germany. A new phase began in which anthroposophic substance and dynamism could *evolve* outward and unfold.

The Stuttgart Waldorf School was symptomatic of this new flourishing, alongside The Christian Community and, somewhat later, endeavors in the field of medicine. Some of the teachers who worked at the school when it opened again after World War II had taught at the first Waldorf school at Uhlandshöhe.[11] According to Johannes Tautz, whom we can regard as the school movement's biographer, around one-third of the original teachers rejoined the newly opened school, including Herbert Hahn, Karl Schubert, Max Wolffhuegel, and Erich Schwebsch. The founder, Emil Molt, was no longer alive, but his spirit still seemed to infuse the place, and his portrait hung in the rebuilt school hall. Inspired partly by sitting with the bodies of deceased colleagues prior to their funeral, Tautz, assisted by Gerbert Husemann, later put together a valuable photograph collection of all the teachers Rudolf Steiner had appointed to the first Waldorf school, along with biographical sketches of each. As the first teacher of German and history after the school's reopening, Tautz wanted to pick up the thread of his predecessor's experiences and insights at the original school. Thus at the beginning of the fifties he sought out Walter Johannes Stein in his exile in London, later becoming his biographer. Tautz compared the encounters he had with Stein over three days with Trevrizent's instruction of Parzival.

Much of the school's original spirit therefore lived for a while in the second Stuttgart school, initially little touched by the tragic events that had split the Society in 1935. Figures such as Emil Bock, who helped The Christian Community to a new, powerful resurgence after the prohibition was lifted, and Jürgen von Grone, who had intimate knowledge of the Moltkes and their destiny, helped set the mood and tone in Stuttgart. Grone was one

---

11   Uhlandshöhe is the district in Stuttgart where the first Waldorf school was located.

of those expelled in 1935. Thus deep, living, and destiny-creating connections were formed with important anthroposophists outside of the Society.

Tautz had many pupils who later became well known in one way or other, including Michael Ende, the popular children's author. He became a lively mediator between the first generation of teachers and a younger, postwar generation.

The first issue of the anthroposophic newsletter in Germany was published in Stuttgart in 1947. Initially edited by Emil Bock, this periodical appeared quarterly and contained high-quality articles. Jürgen von Grone and Fritz Goette later took over as editors. A large Whitsun conference, organized by the Anthroposophical Society, was held the same year. Training courses for priests and teachers were established, and later the Eurythmeum. This period can be regarded as a "golden age" of energetic anthroposophic renewal in Stuttgart, as well as warm, spirited work in the public domain.

The Literary Estate Dispute

However, things in Dornach were not developing in such promising ways. In 1948 Marie Steiner described the expulsions of 1935 as a mistake, but this could not, of course, resurrect key figures in anthroposophic endeavors, such as D. N. Dunlop, Eugen Kolisko, and many others.

At the same time, a new conflict was brewing—how best to manage Rudolf Steiner's literary estate. Steiner's will could not have been clearer; but soon after his death its validity was questioned by some of his pupils, including W. J. Stein, who nevertheless did subsequently alter his stance.

At this point, Albert Steffen and Guenther Wachsmuth became opponents of Marie Steiner, seeking legal control of the literary estate for the Society. Therefore, a few months before her death on December 27, 1948, Marie Steiner found it necessary to found the Estate Association (later called the Rudolf Steiner Estate Administration). Encouraged by Ehrenfried Pfeiffer, she was still able to plan publication of Steiner's complete works (*Gesamtausgabe*, or GA[12]), whose first volumes began to appear in

---

12 SteinerBooks references GA editions as CW, reflecting its English translation, "Collected Works."

1961, the centenary of Steiner's birth. In other words, Marie Steiner had to battle against resistance from her former executive board colleagues to insure that the collected works found their way into the world.

Entirely without authority, and ignoring Marie Steiner's copyright, the Society's executive began to publish Steiner's lecture cycles and books, refusing to acknowledge the position of the Estate Administration. Eventually, the latter had to resort to legal action to enforce its rights. In the course of the lawsuit, the court magistrate in Dornach developed great esteem for Marie Steiner's person and her achievement, stating, "Frau Steiner was central to the movement, if not its very heart." He kept his own counsel as far as the actions of the Society's leadership were concerned, but made the following perspicacious statement: "It is tragic that a Society whose task is to bridge divisions in the world, such as those between East and West, cannot even reconcile differences of view within its own executive."[13]

In June 1952, the Solothurn Supreme Court determined that Marie Steiner had been entirely justified in founding the Estate Association.

Appraising the Deed of Willem Zeylmans

At Easter 1960, Willem Zeylmans van Emmichoven, who had been expelled from the Dornach Society in 1935, along with the Dutch Society over which he presided, decided on an unusual step. In a conversation with Albert Steffen he renewed the Dutch Society's affiliation with Dornach. Some of his friends were surprised, even horrified, since he did this without insisting on the conditions of previous agreements for such a move. These would have included concessions from Steffen over the literary estate question. To Steffen he simply said, "This is what we wish." Lovingly and with a sense of responsibility for Rudolf Steiner's work, Zeylmans wished to prepare the ground for the end of the century with this gesture of unconditional trust in the good powers of striving anthroposophists. His deed was doubtless significant, not the least because it was accomplished by a

---

13 According to an internal report by Henrik Knobel, February 1952. See also *Nachrichten der Rudolf Steiner-Nachlassverwaltung,* October 1952.

man in whose presence, on the evening of November 17, 1923, Steiner took what was perhaps the most difficult decision of his life—re-founding the Anthroposophical Society under his leadership.

Whether Zeylmans' action had a "positive" effect was not dependent solely on this singular action, but even more on the way it was received in Dornach. It would have been desirable if Zeylmans had been invited to join the Dornach executive board, making impossible, or at least very difficult, a relapse into the centralist customs and spiritual pretensions that had led to the split in 1935. The Society could finally have become what Polzer and others had regarded in the 1930s, following Steiner's death, as the only appropriate vehicle—an earthly administrative association that would serve Rudolf Steiner's work in an appropriate and humble way. As Steffen noted in his diary, he believed he "had gained a friend" through Zeylmans' unexpected step; he then added, "However, if he were to become a member of the executive board, this friendship would soon be lost again."[14]

The re-affiliation of the Dutch (and later also the British) Society did not bring the desired benefits; no new tasks or responsibilities were assigned within the Society. Zeylmans gave numerous lectures and worked on the new edition of his important book, *The Foundation Stone*, also writing a monograph on Rudolf Steiner, published in 1961 to mark the centenary of his birth. "The spiritual world no longer gives me any tasks," he said to a friend. In October 1961, he traveled to South Africa, and on November 18 he died in bed. He was found lying with folded hands and closed eyes. All his papers were in order. He died on the day that the Dutch Society was founded, which he had re-affiliated with Dornach more than a year earlier.

⁕

In addition to Zeylmans' book on Rudolf Steiner, the centenary of Steiner's birth was also marked by monographs by Rudolf Meyer and Herbert Hahn. Emil Bock's studies of Steiner's life, which he had first given as

---

14 See *Der Europäer*, year 13, no. 11, September 2009, p. 10.

lectures, were also published as a book. Soon after, the monograph by Johannes Hemleben was published in the Rowohlt series. Significantly, therefore, three priests, one physician, and a teacher engaged with Steiner's biography in this centenary year.

1968: Thirty-Three Years since 1935

At the end of the 1960s, a wave of protest and awakening surged through the student movement in the West. This movement was rooted in a rejection of the power politics of the West and the US, with its strong hold on Europe. To a certain degree, it was based on a clear and truthful sense of the occult background of such political maneuvering. Western cities witnessed waves of demonstrations against the terrible and no longer winnable war in Vietnam. However, the protests remained largely an emotional reaction, while the energies underlying them either degenerated into violence and terrorism or were diverted into one of three directions: psychoanalysis, Marxism, or drugs.

In 1965, an important book by anthroposophist and political commentator Renate Riemeck, entitled *Central Europe: Survey of a Century*, was published in Germany. Alongside its scholarly account of historical facts, it offered broad perspectives and insights into European history over the previous century, including evidence of how Western secret societies had planned World War I. It also referred to Rudolf Steiner's ideas of a threefold society. Riemeck was the foster mother of Ulrike Meinhof. Her book appeared at the right moment to provide the European protest movement with a deeper awareness and conceptual foundation, and to offer it fruitful ways forward and possible solutions. Nevertheless, it remained an isolated phenomenon, receiving no lasting response or support from large parts of the anthroposophic movement. Rudolf Steiner's *Karma of Untruthfulness* (CW 173, vols. 1 and 2), which casts a piercing light on the intentions of the Western lodges[15] and the Roman Curia, was published

---

15 Around this time, literature of varying quality was published in the West on related themes. Caroll Quigley's book *Tragedy and Hope* came out in 1966 and revealed the un- or even anti-democratic background to

(in German) in 1966, but anthroposophists capable of doing so failed to convey its insights to the protest movement in a way that the latter could have understood them. The 1968 protest movement therefore lacked any orienting impulse from Spiritual Science, whose strength had been senselessly fragmented thirty-three years earlier.

The fact that books published by the Rudolf Steiner Estate Administration were not allowed to be sold at the Goetheanum until 1968 shows us the extent to which the Society, supposedly representing Spiritual Science, was again embroiled in useless internal struggles during the very decisive 1960s. This was a full eighteen years after the Society's executive had lost its pitiful court case against the Estate Association—quite rightly founded by Marie Steiner—to which we owe the Collected Works of Rudolf Steiner!

❦

A communication received from the deceased Helmuth von Moltke on February 16, 1921, states, "Europe had to divest itself of its old robes. Now, for a while, it is wandering naked through humanity's evolution." This is an imagination invoking the end of the old centralized state (old robes) and the need for new social garments (threefolding) after a period of "nakedness."

Is Europe's "nakedness" now a thing of the past? Not at all. We have not divested ourselves of the old centralized state; rather, it now wears a double face, like Janus—one in which economic power seeks to be all-powerful, and the other, which the Roman Church seeks to ensoul. These two impulses were already embodied in the founding fathers of the European Union: Jean Monnet and Robert Schumann. Today's EU is entirely under their sway. The first (Monnet) is represented by far-reaching US influences on financial matters, while the second (Schumann) is symbolized in the twelve stars of the EU flag, a "Marian" emblem. The resolution

---

Anglo-American politics. In 1971, Gary Allen published *None Dare Call it Conspiracy*, followed shortly by Antony Sutton's "Wall Street" books. Yet these volumes would have needed a deeper, spiritual-scientific foundation to give the protest movement more sustainable support and orientation.

adopting this symbol was passed on December 8 (1955), the same date that the dogma of Mary's Immaculate Conception was enacted (December 8) in 1854, and likewise the same date as the start of the 1869 Vatican Council, where the blasphemous "infallibility" of the Pope was approved.

Anyone who thinks that Europe is really wearing new clothes has not noticed that the emperor is actually naked. A truly renewed Europe could have come about only with the help of a science of the spirit, something almost entirely lacking in public life during that crucial period at the end of the 1960s.

Pseudo-processes of Involution in the Last Quarter of the Twentieth Century

In relation to social, cultural, and economic affairs, Europe's outward sociopolitical condition at the end of the 1960s reveals a stark absence of any truly strong anthroposophic impulse. Did things improve toward the end of the century? Sadly, the opposite is true. To cultivate more energetic public activity, a further phase of realistic internalization (involution) would have been needed. Instead of this—parallel with immoderate growth of the school movement and other initiatives—we witnessed flights of fancy in the form of misdirected internalization processes. One catchword characteristic of this tendency is "The Christmas Foundation Meeting." Rudolf Grosse, who revered Albert Steffen and was President of the Dornach Society from 1966, fired the starting gun, as it were, for these misguided developments in his book *The Christmas Foundation Meeting as Start of a New Era*. There we find sentences such as the following:

> The Society, as the vessel of Anthroposophy and bearer of the esoteric, spiritual impulses of the Christmas Foundation Meeting, has *remained the place* where Rudolf Steiner still maintains creative connection with his work in accordance with his spiritual task.[16]

Instead of looking toward the end of the century and finally drawing the proper conclusions from the 1935 catastrophe by starting to assume a

---

16 Rudolf Grosse, *Die Weihnachtstagung als Zeitenwende*, p. 149.

humbler administrative role alongside healthy meditative practice, glorification of the Society as such commenced. This was allied with the very dogmatic assurance that this Society was still, as always, the (!) vessel of Anthroposophy and would remain the (!) place where Steiner was still creatively connected. This flies in the face of reason, of any "historical awareness," of any truly spiritual-scientific outlook, and, not least, of the intentions of clear-thinking spiritual pupils such as Ludwig Polzer-Hoditz, Willem Zeylmans, and many others. Centralistic pretensions to "esoteric" ascendancy again burgeoned and blossomed.

The outcome of this misguided esotericism came home to roost in the era of Manfred Schmidt, active in the Dornach executive from the mid-seventies and becoming its president about ten years later. He appended "Brabant" to his name in remarkable resonance with the Belgian Catholic Duchy of Brabant, from which had sprung a figure he also esteemed, Richard Coudenhove-Kalergi, an opponent of any truly anthroposophic impulse for Europe. The following incident, witnessed by the author, clearly signaled the new, Catholic, and centralizing tendency in management of Society's affairs. In 1985, when Peter Tradowsky began work on an edition of Ludwig Polzer-Hoditz's memoirs, he also wished to include Polzer's great speech at the 1935 Easter Annual Meeting as an appendix to the volume. *The president of the Society at the time vetoed this intention.* This is hardly surprising, since the tone of Polzer's speech breathed a very different air—that of spiritual decentralization—from the outlook prevailing once again in the executive board. This intervention left no doubt as to the new direction of the Society's upper echelons—consolidation of spiritual centralism focused in Dornach.

Even the "periphery" was soon infected by this outlook. In 1992, when the author of this book gave a lecture on D. N. Dunlop at the Annual Meeting of the British Anthroposophical Society in London, he ended by suggesting the need for spiritual "peripheralization" within the anthroposophic movement, while retaining central administration. He also expressed the contentious idea that advocating spiritual centralism in terms of Rudolf Steiner's ongoing strong connection with the Society *as earthly society* (as had become fashionable again since Grosse), rather than just with striving individuals, was actually an inhibiting and erroneous Catholic-like view. Indeed, he said that it would be very beneficial to anthroposophic work to live without such a guarantee, which was unworthy of a spiritual movement. In his concluding words of thanks, the general secretary of the British Society at the time replied that, whereas a figure such as Ignatius Loyola did, at a certain point after his death, take leave of the order he founded, Rudolf Steiner remained strongly connected as ever with the General Anthroposophical Society. In other words, to conceive of Rudolf Steiner distancing himself from the Society he founded was a "Jesuitical" idea.

The misguided steps of "involution" also include the brazen attempt in 1993 to inaugurate a "Second Class" of the Michael School, even though Steiner did not even complete the first one.[17]

Failing to Defend Steiner against Accusations of Racism

We must now cast a brief glance at a series of phenomena that demonstrate unequivocally the extent to which anthroposophic work has been weakened by misguided and sectarian processes of involution. These phenomena approached the anthroposophic movement from the public domain.

During the 1990s, Anthroposophy, and Rudolf Steiner himself, were increasingly attacked in the media for Steiner's supposedly racist doctrines, along with hints, at least, of anti-Semitism in his work. This triggered a kind of panic reaction among leading anthroposophists in Holland, the starting point for the worst attacks. They believed they should "save" Anthroposophy only by making admissions to their opponents. Their admissions were void of any objective basis and were, thus, tantamount to an attack that they themselves launched on Steiner. For instance, instead of clearly showing that no racism figures in his work, they claimed that Steiner did not propound any racial doctrines. Additionally,

---

17 Cf. *Der Meditationsweg der Michaelschule*, Perseus Verlag, 2011, p. 452.

a compilation was made on behalf of the Dutch Anthroposophical Society of all Steiner's comments on race, national characteristics, and Judaism, which (removed from their specific context) can be very easily misunderstood. The conclusion of these efforts was to establish that sixteen passages in Steiner's work would be liable to criminal proceedings under today's laws!

The compilation of these passages has become known as the "Van Baarda Report." Modern opponents of Anthroposophy sometimes cite it as evidence of "recognition" by some anthroposophists that Steiner did make "problematic" comments. For instance, this is stated in the educator Heiner Ullrich's biography of Steiner.

In January 2000, opponents of Anthroposophy, who had only a passing acquaintance (if that) with Steiner's work, were given an opportunity in the Foundation Stone Hall at the Goetheanum to express their doctrinaire criticisms of Steiner and Anthroposophy, based solely on a few easily misunderstood passages that they had mostly learned by heart. The discussion was chaired by a civil servant from Basel. Only a single member of the Dornach executive board, who said nothing, was present. In passing, we can see this event as a kind of internal mockery of the spiritual aims implicit in the very fact that the Foundation Stone of 1913 was buried in the earth beneath the floor of this same hall.

A couple of years later, Rudolf Steiner Verlag halted release of volume 32 in the Collected Works, because in one of its essays Steiner defended Robert Hammerling against accusations of racism. The essay contains two sentences it was thought could possibly be interpreted as racist![18]

It is easy to see what has done the greatest long-term damage to Anthroposophy's reputation—not the primitive attacks on Steiner from without, whose substance was not fundamentally new anyway and will surface again in future, but the fearful caving in to these attacks by "representatives" of Anthroposophy. If the decades of review and reflection

---

18   See *Der Europäer*, vol. 4, no. 5, March 2000, pp. 11ff, where this essay was reprinted with a commentary.

on the "Christmas Foundation Meeting," the "Foundation Stone Meditation," the "School of Spiritual Science," along with everlasting assurances of Steiner's "eternal connection with the institution of the General Anthroposophical Society" had been aspects of a genuine involutionary process, such weak and timid actions—which even betrayed, to some degree, the spirit of Anthroposophy—could never have come about. Authentic spiritual deepening and true anthroposophic work would not have led to such a shameful "running with the pack."

The Chantilly Experiment and the Grand Orient's Good Favor

The Chantilly experiment (we'll call it that, since the whole way it was undertaken made it appear to be one event) occurred in 1995. Clearly, ecclesiastical and anthroposophic circles wanted to find out to what extent the two movements could find some rapprochement.

Briefly, although the new center of the Anthroposophical Society in Paris had just been completed, its French members were informed that the spring Annual Meeting would take place at Chateau les Fontaines in Chantilly, forty kilometers north of Paris. The Paris center was too small, it was said. There was no mention of the fact that les Fontaines housed the Jesuit's headquarters in France and the Robert Schumann Institute. The President of the General Anthroposophical Society was due to give the evening lecture. French members who felt unsure about all this asked for some explanation, but no real clarification was forthcoming until an anonymous article[19] was pinned to a bulletin board in Dornach. This clarified the nature of the location and urged participants to conduct themselves in accordance with its spirit.

If it had really been necessary to go to les Fontaines, this would have provided an opportunity to speak about the differences between the anthroposophic and Jesuit paths of schooling. Clearly, however, none of the organizers had such a plan in mind. The President of the executive board withdrew his proposed lecture; soon after, the idea of going to

---

19 Published in *Der Europäer*, vol. 1, no. 9/10, 1997, p. 11f, and in *What is Happening in the Anthroposophical Society (Newsletter)*, February 26, 1995.

les Fontaines was dropped. The French members were informed that the Annual Meeting would take place in Paris, after all. Apparently, the new center was suddenly large enough.

❧

During a conference for Class members in the 1990s, again in Paris, the discussion turned to the planned French edition of Rudolf Steiner's *Texts and Documents from the Cognitive-Ritual Section of the Esoteric School 1904-1919* (CW 265)[20] with its references to Freemason rituals. The then-President of the Society mentioned in this context that a publication of this nature would elicit a warm response in Grand Orient (Masonic) circles. It is known that the President had contacts with Freemasonry. But why state that an anthroposophic publication would meet with their approval? Was this another attempt to sound out the extent to which anthroposophists might agree to collaborate with Freemasons?[21] It is worth remembering here that the Grand Orient Lodge is one of the Masonic groups that has sought to influence the course of international politics since World War I, if not before.

Thus, in a very dubious—because opaque—manner, members of the Anthroposophical Society were encouraged to ally themselves, or at least to feel themselves allied with, representatives of other movements that are spiritually incompatible with Anthroposophy. This was a significant prelude to the new "public visibility" of certain anthroposophic officials initiated at the beginning of the millennium.

Also in the 1990s, at the same time as the events described here were unfolding, *internal doubts* were voiced about Rudolf Steiner's competency as a spiritual researcher. These related in particular to certain comments he had made in his *Observations on Contemporary History*.[22] A

---

20 Published in English as *"Freemasonry" and Ritual Work: The Misraim Service*.

21 This incident was described to the author in a written statement by a person who attended this conference.

22 Comprising three volumes, including *The Karma of Untruthfulness*, CW 173.

representative of the Anthroposophical Society in Great Britain wrote an article published in the Dornach *Newsletter* on March 15, 1992, stating that Steiner's *Observations on Contemporary History* reveal "emotions in Rudolf Steiner that many have previously been unaware of," and that it seems he had sometimes been "influenced" by the "chauvinistic emotions" of some members of his audience.

"Occult Imprisonment" as a Starting Point for a New "Evolution"

Between 1994 and 2000, misguided involution processes within the Society reached their greatest culmination. Members were urged to focus their work on one esoteric "mystery" each year leading up to the millennium. This began with the "mystery of initiative" (1994) and ended with the "mystery of freedom." In this last year, when anthroposophic work was supposedly dedicated to the "mystery of freedom," the President of the executive board suggested to members that the Society, which lacked any effective public influence, was clearly caught up in some kind of "occult imprisonment." This statement by the president (who died soon after) became his highly influential legacy. It was the starting signal for an unthinking rush into the public domain, which increasingly led and still leads—sometimes literally—to an embrace of individuals who know no more (and do not desire to know more) about Anthroposophy than a cow knows about Sunday.

The first appeal to tackle and break out of this "imprisonment" was announced by a member of the executive board in the *Newsletter* of January 19, 2000. In his view, this "break-out" must start from the School of Spiritual Science.

The use of the phrase "occult imprisonment" marked the transition from a phase of pseudo-involution to one of renewed evolution, of work done in the public eye. One need not be clairvoyant to see what kind of evolution could come from so many decades of misguided involution.

"Never mention Steiner"

In Paris once again, at an Annual Meeting of the French Society held exactly seven years after the "Chantilly experiment," this same member of the Dornach executive outlined a program for the future of anthroposophic work. The phrase "Never mention Steiner" was presented, while also proposing such things as critical detachment and the cultivation of psychological factors in members' interpersonal relations. Eight years later, in a supplement to the weekly journal *Das Goetheanum*, he stated that, in relation to Anthroposophy, "change and flux has become our all-determining principle," and expressly questioned the imperishable spirit of Anthroposophy in the following words: "...'eternal values of Anthroposophy'—*if such a thing exists.*"[23]

In this "representative of Anthroposophy," "transience and change" have indeed become an all-determining principle that even overrides eternal values. Apparently, we can therefore now delight in engaging with those who know Anthroposophy only superficially at best, and who attribute the worst kind of nonsense to Rudolf Steiner. Such figures include: Miriam Gebhardt, who proclaims Steiner's research to have been fueled by cocaine; Heinrich Ullrich, who thinks Steiner did not understand Kant; and Helmut Zander, who, in his love-hate relationship with Anthroposophy, cannot study a single page by Steiner with an open mind or any self-detachment and demonstrates this in thousands of his own pages. I leave it to others to list everything he accuses Steiner of and will confine myself to his assertion that all talk of a suprasensory realm is a great swindle, and that Steiner did not pay much heed to the truth—as evidenced, supposedly, by a *single* discrepancy relating to his date of birth.

A great change has indeed occurred since Steiner's hundredth birthday. Back then, anthroposophists published thoughtful monographs about Steiner; now non-anthroposophists, with dilettantish knowledge and slanderous intent, are doing so. Nevertheless, this is not the greatest cause for concern. The worst thing is that an executive board member finds such

---

23 See "Keinerlei Bezugnahme auf Rudolf Steiner...," in *Was will die Goetheanum-Leitung von Rudolf Steiners Geisteswissenschaft heute noch vertreten?* Download at www.perseus.ch.

publications highly commendable. In an interview with the Sunday paper *NZZ am Sonntag* (January 9, 2011), when asked whether he was pleased about the three new biographies of Rudolf Steiner, he said, "Definitely. These are three acknowledged authors and three major publishing houses." Shortly after this, one of his colleagues on the executive board stressed that the Dornach executive was an "organism," despite the marked differences of views between its members, especially in relation to opponents of Anthroposophy. As the most important theorist of the "Christmas Foundation Meeting" since Rudolf Grosse, he propounds the dogma of Steiner's indissoluble connection with the institution of the General Anthroposophical Society.

Yet, from a deeper perspective, perhaps these divergences of opinion are not so great. Seen in terms of the law of evolution, it is clear that a false evolutionary process *inevitably* proceeds from a false involutionary one. In other words, a one-sided, sectarian inwardness ("Christmas Foundation Meeting," Steiner's profound connection with the General Anthroposophical Society as an institution, and so on) will induce a one-sided, superficial outwardness. Thus, we can view both types of one-sidedness— the one more *in*volutionary, the other more *e*volutionary—as *two sides of the same coin.*

The Illusion of Clinging to the "Christmas Foundation Meeting" and the "School"

A certain culmination based on false involution was reached in 2003. An internal "constitution debate" that exerted its debilitating effect through much of the 1990s found a preliminary end in January 2003, with modification of the Society's entry in the Swiss Companies Register, which was revised from "General Anthroposophical Society" to "General Anthroposophical Society (Christmas Foundation Meeting)." Yet, this was only a temporary end of a process that squandered huge spiritual and financial resources. After justified internal protests against the factually unfounded change of nomenclature by the executive—one might even call it attempted false-labeling fraud—Solothurn's Court of Appeal decided in

January 2005 that the supplementary description "Christmas Foundation Meeting" should be removed, and this was done on May 10, 2005. Once again, Anthroposophy's reputation was damaged considerably by these events, which were splashed all over the press.[24]

We can see from this grotesque sequence of events that deluded sectarian ideas and legal actions can go hand in glove, are mutually reinforcing, and actually elicit each other. Seen in terms of Spiritual Science, we find here an interplay of luciferic and ahrimanic powers.

Although opposed by Polzer, this same "duo" was allowed to take center stage back in the 1930s, with very negative results. At the beginning of the 1950s, we had the court proceedings relating to Rudolf Steiner's estate. Fifty years later came another such action concerning the "Christmas Foundation Meeting" epithet.

Anthroposophist Karl Buchleitner commented on the 2005 Solothurn verdict:

> The claim to embody the Christmas Foundation Meeting has greatly hindered anthroposophic work and condemned Anthroposophy itself to inefficacy on the world stage. Something great could still arise, however, if this Society were to retreat from its spiritual pretentions and get down to specific tasks. There is much to be done. The Solothurn verdict could lead to an awakening.

Did an awakening occur? Let us examine this by considering two questions:

1. How was the innovative Munich conference of 1907 remembered in Dornach in 2007?[25]
2. What is the current concept of the School of Spiritual Science founded by Steiner?

---

24 Cf. *Der Meditationsweg der Michaelschule in neunzehn Stufen*, p. 452.
25 The Munich Conference of May 1907 offered the first attempts of incorporating esoteric insights in art. Eduard Schuré's mystery play *Holy Drama of Eleusis* was performed. The conference hall was also decorated as a Rosicrucian Temple with seven apocalyptic seals.

In the spring of 2007 a container filled with dried banana peels stood for several months in the entrance hall of the Goetheanum, a creation by Englishwoman Shelley Sacks, a student of Joseph Beuys. Her "artwork" was touted as "social sculpture." An exhibition entitled "Joseph Beuys and Rudolf Steiner" was set up in the archive offices of the Rudolf Steiner Estate Administration. Both events were, by their very nature (undoubtedly not consciously intended) a mockery of the healthy new anthroposophic art impulse that came to public attention for the first time in Munich, from which the Goetheanum building later emerged.

How do things stand with the School of Spiritual Science established by Steiner, for whose members Steiner gave the nineteen lessons of the First Class? In Ludwig Polzer's view, the School was killed off by the expulsions of 1935. Charles Kovacs, the clear-sighted anthroposophist and painter, also placed the beginning of the end of the School in the 1930s, and could not understand why the Dornach executive still refused to recognize this in the 1980s. Both these figures, of course, are representative of many others who hold similar views.

Carl Unger wrote of the psychological and spiritual background to pseudo-esotericism, which is usually associated with secrecy or conditional, restricted access:

> Modern esotericism must be free, for it can be Christian only in this way. Esotericism bound to old traditions is something luciferic. An old, not a new, impulse—the aim of securing superiority over others—is behind efforts to maintain secrecy. This works like a poison in human society.[26]

Anyone who today still holds and promotes the view that access to the Michael School's path of meditation (First Class texts)—which have long since been published!—can be allowed only after presentation of a special members' card from a School of Spiritual Science that no longer exists, is continuing to help produce such poison.

---

26   Carl Unger, *Schriften,* vol. 2, p. 238.

Refusing to credit the reality of certain facts—which Polzer already spoke about—perpetuates a false involutionary process into our present time, and, as the described phenomena show, can only trigger further unhealthy evolutionary processes.

Buchleitner's twin hope that a number of catastrophes would finally teach us to "retreat from spiritual pretentions and get down to specific tasks" has, therefore—apart from the courageous achievements of a very few anthroposophists—so far remained unfulfilled. People have been unable to decide either to relinquish the corpse of the School or to get down to "specific tasks," such as proper ways of dealing with opponents or energetic publication of the results of spiritual-scientific research. As regards the latter, the reverse has often happened: academic standards or qualifications have increasingly been introduced *into* or imposed *upon* anthroposophic institutions.

Taking Stock

The mutually inducing erroneous processes of involution and evolution in the development of Anthroposophy since Steiner's death have led to a desolate situation today: an anthroposophic movement governed largely by *both* these unhealthy processes—albeit with varying emphases—and now stuck in a kind of stagnation.

On the one hand, Steiner's work is available throughout the world as never before, downloadable onto a hard drive measuring just a few square centimeters. On the other hand, *thinking* engagement with and assimilation of Anthroposophy has—again, apart from a few exceptions—sunk to rock bottom, as can be seen by glancing at the bibliographies of those "acknowledged authors," as well as by perusing certain volumes produced by supposedly anthroposophic publishers.

Two comments found in Helmuth von Moltke's post-mortem communications seem particularly noteworthy in this context, both received October 26, 1920. The first states: "The imminent fate of the 'spiritual movement' will be to stand there like a plucked chicken. All its feathers will be pulled out." Here is a picture of the intellectual plundering of anthroposophic substance, made still easier now by the digital Collected Works and Internet search engines. Through such intellectualization, spiritual substance loses its innate impetus.

Moltke's second comment states: "The 'spiritual movement' is spiritual substance without a reflection in human heads."[27]

Here the Moltke individuality experiences the objective spiritual substance of Anthroposophy—in a sense, its "eternal value"—but also witnesses how humanity fails to integrate it into its *thinking consciousness*. This is certainly a radical statement, but it holds true today even among some sections of the "anthroposophic movement."

It could be objected that, for instance, the school movement has expanded further, into Eastern Europe and even to Asia. In Hungary alone twenty-seven schools have been established since the turn of the millennium. Nearly one thousand Waldorf schools are in existence today. And hasn't the medical movement also spread internationally? Then there is the biodynamic movement, too, reaching as far as Nepal. Surely the current state of play is not so negative.

Certainly we can discern expansion in these fields, and within certain bounds this is positive—yet only to the point where we ask whether and to what extent this proliferation is accompanied and sustained by healthy processes of involution or inner deepening in an *anthroposophic sense*. Expansion alone will not be important in the long term. Let me clarify this with an example. Ehrenfried Pfeiffer once reported a conversation he had with a leading Jesuit, who told him that biodynamic agriculture would be the only sound basis for a future social order. Pfeiffer asked,

> "Do you realize that biodynamics originated with Rudolf Steiner, whom the Catholic Church attacked?" The man replied, "Oh yes, we're fully aware of that." Then I continued: "He also taught about reincarnation," to which the answer was, "There's nothing in the Bible that contradicts the idea of reincarnation."

---

27 Thomas Meyer, *Moltke*, vol. 2, p. 255.

Pfeiffer concludes this account by saying, "I cannot dwell further on this here. All I'd like to say is that, if we don't take Steiner's teachings seriously, then others will."[28] My own addendum to this is that they will do so *in their own way*. Here Pfeiffer suggests that adopting and realizing something that originates in Anthroposophy is not enough. It also depends on *who* does this, and *in what* spirit.

The plucked feathers can also be used by people who serve beings quite other than Anthroposophy.

⁂

When asked in a private conversation with Walter Johannes Stein how one could defend oneself against the mental disorders so rife today, Rudolf Steiner replied:

> There are three enemies of the psyche: vanity, ambition, and untruthfulness, all of which have bad effects in daily life. However, in a spiritual movement, their effect is devastating. If people are on their guard against these three, they need not fear for their psychological health.[29]

He impressed the same thing, almost word for word, on the priests of The Christian Community, but also warned them against impulses to anger.[30]

These three (or four) fundamental vices are also what have led to false processes of involution and evolution within the anthroposophic movement. The author hopes that a history of the development of Anthroposophy in the world will one day be written, or at least considered, from *this* perspective. A great deal of obstruction during Rudolf Steiner's life, and still more after his death, must be attributed to the influence of these four. Much of the inner or outer developmental distortions here described arose

---

28 Ehrenfried Pfeiffer, *Ein Leben fur den Geist*, p. 22.
29 Printed in: *Mitteilungen aus der anthroposopischen Arbeit in Deutschland*, no. 46, 1958.
30 "Lectures and Courses on Christian Religious Work, Vol. 3: Lectures at the Founding of the Christian Community," Sept. 9 1922, CW 344 (not yet translated into English).

from vanity, not to mention the other three "dis-graces." A huge amount has simply been conceitedly squandered in this way.

Domes of the Future

After this perhaps sobering analysis, let us now turn to the future, taking our lead from certain comments by Rudolf Steiner. One states that domed buildings will arise everywhere in Europe in 2086. He made this comment on March 7, 1914, to a group of anthroposophists in Stuttgart. This was during the very early building phase of the Goetheanum's first cupola in Dornach, a few months before the outbreak of World War I. According to a very sketchy transcript, Steiner said:

> Confusion and devastation will hold sway as the year 2000 approaches. And no single piece of wood of our building in Dornach will be left standing. All will be destroyed and ravaged. We will look down upon this from the spiritual world. However, when the year 2086 arrives, everywhere in Europe buildings will be seen arising dedicated to spiritual goals, constructed in the image of our Dornach building with its two cupolas. The golden age for such buildings will have arrived.[31]

Taking the strikingly precise reference to the year 2086 in relation to 1914, we find that the year 2000 is an axis of reflection lying exactly midway between them. Anyone who was not completely asleep at the time knows, of course, that 2000 fell in a period of catastrophe. In 1999, thanks to NATO's illegal intervention, the bloodiest phase of the war in Yugoslavia began, followed on September 11, 2001, by the first global war of the third millennium. Thus, the year 2000 was flanked by these two events or sequences of events. The old wooden Goetheanum had long since been destroyed, of course, while the new, concrete building still stands...but we have already seen how much Anthroposophy was practiced within its walls around the turn of the century.

---

31   Rudolf Steiner, *Architecture as a Synthesis of the Arts* (previously published as *Ways to a New Style of Architecture*), CW 286.

Moltke's postmortem communications also contain a comment that might relate to the period Steiner referred to in 1914. Received on February 8, 1918, it runs: "In the twentieth century much materialism will prevail and will increase further in the twenty-first century. But everywhere there will be centers of spiritual will and action."[32]

This 1914 communication leads us to ask whether the prophesied "golden age" will dawn only after a further global catastrophe. There is a whole series of other prophesies that should be taken seriously—for instance, one by the Bavarian seer Alois Irlmaier—which speak unmistakably of a third scenario of devastation.[33]

But there is even no need to seek out such prophecies. The fact is that neither the wider world nor the anthroposophic movement, which should inform itself with beneficial impulses, have drawn the necessary conclusions from the twentieth century. This must leave all reasonable people expecting further catastrophic lessons from world-historical powers. Moltke's comment could tell us that prior to a forthcoming world catastrophe, and even during it, anthroposophic spiritual work could be undertaken on a small scale at least, in homeopathic dosage, as it were. This would mean an emphasis on involuntary, internalizing activity, which can thereby shine out all the more spiritually into the wider world.

The era of new domed buildings will be one during which the Foundation Stone laid in 1923 will enable people to undertake new, individualized, *outwardly directed* work. In the same way that many cupolas will have arisen from the original one, so the one Foundation Stone will live in many human beings in individualized form. To both phases—both the preliminary one suggested by Moltke's communication as well as the actual golden era of new domed buildings itself—Polzer's phrase will apply in tangible form: "The Goetheanum exists wherever esoteric work is undertaken as Rudolf Steiner intended."

---

32 Thomas Meyer, *Moltke*, vol. 2, p. 166.
33 Wolfgang Johannes Bekh, *Bayrische Hellseher*, Munich, 11th edition, 1998.

In view of the lack of much hope in the current situation in the "wider world," as well as in the world of the anthroposophic movement, both statements are certainly capable of kindling our will so that we do not succumb, as if hypnotized and petrified by the Medusa gaze of current events.

In preparation for the not so distant future at the end of *this* century, it is clear that the involution and evolution processes of anthroposophic spiritual-scientific work must be harmonized in a way that has not yet been forthcoming since Steiner's death. While many people one-sidedly sought outward development and public recognition, others withdrew into a navel-gazing esotericism. In fact, the fundamental one-sidedness of all modern times consists of an *over-valuing of the evolutionary dynamic*, as Steiner told the priests on October 2, 1921: "Today, in our modern civilization, we live almost entirely in adherence to evolutionary values. It is very necessary that we return to involution values once more, by nurturing sacramental qualities."[34] But for Steiner himself, the sacramental had already begun with our *thinking* and *perception*.

The development of the Cistercian order offers a historical precedent for relatively harmonious processes of involution and evolution. The order spread by moderate degrees, and was always sustained and governed by a corresponding inwardness compatible with those times. This was the secret of its successful and sustained growth through many centuries, and of its spread through the whole of Europe, as it then was.[35]

The Connection of Anthroposophy with the True German Spirit

Below I wish to clarify a couple of grave misunderstandings and to develop a few future perspectives connected with Anthroposophy's further development.

---

34 Rudolf Steiner, "Lectures and Courses on Christian Religious Work, Vol. 2: Spiritual Knowledge—Religious Feeling—Cultic Doing," CW 343 (not yet translated into English).

35 See Ekkehard Meffert, *Die Zisterzienser und Bernhard von Clairvaux*. Something similar must be sought in the anthroposophic movement of the future.

It is a historical fact that Rudolf Steiner developed Anthroposophy in attunement with the intention of the Time Spirit Michael. However, at the same time, he also developed it in accordance with the aims of the true German Spirit who is "intimately allied" with Michael.[36]

This Spirit of the Germanic peoples, still a young Spirit, received his national tasks from Michael when the latter became the prevailing Time Spirit in 1879, and is the guardian angel of the Bodhisattva who was elevated into Buddha. This was first pointed out by Karl Heyer in his important book, *Wer ist der deutsche Volksgeist?* ("Who is the German Folk Spirit?"). This Folk Spirit still has a task that will last for over a thousand years, as Rudolf Steiner said on January 19, 1915. Steiner's description of this Spirit can show us the true task of the German peoples:

> The mission of the German peoples is that ultimately its endeavors must inevitably flow back with it into spiritual life. Yet this means nothing other, spiritually speaking, than that the German peoples are called upon to connect inwardly with what arises in the world through Michael's leadership.[37]

The rejection of Spiritual Science on German soil in the 1920s—as symbolized starkly by the attempt on Steiner's life in Munich—obstructed real engagement with this task for decades, at a minimum. Yet, everything leading in Germany to World War II and the Holocaust should not be attributed to the true German Folk Spirit but, on the contrary, to its utter absence.[38]

Here arises a misunderstanding that circulates even in some anthroposophic quarters—that, owing to the Holocaust, the German Folk Spirit no longer has any task and, in a sense, has "come to an end." *This Spirit* has not come to an end, but rather large swathes of the German people have lost their connection with it or, to be more accurate, did not inwardly

---

36 January 19, 1915, *The Destinies of Individuals and of Nations*, CW 157.
37 Ibid.
38 It is an important task of spiritual-scientific research to discover which spiritual entity filled the vacuum left by the absent spirit of the nation.

connect with it. What Steiner said in a public lecture in Berlin on January 14, 1915,[39] in the midst of war remains true despite all pseudo-Germanic nationalism.

> The German Spirit has not yet brought to fulfillment
> Its active work in world evolution.
> Concerned for the future it lives full of hope,
> Hoping for future deeds, and full of life;
> Within its being's depths it feels the might
> Of hidden nature that must emerge and ripen.
> How can the power of enmity allow
> An uncomprehending wish for its demise
> As long as life is manifest, sustains
> within this Spirit's roots creative power?

It is essential to distinguish between Germanic Spirit and "German" reality in the twentieth century. In a conversation with Stuttgart solicitor and anthroposophist Bruno Krueger, Steiner said, "Anthroposophy is and remains connected with the German Spirit."[40]

Those who read anything even remotely connected with the Holocaust and World War II into this phrase will inevitably remain "uncomprehending" in the above sense. In his conversation with Krueger, Steiner then added, "The German Folk Spirit has descended upon its people two times: at the time of Walther von der Vogelweide in the Wartburg region, and again at the time of Fichte, Schiller and Goethe. Now, as a third occasion, the Germanic peoples must intentionally raise themselves to this Spirit." This self-raising did not occur to a sufficient degree, but it must happen if the "future deeds," for which the German Spirit lives "full of hope," are at last to become reality.

It is another question whether this must take place within the geographical area of Germany, or even whether it can any more. It is apposite

---

39 Rudolf Steiner, *Aus schicksaltragender Zeit* ("Out of Destiny-Burdened Times"), CW 64 (not yet in English).
40 Bruno Krueger, *Leben und Schicksal*, p. 39f.

here to recall the great poet and thinker Fercher von Steinwand,[41] who appeared in spiritual form to Rudolf Steiner during the dark days when the latter was working on German soil—as if to comfort and admonish him to attend to the still uncompleted mission of the true German Spirit. Steiner referred to him at that point in Munich as the "Leader of the White Lodge of the German-speaking peoples."[42] All talk of German culture must be rooted in this picture and not in its opposite, which was to assume tangible form soon after.

In a presentation Fercher gave to the King of Saxony in 1859, he outlined a picture of German culture scattered across the globe, albeit in the sense of degeneracy such as he perceived in the gypsies. He warned against the decline to which the German people—though not the German Spirit itself—was susceptible, and which might come about precisely if they were not willing to heed the German Spirit.

Another great German, Goethe, spoke of how the Germans would only work in a way beneficial to other nations once they had been scattered through the world like the Jews. His actual words to Chancellor Mueller in 1808 were, "Germany is nothing, but every single German is a great deal; and yet the Germans imagine the very reverse to be true. The Germans must be transplanted and scattered through the world like the Jews, so as to develop the mass of good in them for the benefit of all nations."[43]

There is something remarkable here. Fercher, who was born on the same date (March 22) that Goethe died,[44] takes a parallel used by Goethe but alters it to warn of a possible decline, whereas Goethe emphasizes the

---

41 Austrian poet (1828–1902), born in Carinthia, died in Vienna. Rudolf Steiner recounts his relationship with Fercher in his *Autobiography:* "I view it as one of the important events in my youth that I was privileged to know Fercher von Steinwand. His personality had the effect of a sage who reveals his wisdom in true poetry" (p. 68).
42 See chapter 18, *Milestones (Wegmarken).*
43 Goethe, *Gedenkausgabe*, vol. 12, 1949, p. 527.
44 Goethe died on Mar. 22, 1832, four years after Fercher was born.

positive aspect of such a development. At that dark moment in Munich, Fercher appeared spiritually to Steiner—no longer to warn, but as the *guardian* of the true mission of German culture, just when this mission is being betrayed or forgotten by the German people.

An unpublished poem by Karl Julius Schroer embodies a beautiful, but little known, characteristic of the universal spiritual mission of the German people. Here Schroer completes a well-known fragment that Friedrich Schiller composed on "German Greatness":

> Not to momentarily dazzle
> But conclude the spiritual battles
> That the world has long waged:
> Reconciling all division
> *Thus* victorious is the mission
> That sustains its coming age.[45]

We see already in Goethe that fulfillment of the future mission of the German Spirit is no longer bound to German *territory*.

Following the collapse of a great majority of the German people into the chasm of anti-Germanism, we can lead on from Goethe and Fercher to ask, "Is fulfillment of the as-yet uncompleted mission of the German Spirit still exclusively bound up with people of Germanic descent?" Fichte already knew that one is not a true German by birth, but can only *become* one. Surely this also means that "becoming German" in a good, spiritual sense is also possible for people of quite other national and linguistic origins. Indeed, the fact that so many "German Germans" did not initially take up this task—to the detriment of the whole world—means that fulfillment of the mission of the German Spirit can draw on this *possibility* all the more. All such "elective Germans" would include those who find, or will find, their way to Rudolf Steiner's Anthroposophy in an honest and judicious way, since the latter "is and remains connected with the German Spirit." In this sense, a person from Japan who penetrates

---

45 The entire poem was first published in *Der Europäer*, year 9, no. 5, Mar. 2005, pp. 5ff.

the spirit of Anthroposophy would actually come far closer to the German Spirit than those "Germans" who, if they outgrew materialism at all, turned to ancient Asian spirituality.

Anthroposophy and the German Language

Anthroposophy is and remains tied to the German Folk Spirit. To what extent does this apply also to its connection with the German *language*? The Spirit of the German language is connected with the German Spirit in a manner similar to the way the German Folk Spirit is connected with the Time Spirit, Michael. This is not altered by the fact that the German language has also been misused by the anti-spirit of Nazism. Rudolf Steiner's comments on December 18, 1916,[46] on the nature of the Spirit of the German language, show that, in comparison with the other Spirits of European languages, German is particularly adapted to enable us to experience thoughts inwardly prior to, and independently of, linguistic expression, thereby nurturing our capacity for pure thinking. By contrast, the Romance languages tend to hinder this capacity by adapting thoughts to words. In English thought even becomes completely subordinate to the word. With respect to the German language Steiner says:

> It is a peculiarity of Germans that their thoughts stop short of their words. It is because of this fact that German culture has possessed philosophers such as Fichte, Schelling, and Hegel, who could not have existed anywhere else. A German does not bear a thought right into words, but retains it as thought.

The following basic characteristic of the German language is, at the same time, a core concern of the whole of Anthroposophy, as expressed in the motto cited earlier: "The essence of German is to establish a union between the spiritual *per se*, and the spiritual in thought." The fact that Anthroposophy also appeared in the world in the linguistic garb of idealistic philosophy thus reveals its deep justification. For this reason, a

---

46 Lecture 7, *The Karma of Untruthfulness*, vol. 1, CW 173.

"correct translation," especially from German, "is not possible, and is always only an approximation or substitute."[47]

The Spirit of the German language is, additionally, available for new, individual forms of thought in a way that neither French nor English allow. Only the Russian language possesses a somewhat greater creative, formative capacity, indicating the future mission of that language. However, one has to wrest, consciously and determinedly, new expression from the Spirit of German, in the same way that Anthroposophy must also be won by the thinking "I." This is particularly apparent in Steiner's mantric verses, from his *Calendar of the Soul*, through the Mystery Plays, to the mantras that form part of the meditative path of the Michael School. It is no mere chance that Anthroposophy's creative texts, especially the most profound, have appeared in the world in the garment of the German language. Likewise, it was not accidental that Homer's great epics arose in the Greek language, nor that Dante's *Divine Comedy* was written in Italian. It is clear from this that knowledge of the German language can, without doubt, *make it easier* for people to understand Anthroposophy, and will do so in future as well.

George Adams-Kaufmann, the gifted, brilliant translator of Rudolf Steiner's lectures in England, wrote in his memoirs that almost all the meditations that Steiner gave his pupils were in German, and added,

> ...many of them [his pupils], while they could scarcely speak or even understand the language in trivial and profane intercourse, became at home in it as a medium of Spiritual Science and above all, of meditation. This experience accords with what Dr. Steiner himself foresaw—namely, the possibility of German becoming to some extent a universal language, not for external intercourse, but as a vehicle of spiritual life, as other languages—Sanskrit, Greek, and Hebrew, for example—have been in earlier times. At one of the conferences held in Dornach late into the night during the time of the "Threefold" movement, I heard him speak to this effect...

---

47 December 18, 1916, *The Karma of Untruthfulness*, vol. 1, CW 173.

Adams continues, "...though if I understood him rightly, the possibility was contingent upon historic events that are to this day undecided; moreover, if fulfilled, it would mean rather a sacrifice of life for the German nation than any access of external greatness."[48]

No doubt these are important future perspectives in regard to Anthroposophy's further spread over the coming centuries. People today, whatever their mother tongue, take it as self-evident that international air traffic and global commerce are conducted in English. Yet, a time might come when acquiring at least a few basic elements of the *language of the Spirit's flight* will be regarded as equally self-evident for meditation and for easier, fuller engagement with the substance of Anthroposophy. Wouldn't that be a better idea than laboring over various surrogate versions of the original and wondering which is better? Perhaps the future here will lie with dual-language editions of Steiner's work. But such means will become possible only once a study of history that accords with the Spirit has come to show that the true, spiritual nature of German culture—as exemplified in Fichte through to Steiner—can no longer be associated or even confused with the shadow side of Germany and its abysmal deeds. Once the true German Spirit is recognized in its indissoluble connection with Anthroposophy, the German language will also come to be valued as being especially appropriate for serving both.

The Vessel of the Anthroposophic Movement in the Future

The anthroposophic movement of the future will need a vessel in the form of a Society capable of harmonizing the involuntary and evolutionary processes of anthroposophic activity that were disrupted during the twentieth century. This can come about only through authentic "creation out of nothing" or, in other words, through genuinely free deeds. Such a vessel was already envisaged by D. N. Dunlop when he wrote to his younger friend and colleague Walter J. Stein, after the latter emigrated

---

48 George Adams, "Rudolf Steiner in England," found in *Rudolf Steiner: Recollections by Some of his Pupils*, The Golden Blade, 1958, p 13; also *Wir erlebten Rudolf Steiner* (ed. K. v. Poturzyn), Stuttgart 1957, p. 22.

from Nazi Germany to England in 1932. In a letter written seven years after Steiner's death, he suggested the need to reflect on a future perspective for the Society. At the time Dunlop wrote this letter, he was General Secretary of the British branch of the Society, and in that office did everything possible to nurture the Society in England. However, with growing concern he could also see how the Dornach Society was increasingly heading down a sectarian cul-de-sac, with inevitable negative repercussions for the way Anthroposophy was represented in the world. This was the period of ever more militant conflicts in the Society, which led to the expulsions of 1935 in which he, too, was caught up. On June 16, 1932, Dunlop wrote the following:

Dear Dr. Stein
    I feel very strongly that an effort should be made during the next year or two to form an
*International Association
for the
Advancement of Spiritual Science.*

A preliminary prospectus should be prepared to circulate widely in all countries, and when the foundation is laid a Conference should be called. This should be guided and controlled by Anthroposophists who feel the call and the need of humanity everywhere, and who feel how inadequate the General Anthroposophical Society (as it is now controlled from Dornach) has become.

Will you think about it and see if you can get the impulse for a preliminary prospectus and we can speak of it when we meet in London. Greetings,
        Yours,
        D. N. Dunlop

No such prospectus has been found, and nothing further is known about this project. Three years later, the initiative came to an end in practical terms with the expulsions and Dunlop's death soon after.

Nevertheless, the seed, formed in deep concern about the further development of Anthroposophy, did not die. It continued ripening through all the upheavals, and we will need to cultivate it in the future. We should reflect that this was not an impulse *against* the Anthroposophical Society, involving any kind of personal ambition. D. N. Dunlop was simply too great for that. Instead it was a seed, developed from insight into the current situation, for saving and preserving the anthroposophic impulse far into the future. The Society of those days did not save it, nor can it be fully saved by today's Society. While it is true that, in the last two decades, much has been said in the Society about openness to the world, and worthwhile global activities have indeed been undertaken, nevertheless certain sectarian esoteric tendencies continue to operate undiminished. The most primitive opposition to Steiner and his work has been met for many years with a misguided and supposedly "Christian" stance, or even with blindness to reality.

The International Association for the Advancement of Spiritual Science, which Dunlop considered necessary, will have the function of including and encompassing the best parts of the Society along with people from quite different movements: everyone, in fact, who truly connects with Anthroposophy. It might well even bear a quite different name.

We Still Have Four Hundred Years

Anthroposophy has come to all humanity as a new light of the spirit, not just to a group of the "elect." It is the Michael-Christ message *for our time*. The way it spreads can accord with human dignity and its own true nature if it finds people who want something more and different than the Pharisees to whom Christ, speaking of their stance toward his forerunner John, said in the temple, "He was the light, burning and shining, and you wanted nothing more than to bask for a while in this light" (John 5:35). Rudolf Steiner, the originator of Anthroposophy, was similarly a preparer of the way.

In an esoteric lesson of February 12, 1911, Steiner made a significant comment about the future period during which Anthroposophy—then still called "Theosophy"—can still spread to all humanity. Compared to the great evolutionary epochs of human history, this is a relatively short span of time. He said:

Since November 1879, a small handful of people have grown mature enough to take up the teachings of Theosophy. This remains just a small flock so far, while other people in modern times are as yet incapable of appropriating teachings, which they regard as empty musings or fantasies, or which even anger them.... We still have roughly 400 years left when we can make these teachings accessible to all people in the form of Theosophy. And so that everyone will have an opportunity for this, those who have rejected these teachings in their current incarnation will be born again within the next 400 years. *However, for this to happen a group must exist who represent Theosophy in the right way.*[49]

This period clearly extends through the whole Michael era, lasting around 350 years, which will be succeeded by the Age of Oriphiel in 2230. About thirty years had passed since the beginning of the Michael Age when Steiner made this statement.

Thus, Anthroposophy can continue to take effect in the world, or be renewed, roughly until the end of the Michael Age. It will be of greatest importance during this Michael era that a second, strong wave of anthroposophic work is prepared, unburdened by the false processes of involution and evolution at work in the previous theosophical-anthroposophic movement. It is only during a Michael Age that spiritual *cosmopolitanism* can come into its own.

Now I would like to outline briefly how a certain tendency of this second wave of the anthroposophic movement might be prepared.

A New Experience of the Seasons

The future renewal of worldwide anthroposophic work will include the need to take up an impulse that so far has existed only in germinal form: the creation of new, seasonal festivals to help human beings increasingly experience the etheric Christ, who can be found today in seasonal processes and in the whole cycle of the seasons. Friedrich Rittelmeyer once asked Rudolf Steiner, "What can one do to prepare for Damascus-type

---

49 Rudolf Steiner, *Esoteric Lessons: 1910–1912*, CW 266/2 (author's italics).

experiences of Christ?" Steiner replied, "This is possible only by experiencing Christ in the cycle of the seasons."[50]

However, the cycle of the seasons takes place in polar opposite ways in the northern and southern hemispheres. During the year's process of evolution in the northern hemisphere, the antipodes are involved in the process of involution, and *vice versa*. The very first edition of the *Calendar of the Soul*, published in 1912, takes account of this polarity with a dual assignment of the 26 letters of the alphabet to each of the 26 weekly verses. For instance, when the Easter verse "A" begins our meditative experience of the seasons in the northern hemisphere, this corresponds to contemplation of the corresponding or counterpart verse "A'" in the southern hemisphere, and so forth.

By meditating *simultaneously* on one verse and its counterpart we can live our way into the dual stream of time, knowledge of which was of such key importance to the nineteen-year-old Steiner. In this way, a polar sense of natural processes, where the etheric, cosmic Christ is today at work, can awaken within us a relation to the whole globe.

It is clear that Steiner's answer to Rittelmeyer also applies to an experience of the polar opposite seasons in the southern hemisphere. While the historic Christ entered the "stream of earthly being" at a particular point in the northern hemisphere, his reappearance since the 1930s of the last century is taking place in the natural processes of *both* hemispheres.[51]

The Foundation Stones for the Mystery Centers of the Future

In a world where such global Christian sensibility can arise, new Mystery centers can also emerge throughout the world from the Foundation Stones enshrined in the hearts of individual human beings. These Foundation Stones are nothing other than images living in each human soul of the meditation that Steiner laid into the hearts and souls of those present during the "ideal, spiritual founding" of the new Society and the new building

---

50 F. Rittelmeyer, unpublished notebooks, Perseus Verlag archive.
51 Cf, articles by G. Aschoff, G. Suwelack and A. Anderson in *Der Europäer*, year 16, Feb. to June 2012.

in 1923. The first "builders" were the present members at the time, to whom he said, at the end of the Christmas Foundation Meeting and only a few hours after an attempt to poison him:

> Carry into the world your warm hearts where you have embedded the Foundation Stone for the Anthroposophical Society. Carry these warm hearts into the world to work there with energetic healing power. And help will come to you, so that what you would direct with single purpose can illumine your heads. Let us undertake this today, with all the strength we can muster.... *If we prove ourselves worthy of this, a good star will shine over the will that is kindled here.* My dear friends, follow this good star.[52]

The history of the anthroposophic movement and Society after Steiner's death soon revealed developments wholly *unworthy* of these original aims. However, since 1935, the "good star" has shone over *all* whose endeavors are in harmony with the Foundation Stone meditation, whether they are members of the Society or not. This is because since then, the Goetheanum is "wherever people work esoterically as Rudolf Steiner intended," as Ludwig Polzer-Hoditz wrote in December 1935. In the penultimate sentence he spoke at the Christmas Foundation conference, Steiner had already tied the sway of a good star over the Society and Goetheanum building to a clear *"if."* Only when we harbor illusions can we see developments after Steiner's death as being adequate fulfillment of this *"if."* Polzer-Hoditz drew the consequences of this in his Michaelic speech during the 1935 Annual Meeting, saying:

> The Foundation Stones that rest in strong hearts are no longer tied to a particular location and a single building. They must become the Foundation Stones for the Mystery centers of the future at diverse locations. Those who will sow the seeds for these Mystery centers can only be called to do so by their destiny, directly by the spiritual world.

---

52 Jan. 1, 1924, *The Christmas Conference for the Founding of the General Anthroposophical Society,* CW 260. Also published as *The Foundation Stone*. Author's emphasis.

Helmuth von Moltke, an individual significant for both the past and future of European developments, was not a member either of the Theosophical or the Anthroposophical Society. He enshrined this Foundation Stone in his soul just a few years after his death—in 1916, at the Uriel season. On January 13, 1924, the Moltke individuality gave from the spiritual world a kind of esoteric commentary on the Foundation Stone meditation from the Christmas Conference, which was witnessed by his still living wife:

> There "she" sits in the Goetheanum. Often "her" thoughts are such that my soul can be present with her. Yes, if only this were heard: "Practice spirit remembering," "Practice spirit awareness," "Practice spirit beholding." But human beings will only hear it when the Michael Spirit succeeds in finding in the astral light the trails leading to the spirit altar where the astral flame burns that Ahriman fears. No doubt this will take until the end of the century. For, as yet, the eyes are not there that could perceive the Christ walking in the ether light. Eyes filled with the divisiveness at work in humanity will not be able to have such vision.[53]

The end of the twentieth century has already passed and we stand at the beginning of the third millennium. Many Foundation Stones will be needed to establish the Mystery centers of the future. Despite all diversity, these will have two founding impulses in common: knowledge that the new working of Christ penetrates the whole earth, and all humanity that it sustains, and the knowledge that Rudolf Steiner's Anthroposophy is the most effective means of serving this new Christ impulse.

---

53 Thomas Meyer, *Moltke*, vol. 2, p. 291. This communication was received on the day when the Foundation Stone meditation appeared in the members' newsletter.

Appendix 1

A Chronology of Relevant Events

Only dates especially relevant to this volume have been included in this timeline.

1861   February 27: Birth of Rudolf Steiner

1868   Clairvoyant experience in the waiting room at Pottschach

1875   November 17: Founding of the Theosophical Society in New York

1879   Autumn: Encounter with the "unknown master" and with Karl Julius Schroer.

      Rudolf Steiner passes through his first moon node

      November: The Michael Age begins

1881   January 10/11: Birth of the "I"

1888   Summer: Meets Fercher von Steinwand

      November 9: Wilhelm Neumann utters the words "Thomas Aquinas"

1889   End of January: Seemingly out of the blue, Schroer exclaims "Nero!"

      Beginning of the Weimar period and work on Goethe, until 1897

1899   February 19: End of Kali Yuga

      Tumultuous spiritual experiences around the turn of the century: Steiner stands inwardly before the Mystery of Golgotha

1900   Winter: In Berlin, Marie von Sivers first hears a lecture by Rudolf Steiner

1901   November 17: Marie von Sivers asks about an esotericism suited to the West

1902   First conversation between Ita Wegman and Rudolf Steiner

	October 20: Rudolf Steiner becomes General Secretary of the German Section of the Theosophical Society
1907	Whitsun: Munich Congress. Decisive conversation with Ita Wegman.
	Performance of Schuré's Play about Eleusis. Artistic impulse, Rosicrucianism
	Esoteric revelation in Barr, 28 years after he met the "Master"
1909	Works on *Occult Science*, which is published 28 years following birth of the "I"
1912	December 28: Founding of the Anthroposophical Society in Cologne. Steiner is not a member of it, only a teacher
1913	February 4: Autobiographical lecture at the Annual Meeting in Berlin
	September 20: Laying of the foundation stone of the first Goetheanum building in Dornach
1914	June 28: Lecture on architecture on the day of the Sarajevo assassination
1916	June 18: The death of Helmuth von Moltke. The beginning of his post-mortem communications
1917	July: First discussions on threefolding with Count Otto Lerchenfeld, Ludwig Polzer-Hoditz, and Walter Johannes Stein in Berlin
1918	November 9: Abdication of Wilhelm II. Germany becomes a Republic
1919	June 1: Five-hour discussion with Wilhelm von Dommes. Moltke's pamphlet is pulped
1920	September 26: First gathering in the first Goetheanum
	September 27: Start of the first School of Spiritual Science course
1922	May 15: Lecture in Munich disrupted by right-wing extremists. Fercher von Steinwand appears to Steiner in spiritual form
	December 31: The first Goetheanum is destroyed by fire
1923	November 17: Steiner makes the decision to re-found the GAS under his leadership, following a request from Ita Wegman at a conference in The Hague
	November 18: Founding of the Dutch Society

A Chronology of Relevant Events

	December 24: The Christmas Foundation Conference begins with three ritual knocks
1924	January 1: Attempt to poison Steiner, at around 5 p.m.
	September 28: Steiner's last address
1925	March 30: Steiner dies at 10 a.m.
1935	April 14: Dornach Easter Annual Meeting; expulsion of Ita Wegman, Elisabeth Vreede, and the English and Dutch branches of the Society
	Speech by Ludwig Polzer-Hoditz
	May 30: D. N. Dunlop dies
	November 1: The German branch of the General Anthroposophical Society is banned in Germany
	November 17: The three-member executive board of the General Anthroposophical Society (M. Steiner, G. Wachsmuth, A. Steffen) sends letter to Adolf Hitler seeking annulment of the order dissolving the German Anthroposophical Society.
1936	May 30: Ludwig Polzer-Hoditz resigns from the Society
1943	March 4: Ita Wegman dies
	August 31: Elisabeth Vreede dies
1945	October 13: Ludwig Polzer-Hoditz dies
	October: The Stuttgart Waldorf School reopens
1948	Spring Annual Meeting: Marie Steiner states that the expulsions of 1935 were a mistake
	December 27: Marie Steiner dies
1952	June 17: Solothurn Supreme Court recognizes the Estate Association (Rudolf Steiner Estate Administration) founded by Marie Steiner; this verdict is not accepted by Albert Steffen and Guenther Wachsmuth; the Society boycotts books published by the Estate
1960	Easter: Willem Zeylmans von Emmichoven re-affiliates the Dutch Society with the General Anthroposophical Society
1961	Centenary of Rudolf Steiner's birth. Anthroposophical authors publish assessments of his life and work

1961	November 18: Willem Zeylmans dies
1963	March 2: Guenther Wachsmuth dies
	March 30: George Adams-Kaufmann dies
	July 13: Albert Steffen dies
1968	For the first time, books published by the Estate Administration are allowed to be sold at the Goetheanum
1976	Rudolf Grosse's book *The Christmas Foundation Meeting as Start of a New Era* is published; also the book by Margarete and Erich Kirchner-Bockholt entitled "Rudolf Steiner's Task for Humanity and Ita Wegman," the latter 33 years after Ita Wegman's death
1993	February 23: In advertisements published in the press, the executive board of the Dutch Society distances itself from any possible "racial doctrines in Steiner's work."
	Michaelmas: Experiment of a "Second Class" with annual themes leading up to 2000 ("The Mystery of Freedom")
1995	February/March: The "Chantilly experiment"
2000	January: Opponents accuse Steiner of racism in the Foundation Stone Hall
	The Society is said to be in "occult imprisonment"
2003	January: The Society is entered in the Swiss companies' register as the General Anthroposophical Society (Christmas Foundation Meeting)
2005	May: The supplementary designation "Christmas Foundation Meeting" has to be removed again following a decision by Solothurn Supreme Court. The Society must be re-registered under its old name
2011	150th anniversary of Rudolf Steiner's birth. Opponents write biographies of Steiner and his work, which are welcomed as a positive development by many members and some members of the Society's executive board
2086	Golden age of domed buildings in Europe
2230	End of the Michael Age; beginning of the Age of Oriphiel

Appendix 2

THE "MEMORANDUM"

Concerns in the Anthroposophical Society, 1925–1935

Between 1980 and 1991, for the purposes of this present study and as part of a documented biography of Ita Wegman, I made a close examination of the following publication drafted by Gunther Schubert, scrutinizing both its historical accuracy and its method of presentation. The observations I made during this process lead me to refrain from portraying the text in any particular light, as I prefer to leave readers free to judge it for themselves. The appended pieces by W. Zeylmans, L. Polzer, and O. Schmiedel contain replies, refutations, and commentaries in response to this "Memorandum." These people, who actually witnessed the events in question, have a major contribution to make to an assessment of the work's truthfulness and method of presentation. Lilly Kolisko characterized it in 1961, in her book Eugen Kolisko: Ein Lebensbild *[Eugen Kolisko: A Biography]. The "Memorandum" appeared on time, three weeks before the Anthroposophical Society's Annual General Meeting of April 14, 1935 (in the week beginning March 25 and not, as appears on the title page, February 1935), and was available for purchase in the Goetheanum and from the book tables of anthroposophic groups throughout the world. The 2,000 or so members expelled in 1935—"a bare tenth of the total membership") were dismayed to learn of this book. These people, however, were unable to respond publicly to it, because the* Newssheet *of the General Anthroposophical Society no longer accepted their contributions. Other people unaffected by the expulsions also protested against the "Memorandum." However, its perfidious method of presentation was hard to see through, even by those who had considerable powers of judgment. As an example, I will quote a letter Friedrich Rittelmeyer wrote to Albert Steffen on April 10, 1935.*

Dear Albert Steffen

Stuttgart, April 10, 1935

You are no doubt aware of the reason for my letter to you today. I would like to preface it by saying that I am not involved in any move to "mediate" in this matter. If my name is mentioned in any such context, it is without my consent. As far as I can see my only option in this affair is to turn directly to you.

The Memorandum of the twelve lies before me. It presents a shocking picture as it stands. There is a good deal that I myself did not experience. If this is all true, for example in regard to Dr. Wegman, then it represents a truly sad episode in the history of the Anthroposophical Society and the anthroposophic movement. I did witness some of what is described, for example her defense in the Einsingen matter in 1930, which made a very unfavorable impression on me. On this occasion, whether intentionally or more instinctively, she blurred the truth, failing to sense her responsibility or perceive the seriousness of the situation. After witnessing this I can fill in the rest of the details for myself.

I must say that in all these years I had little contact with Frau Wegman. In 1925, after the death of Dr. Steiner, I initially looked to her as the person whom one should respect and support in matters connected with the Class Lessons. At that time I also spoke with Frau Dr. Steiner, who—I can remember her words exactly—expressed a similar expectant and self-restrained attitude. After the "Leading Thoughts" (*Leitsätze*) appeared, and the Class Lessons were held without the consent of the whole *Vorstand* [executive board], I went to Frau Wegman and held a first conversation with her, which was in fact the only one we had relating to decisive Society matters. In that conversation I told her that I could not agree with what she was doing, and in particular that the only esotericism possible was one that proceeded from the will of the whole *Vorstand*. I advised her to hold herself back from these things for a few years, for if the guiding powers really intended to entrust her with them, they would find a way of arranging it. The errors of judgment that had been made now meant that she should restrain herself, I said. She did not agree. In subsequent years

I repeatedly told her friends that, if forced to choose between Frau Dr. Steiner and Dr. Wegman, I would not hesitate for a moment. My objective choice would come down on the side of Frau Dr. Steiner.

I can say all this since my position in Dornach, as far as I can see at the moment, has not always been judged correctly. I am completely free, and basically alone and independent.

Yet I have to say that when I examine the Memorandum, I find it slanted in respect to all the matters that I myself experienced in a way that will give members a false impression. I will only refer to passages where my name is mentioned, of which I feel most competent to speak—not because I wish to emphasize the importance of my personal involvement, but because it is in these matters that I have the greatest right and duty to express a view.

1. First a small detail. On page 134 [194], it says in parentheses: "Dr. Rittelmeyer however agreed that criticism of the Hanover conference was justified." The truth is that on learning about it—for I am not told about every local event—I immediately wrote to the Dornach *Vorstand* to say that such a matter could not be condoned if it really had occurred as described to me. It was not necessary to force an "acceptance" from me. Neither was it a Christian Community conference, but rather a course held chiefly for female welfare workers, with possible attendance by Christian Community members, at which Bock spoke from a pastoral care perspective. A quite false impression is created by saying this was a "conference" of the Hanover Christian Community, "in which lectures were held exclusively on themes such as sexuality, crime, drugs, and so on." Although the Memorandum does not accuse either me or the Christian Community, its method of presentation should still stick to the truth in such matters. It would inspire more confidence if it did.

2. Page 68 [123] mentions events in the German executive council following Dr. Unger's death. At the time, Herr Leinhas talked at length about the fact that Dr. Unger had made his remaining in the German executive council after Stein had left conditional upon there being no one else who shared Dr. Stein's view about [Rudolf Steiner's] will and testament. In

the first *Vorstand* meeting after Unger's death, we spoke above all about how we might fulfill this, Dr. Unger's legacy, even after his death. One after another we declared that we actually did not share this discredited view, and communicated this fact to everyone in the German branches, initially offering our resignation to the Dornach *Vorstand*, and only continuing with the running of administrative affairs. Dornach then accepted and officially recognized us. Yet on page 68 [240] one reads, "His sudden death, though, provided a pretext for speaking of the need for "restructuring the German executive council.... This reorganization consisted only in no longer having to take account of the view represented by Dr. Unger, giving free rein instead to the influence of Dr. Kolisko." This is the opposite of the truth. I must object to it in the strongest terms, inasmuch as it applies to me. It is nonsense to say that we were all under the sway of Dr. Kolisko—an extraordinary idea to suggest about people like Leinhas, Dr. Palmer, and me, all older than Kolisko, and longer-serving members of the Society, who had their own anthroposophic conscience! People who were not there have taken it upon themselves to describe what happened! In fact, to ensure that we acted in Dr. Unger's interests, we elected Dr. Piper and Stockmeyer to join us. No mention is made of that. All those involved will strongly object to being described in these terms.

3. Page 47f [100f] mentions the "Declaration." On page 51 [104], it says, "Details of the origin and writing of the Declaration have never been fully cleared up, since they were shrouded in darkness and secrecy in a way very similar to that surrounding the earlier founding of the World School Association, and the subsequent writing of the 'Statement of Intent.'"

The truth is that I gave a full and detailed description of the origin of the Declaration at the Extraordinary General Meeting of the German Society on April 6, 1927, in Stuttgart, before roughly a thousand members, and in the presence of Frau Dr. Steiner and Dr. Poppelbaum. So much for the "darkness and secrecy" in which these things were intentionally "shrouded." The wording was mainly by me, and came about in the following way. On several occasions Dr. Stein attempted to get me to make a statement of some kind about Arenson. I refused. Finally I said to him:

The "Memorandum"

"I am more concerned that you should behave properly. Let me give you a few points to consider that might ensure that your behavior has a beneficial influence. You can then pass this on to your friends and discuss it with them." He asked to be allowed to take it down in shorthand, and I had nothing against this. This is how the three points on page 53 [106f] came about. After some time Dr. Stein came to see me again to say that his friends were in agreement with my points, and to ask whether one could not make a general declaration out of them. I replied that even though the points had, of course, expressed my true opinion, I could only participate in such a declaration if signatures were gathered from the whole society and not just from one group, and above all if Dr. Unger and Leinhas were told about it, and asked for their signatures. This was agreed. Since I wanted to avoid things taking a wrong turn, I gave my friend Werner Klein, in the presence of Herr von Grone, the task of seeing that everything was conducted properly and satisfactorily. I myself had to leave then, to keep a lecturing appointment. Unfortunately, Werner Klein did not see things through properly, and perhaps I should have realized this would happen.

When the "Declaration" appeared some days later, the signatories were almost solely from the Wegman group. When I asked about this, I was told that people had made efforts to get other signatures, but had been unable to obtain them. Leinhas was away at the time and therefore unavailable. Dr. Unger had been asked but in quite the wrong way. Under these circumstances Michael Bauer and I should have been allowed to retract our signatures. Later I often told the signatories that this had made it extraordinarily difficult for me ever to put in a word for them in future. I did, though, whenever I could with good conscience. In the German executive council we discussed all this very thoroughly, and with Herr Leinhas as well, who had attacked me so stridently in public. After this discussion, all of us, including Dr. Unger, decided that we must work together in spite of these events, and must try to surmount the gaping discrepancies between us by finding common ground in Anthroposophy.

Given the atmosphere of distrust that so strongly prevailed, it was easy for the "Declaration" to be seen in a different light from that originally intended. Yet even the very first sentence—for example, where it says, "views have been expressed about Dr. Steiner's life and work continuing"—has nothing whatever to do with Frau Dr. Steiner and Arenson, but applies much more to the other circle. This sentence, "Even if we ourselves have given rise to something that is in opposition to the view presented here, we must condemn it," was expressly added by me to lay an obligation upon Dr. Stein. I said to him at the time that if he signed it he must keep to it, as well.

Even if I admit that the way it was launched left the Declaration open to another interpretation, I still find it painful that, without any mention of my explanations, the following passage by Frau Dr. Steiner—which clearly refers to me—has now been fixed for posterity: "The 'clarifications' and 'admonitions'... have been written in blindness, and can only be excused, if at all, perhaps, as a well-meaning attempt to intervene where accusations are loudest by someone unfamiliar with the actual facts and their origin, who has been subject to a certain influence."

Now read, please, what it says on page 52 [106] of the Memorandum: "The insincere... assertion that views about Dr. Steiner's continuing life and work have been propounded, whereas in fact such views have only surfaced in the authors' own circle.

The whole thing was nothing other than an attack on the supposed power-lust of Frau Dr. Steiner, and on Herr Dr. Steffen.... It was a declaration with a purely Alexandrian slant..." and so on. Such things really ought not to be possible after the public explanations that were given in good faith at the time.

I also consider it absolutely unacceptable that all sorts of judgments were made about the Declaration before it was ever circulated, which naturally prevented anyone from forming an unprejudiced opinion about it. Reading between the lines [of the Memorandum], it is fairly clear that there is not much to object to in the [Declaration's] wording. Yet the signatories—and I must say this for the sake of truth, even if I was the one who suffered most from the affair, and, like Michael Bauer, may appear to many as a well-meaning dupe—never intended it, either consciously or unconsciously, to be viewed in the way it is now represented.

I have had to go into some detail on these few points, and ought perhaps to add still more details. For instance my memory of the General Secretaries meetings, which I myself attended, is in many respects quite different from the way they are described here—described, mind you, by people who for the most part were not present. Most important of all, much else occurred [which is not mentioned]. If one is going to tell all sorts of stories about one side, such as remarks made by unnamed persons, let me say that I remember hearing extremely odd things on the other side, which, for the time being, I do not care to mention here. There is also a great deal I might say about the battle waged against the old German executive council, which would radically alter the picture presented in the Memorandum.

Nevertheless, for the sake of brevity I must limit myself to dealing with the three points that no one can dispute my right to discuss and toward which I feel a particularly strong historical obligation.

Can you blame me, my dear Herr Steffen, for having the greatest reservations about the Memorandum, if those aspects of it I am in a position to assess are of such a nature? Can you blame me if I regard a bias of this kind within the Society—shortly before the Annual General meeting—as an improper basis for taking such far-reaching, fateful decisions? Can you blame me if I am unable to regard the authors of the Memorandum themselves as objective enough to see and discover the truth? As someone who is in a position to form a judgment about what occurred, I have to reject the historical validity of the Memorandum, and regard it as a misfortune for the Society. I agree that Kolisko's errors—of which I am well aware and about which I have spoken to him quite openly more than once—must be met with the greatest severity, as long as the mistakes and offenses of his opponents are treated with similar justice and openness. Is that really the case? The Memorandum no doubt contains a great deal that is accurate, but presents it in such a way that these opponents are seen in far too favorable a light, which will just make them talk all the more. That is what will really damage the Society. Less in Dornach perhaps, but certainly in the public arena.

The Memorandum is what I have closest to hand. Under these circumstances I definitely do not wish to make specific proposals for the Annual General Meeting. I would then have to stand up for them personally, which I am unable to do. However, let me say the following, my dear Herr Steffen, so that you at least are in no doubt about my position:

1. I recognize that the Society must protect itself against Anthroposophical Society membership cards being issued without the approval of the *Vorstand*. If the "free anthroposophic groups" demand that such membership cards are accepted as valid at the Goetheanum, they are demanding something impossible.

2. I recognize that *Vorstand* members must be able to work together. If they are unable to, for whatever reasons, ways must be found to create a *Vorstand* whose members can work together, which can really lead the Society and guide its important tasks. This is why I was, and am, prepared to recognize the *Vorstand* composed of three members as the *Vorstand* of the General Anthroposophical Society, which does not mean, however, that I am necessarily in agreement with all of its measures.

3. Anything that goes beyond the scope of these absolute necessities for the life of the Society should, in my opinion be avoided. In particular, I do not find in that part of the Memorandum that makes a positive impression on me any compelling reason to exclude members from the Society whom Rudolf Steiner himself both recommended and commended to our care, who for their part are earnestly committed to Anthroposophy. As far as I can judge, their departure would damage the whole anthroposophic movement so severely that it might well be unable to fulfill its task for humanity. It is therefore my fervent wish that ways and means be found to avoid this.

This is neither weakness nor softness on my part. Nor is it misguided humanitarianism or false tolerance. Since I feel quite alone in this matter, and neither have nor seek a single ally, it would be far easier for me just to keep quiet. I am compelled to speak out, though, by my conviction that this moment is of decisive importance for the fate of Anthroposophy.

The "Memorandum"

This letter is not intended for public consumption by the members of the Anthroposophical Society. I see no other possibility, dear Herr Steffen, than to turn to you personally. May you succeed, in this dark hour, in finding the right way forward!

With heartfelt greetings
Friedrich Rittelmeyer

One can see from this letter (which, incidentally, contains some noteworthy turns of phrase) that even someone such as Rittelmeyer was not aware at the time that the Memorandum actually derived from the intentions and views of Steffen and Marie Steiner. He recognizes the new "Vorstand composed of three members" and, at the same time, expresses the view that expulsions should be avoided. The Memorandum and the effect it created on April 14, 1935—grounds that it provided for the exclusion of roughly two thousand members from the General Anthroposophical Society—have since then remained a taboo subject in the annals of this Society. Emil Leinhas gives an accurate picture of the effect of these events of 1935 in his 1940 obituary for Eugen Kolisko, writing that the Anthroposophical Society gradually gave up all serious attempts to realize its mission of working for a comprehensive renewal of culture.[1] Since the Memorandum has continued to exert a considerable influence on people's judgments about Ita Wegman right up to the present day, it is necessary for all who wish to examine the basis of their judgments to make a thorough study of it.

E. Zeylmans

---

1   Cf. Eugen Kolisko, "Bilder aus seinem Leben und Wirken," Stuttgart, March 1940, p. 41f, vol. 8 of the series *Pioniere der Anthroposophie: Eugen Kolisko, Auf der Suche nach neuen Wahrheiten*, Dornach, 1989, which prints most of the obituaries from the 1940 commemorative book, omits Leinhas's contribution about Kolisko.

Memorandum

Matters of Concern in the Anthroposophical Society, 1925 to 1935

Printed as manuscript for members of the Anthroposophical Society only and submitted to them by

Dr. C. Bessenich
Paul Bühler
Dr. E. O. Eckstein
C. Englert-Faye
Dr. Otto Frankl
Dr. Emil Grosheintz
Ehrenfried Pfeiffer
Dr. Hermann Poppelbaum
Paul Eugen Schiller
Gunther Schubert
Dr. Richard Schubert
Jan Stuten
Dornach, Switzerland
February 1935
All manuscript rights reserved;
Reproduction of individual passages also strictly prohibited [page 2]

Preface

In what follows the reader will find a description of events that have been of fundamental significance for the way that the General Anthroposophical Society conducts its affairs. Difficult problems, which surfaced from 1925 onward, have been provisionally resolved since the Annual General Meeting of 1934, where it was acknowledged that decisions jointly made by the three *Vorstand* members, Herr Steffen, Frau Dr. Steiner, and Herr Wachsmuth, are binding for the Society. Much occurred prior to this measure that justified taking such a step, and anyone who tries to understand these things would wish to be able to look back at what happened and examine it closely. It is therefore quite understandable that many who knew either little or nothing of former events should express the wish for a clear, consistent account of what occurred in the Society after Rudolf Steiner's death.

It was an awareness of this need that, last summer already, led several colleagues at the Goetheanum to try to draw up such an account, so as to help clarify the present situation. Herr Dr. Poppelbaum joined this initiative, since people had often asked him to write a report of this kind.[2] That is how the account contained in the following pages came about. A few colleagues first made a written draft, which, at a series of joint meetings, was expanded into its present form.

It was no easy task to work through the available material. In addition, the nature of the events was such that not everything had been recorded in writing. It also frequently happened that the moods, feelings, and divergent opinions of different groups of members exacerbated the whole situation, which therefore remains difficult to understand for those who were not present.

It is difficult to give an account of things that, still to this day, remain painful and often enough shameful. Our task, which truly gave no pleasure to anyone, was made more difficult by the fact that there are groups of people who not only consider it unnecessary to bring up the past, but who are immediately suspicious of anyone who dares suggest that present effects are rooted in past causes.

It is characteristic of the present situation that people have found it necessary to argue about whether the history of the last ten years ought to be spoken about or not. If, as some claim, looking back at past events is really so unimportant for judging the current situation, members might surely be allowed to form their own views on whether to do so or not. However, to be sure that the past is finished and done with, it is essential

---

2   He did present an initial, short report, and at the same time worked on this Memorandum with the others.

to be sufficiently aware of the facts, and in many quarters this is far from the case. Why should people not be allowed to know these facts? A great deal of damage has already been done because members were not properly informed, and even—supposedly to safeguard the positivity of their outlook and work—wished to be left in the dark. Yet this did not stop them playing a part in decisions upon which they could bring no personal insight to bear, simply trusting blindly in the authority of others.

Facts can be ascertained and opinions can be formed about them. There will be different opinions about the same facts, and no one disputes the right of individuals to stand up for their own honest convictions. However, an opinion has value only if it is based on actual facts. What is truly cause for concern is when the facts themselves are distorted and that distortion forms the basis for opinions. This may indeed stir up dissent and rebellion, but hardly allows people to find any common ground with those who see things differently from them. The so-called Statement of Intent showed this clearly.

Goethe coined a phrase that may sum up our efforts in producing this account of important events of the last decade: "I can promise to be honest and upright, but not to be impartial." This document arose in circumstances in which everything now depends on having the will to realize and implement what one sees as right. The demands of impartiality will indeed be fulfilled if we keep our promise to be honest and sincere. If anyone should describe this Memorandum as a polemical treatise, a call to battle, we could raise no objections: it does not deal with a dead past but with events whose consequences are still doing harm to the life of our Society.

It must also be born in mind that this Memorandum does not in the least set out to be a "history of the Anthroposophical Society." It deals only with the most unpleasant chapters of this history. The shadows cast should not alarm us, nor induce us to regard everything as hopeless. On the contrary, in spite of the appalling difficulties, people were able to continue working; their strength did not fail. Not only does the Goetheanum still stand, but in the unbroken succession of major conferences held there, every last seat is filled. Inasmuch as the future depends on inner conditions, it will always be assured as long as we build upon the foundations of truth. It lies within the freedom of each one of us to do so.

1925

The death of Rudolf Steiner was an immeasurable loss to the Anthroposophical Society, and inevitably threw up the question of how the Society would be led and managed in future. It would have been strange indeed if this central question had not assumed decisive importance for the Society's further development. At the same time it is easy to understand that fundamentally divergent answers to this question led to deepening disagreements, whose consequences could only grow more and more severe. If we can show that conflicts always focused on this point, and that the people involved were always the same ones, then we have something of a thread to which we can hold fast in guiding ourselves through the many confusing events of recent years. These events were mostly just the visible expression of those basic differences of opinion, which continually reignited the same old conflict again. All this began in the time immediately after Rudolf Steiner's death, and that first year needs to be described in more depth and detail than is necessary for subsequent years.

To begin with, most members were not too worried about how the Anthroposophical Society would be led. That Rudolf Steiner could no longer preside over its affairs, as he had done since the Christmas Foundation Meeting of 1923, was felt as a heavy blow of fate, as was the fact that no one was capable of continuing his immense life work. These people did not doubt that the *Vorstand* members, chosen by Dr. Steiner as his colleagues, would manage the Society as he would have wished, to the best of their ability. People's trust in the esoteric *Vorstand* ruled out any fear that the Society's future might be in jeopardy. They had, it is true, only hazy ideas about the esoteric nature of the *Vorstand*, but this itself strengthened their conviction that the right thing would be done. They expected *Vorstand* members to work together at the Goetheanum to draw up guidelines for ongoing work, and hoped to be able to channel and transform the enthusiasm that, in his last phase of activity, Rudolf Steiner had more than ever before engendered, into strength for carrying out this—now much more difficult—work. No one imagined that the members of the *Vorstand* would ever find it impossible to work together. It was only after many bitter experiences that people finally realized it was no longer even right to demand this cooperation. In later years, only members who knew nothing about what had gone on could possibly still demand it.

For other circles of members Rudolf Steiner's death had been equally painful, but they formed a different and very decided opinion about how the Society should be led in future. These circles also recognized the five-member *Vorstand* as the head of the Society, placing great emphasis on its esoteric character, but pointed out the distinction between leadership of the Society and leadership of the School of Spiritual Science. Rudolf Steiner himself had presided over the Society and the School of Spiritual Science. After his death the *Vorstand* took over leadership of the Society; and most members thought it should also lead the School of Spiritual Science—the heart of anthroposophic work, and, in particular, the place where esotericism would be nurtured and practiced. The other circles mentioned above, however, opposed this view, demanding that Frau Dr. Wegman should be recognized as leader of the School. The very way that they themselves granted this recognition showed that they regarded Frau Dr. Wegman as the real leader of the Society, even if she did not bear that official title. The special esteem in which they held her appeared, in their eyes, to give her the right to take important decisions by herself. The other *Vorstand* members were thus expected to subordinate themselves to a person regarded as the successor to Rudolf Steiner, and help to realize the aims set out by her. The actual course of events clearly demonstrates that certain members considered this a means by which they themselves could influence the aims of the Society.

In these circles, too, therefore, people looked forward to a harmonious cooperation between all the *Vorstand* members, not least because its very esoteric character was thought to imply an obligation to come to unanimous decisions about matters laid before it. In other matters, however, people felt they had the right to communicate only with the supposed leader of the School. When, as soon happened, this attitude met with resistance from some *Vorstand* members, and growing numbers within the Society itself, this was seen as evidence of their esoteric immaturity, lack of judgment, or even ill will.

Yet the real reasons for placing Frau Dr. Wegman on such a high pedestal were not actually based on this rather theoretical view of the relationship between Society and School, nor on the interpretation of certain statements by Dr. Steiner supposedly expressing his wish for Frau Dr. Wegman to assume a special position, and least of all on her demonstrable achievements. They actually lay elsewhere entirely. Some members, partly through their studies of lectures by Dr. Steiner, partly, they claimed, though their own karmic research, had come to a conviction that made a deep impression on certain others. They believed that the individuality of Alexander the Great, described by Dr. Steiner on many occasions and in particular at the 1923 Christmas Foundation Meeting, had incarnated among the members of the Society. Not only that, but all of Alexander's commanders were also thought to have appeared—as these same members conducting karmic research. Thus this circle regarded the question about the future leadership of the Society as settled, supposedly for the deepest esoteric reasons. Since Dr. Steiner had also spoken of the importance of this historical individuality for the life of spirit, these circles felt they could rest assured that, after Dr. Steiner's death, a second leader of the anthroposophic movement was active in the earthly realm.

The combination of this supposed reincarnation of so many of Alexander's former commanders with the so-called "esoteric appointments" that were thought to have come about through the 1923 Christmas Foundation Meeting gave rise to a quite particular attitude.[3] On the one hand, all actions and words of Frau Dr. Wegman and some of her colleagues were invested with infallibility, and, on the other, members were expected to fall in with and subordinate themselves to this, rather than forming their own reasoned judgments. The much-vaunted free life of the spirit,

---

3   Concrete examples are contained in accounts of the events of 1930.

when imbued by an esotericism of this kind, increasingly became belief in authority and dogmatism. This sect-like mood gave rise to the view that the esoteric leader did not need to give an account of herself for anything, and that the esotericists should be told only what they could understand, and what it was permissible for them to hear: "Important matters can only be discussed in an intimate circle." At all events, this led to a state of affairs in which the fiercest battles often had to be fought in the Society just to find out what was actually going on. It was hardly ever possible to gain complete clarity, for someone like Dr. Kolisko invariably stood up and said, "We are not on trial here. We object to such questioning." Such secrecy and intentional covering up of the facts were a major reason for the failure to find common ground. The greatest confusion was caused by facts being hidden, or only half-known, or twisted.

To find the cause of all the years of conflict we need to ask the following question: How was it possible that no general consultation took place, no shared view was sought, about a change in the Society as decisive as that brought about by Rudolf Steiner's death? The history of those first months supplies an answer. As the views already described demonstrate, some members thought things would sort themselves out, while others built up a dogmatism that was not open for discussion, and that instead sought allegiance from others. Of most critical significance was the fact that, before consultation and agreement ever took place, a state of affairs was created that made consultation impossible, and led to endless conflict instead of proper communication. The thoughts and intentions of each of the *Vorstand* members also became apparent in relationship to this state of affairs.

An attempt to hold a discussion within the *Vorstand* about leadership of the Society revealed very divergent perspectives. Frau Dr. Wegman and Fräulein Dr. Vreede held the strong view that it was unnecessary to name a new chair, that Dr. Steiner should continue to be this, and that everything could remain as it had been. Frau Dr. Steiner thought that Rudolf Steiner would certainly continue as esoteric leader, but that he would be unable to deal with affairs of the physical plane, which are such a major, and frequently so unpleasant, part of a chair's task. She thought it was clear that the deputy chair, selected by Dr. Steiner as the most outstanding anthroposophist, ought now to take over the difficult office of chair. Since Herr Steffen remained extremely cautious and reticent, Frau Dr. Steiner was outvoted, and could only add that she was sure that outer conditions would necessitate naming a new chair.

The way that this session went showed there were radical differences of opinion. But in the *Mitteilungsblatt* [news bulletin], no. 17, April 26, 1925, Frau Dr. Wegman nevertheless wrote:

> But those of us whom he had chosen as *Vorstand* were clear that we should not leave the position he had assigned to us. It was clear to us that it is our holy task, if we wish to take seriously what the Master passed on to us from the world of spirit, to remain in our grouping around him, so that, although he cannot be with us in the physical world, he can remain among us and work through us. This mood held sway in us. Thus we continue to regard Rudolf Steiner as the leader and chair of our *Vorstand*, and all *Vorstand* members as holding those functions he assigned to them.

Who could doubt, reading this, that the words *we* and *us* referred to the *Vorstand*, and that it was unanimous on these issues? Yet Frau Dr. Steiner and Herr Steffen read, with surprise and displeasure, this view attributed to them that there should be no new chair for a Society that clearly had to work in the physical world and could not deny its very real loss. In the next *Mitteilungsblatt*, no. 18, it was however at least possible to publish a statement signed by all the *Vorstand* members, which declared in general terms that the *Vorstand* believed it to be "its duty to retain its functions, and to continue to work in the spirit of Rudolf Steiner, whom we know remains at the heart of the *Vorstand*." There was no mention of the office of chair for a long time after that.

From May 1925 on, letters "To the Members" appeared in the *Mitteilungsblatt*. These were written by Frau Dr. Wegman, and appeared to be a continuation of Dr. Steiner's letters. Then came the "Leading

Thoughts," which were likewise supposed to be a continuation of Dr. Steiner's "Leading Thoughts." There were a number of members who either believed or were sure that spiritual research had not necessarily come to a sudden end, and for whom it was self-apparent that Frau Dr. Wegman would have the capacity to replace Rudolf Steiner and his activity, and should therefore be viewed as his successor. Frau Dr. Wegman's manner and appearance only strengthened this view in the minds of the members who already held it.

The other *Vorstand* members only ever saw the letters and "Leading Thoughts" when they appeared in print in the *Mitteilungsblatt*. It was also by this means that they learned the news, one day, that Frau Dr. Wegman had traveled to Paris at the end of May and had there begun to give esoteric classes for the first time since Rudolf Steiner's death. They also learned that Fräulein Dr. Vreede had been with her in Paris, and had herself given a lecture, and that Dr. Kolisko had also held study sessions on the "new Leading Thoughts." In her report Frau Dr. Wegman tried to imitate every detail of the style of Dr. Steiner's accounts of his travels.[4] Here she wrote as follows:

> When our Master Rudolf Steiner left us behind on the physical plane, one of the most important questions facing the *Vorstand* was how to continue with the development of esotericism, which since the Christmas Foundation Meeting had once again assumed a position of central importance within anthroposophic endeavor. It was clear that our first task was to protect the esotericism that had been given us, and through its repetition bring the powers that lie within it to living activity in the members.

More than this, it was actually the view of the other *Vorstand* members that no one at the time was capable of giving new esoteric impulses though their own efforts. Since things could therefore only be repeated, there was little point in assuming unnecessary "rights" for oneself in this regard. Nevertheless, there were efforts underway to have Frau Dr.

---

4   *Mitteilungsblau*, no. 24, June 14, 1925.

Wegman recognized as sole leader of the School of Spiritual Science. She herself made this claim. In the travel account referred to, she made the following interim statement:

> When Dr. Steiner founded this First Class of the School of Spiritual Science, he appointed me as colleague. At that time the new pupils, those who had not yet received any esoteric instruction, promised to be faithful members of the School. It is for that reason that I did not feel myself free of these responsibilities after the death of Rudolf Steiner. On the contrary, I felt myself more than ever responsible, for I could not but regard the arrangements that Dr. Steiner had made as realities of the world of spirit. And so it became my task to begin again with the esoteric lessons of the School of Spiritual Science given by Rudolf Steiner. And to my great satisfaction it was possible, in Paris, to take the first step in this direction.

In spite of the stylistic confusion of this passage, it clearly shows the standpoint that Frau Dr. Wegman adopted at this time, one to which she continued to adhere. Yet when the First Class was originally founded, Frau Dr. Wegman had been appointed in just the same way as the other members of the *Vorstand*. The only difference in function that she exercised was to act as secretary in the sense of taking down inquiries meant to be submitted when a Class member wished to pass on the content of Class lectures to another who had not been present. (Dr. Steiner however also at times gave this intermediary role to other *Vorstand* members when the Class Lessons were held elsewhere and the secretary was not present.) She was never "appointed" as such. Making claims to being specially "appointed" and to having a "mission" became characteristic of the attitude of Frau Dr. Wegman and her colleagues, as well as that of Fräulein Dr. Vreede. Herr Steffen, Frau Dr. Steiner, and Herr Dr. Wachsmuth always categorically rejected the idea that they had been appointed specially in some way by Rudolf Steiner or had been given a certain mission. Dr. Steiner only ever spoke of tasks, obligations, and responsibilities. Frau Dr. Wegman alternately expressed and dismissed the view that she was the surviving colleague of the two original leaders of the School.⁵ The account of later events will show the great difficulties this gave rise to. As far as the promise [to her] to be faithful members of the School is concerned, this is only correct in as much as there were some cases where Dr. Steiner wanted to seal such a promise by having the new Class members shake hands both with him and with Frau Dr. Wegman who stood beside him. To assume special rights from this fact was not justified, for the simple reason that the overwhelming majority of Class members were accepted into the School in quite another way by Dr. Steiner in Dornach, and these pupils never entered into such a promise with Frau Dr. Wegman.

After the Paris trip there followed a visit to Prague in June 1925. Since most of the members here rejected the clearly expressed demands to recognize Frau Dr. Wegman as esoteric leader and guide, this gave rise to confrontations and disagreements between members. This was all the more regrettable because it eventually led to the Czech members who supported Frau Dr. Wegman forming a splinter group that split off from the rest of the movement. As long as Dr. Steiner had been alive such national differences of opinion could always be avoided. Frau Dr. Wegman, in contrast, asked the Czech members whether, as Czechs, they had any complaints about the Germans. At the same time she wrote rapturous articles in the *Mitteilungsblatt* about the cosmopolitan Michaelic impulse.

If, in that summer of 1925, people had kept a grip on reality and waited for actual abilities and achievements to be recognized beyond doubt by all sensible members, all difficulties could have been avoided. Outer conditions for continuing healthy development were also provided when Dr. Steffen enabled Frau Dr. Wegman to start Class lecture readings in Dornach. He briefly introduced her himself, expressing the agreement of the *Vorstand*, and saying that Frau Dr. Wegman would carry out her activities by right of being *Vorstand* secretary. But people did not at all want to accept such a solution. Other, further difficulties arose.

---

5   Seemingly dismissed at least, in February 1926 [page 92], and passionately asserted in November 1930 [page 158].

All of this gave rise to increasing unrest amongst members. The *Mitteilungsblatt* continued to publish pieces by Frau Dr. Wegman. The new "Leading Thoughts," even in their style, seemed amateurish; and members found it hard to credit that the *Vorstand* was offering these to the Society, as some people claimed. It soon became apparent that this was hardly a "new revelation"; and people took offense at the letters and essays by Frau Dr. Wegman, for without making their source sufficiently clear, these were often nothing other than a repetition of unpublished lectures that Rudolf Steiner had given before he died, but watered down and full of mistakes. Should we let this pass as spiritual research? Many did and demanded that others should, too.

In the *Mitteilungsblatt,* no. 26, June 28, 1925, Frau Dr. Wegman described the members who had dared to criticize her as a group who began to scold, to scold in a coarse manner, abusing individualities, people of character (!),[6] quite forgetting the noble figure of Rudolf Steiner who was well aware of what he was doing when he appointed the members of the *Vorstand* to their various functions, actually attacking him by doubting his insight.

This way of appealing to positions "appointed" by Dr. Steiner, and using the name of Rudolf Steiner as a shield with which to keep at bay every criticism of one's own inadequacies, did not improve Frau Dr. Wegman's standing. Apart from this her words were intended to awaken the false impression that the whole *Vorstand* was under attack, and that this *Vorstand* was responsible for the new Leading Thoughts.

Although she wrote in the very next *Mitteilungsblatt:* "The negative attitude of certain members is in such a minority that one can disregard it," she nevertheless continued to justify herself. In the *Mitteilungsblatt,* no. 30, July 26, 1925, it says:

> The continuity of our work could not be sustained by repeating the "Leading Thoughts" that had already been given. These classical Leading Thoughts, which in so marvelous a way contain

---

6   German = *Persönlichkeiten.*

all the teachings of Anthroposophy, should remain as a whole, a wonderful study material accessible to everyone. By continuity was meant that the living word should once more resonate between people, through the *Mitteilungsblatt*. Not in a random way, but by drawing on Rudolf Steiner's treasure store of wisdom, so that important aspects of our current, altered situation might be emphasized and illumined. The situation has changed by virtue of the fact that the store of wisdom, which our leader used regularly to draw for us from the world of spirit, is for the time being closed off. This means that our work can only be furthered at present by giving prominence to particular aspects from this store of wisdom that are of significance at a given moment. There are many things that continue to lie concealed within the lectures and essays—much that was long ago expressed but could, only later and in certain circumstances, be understood properly and then enter human consciousness.

If we disregard the unclarities and contradictions once more contained in this passage, we still have to ask what this important thing was that the Society needed to come to understand after the death of Dr. Steiner, so as to ensure the continuity of anthroposophic work. If we read the same essay further, we arrive at the answer: Alexander and his followers, Alexander and Ephesus, Alexander and Michael! The same theme had also formed the chief content of many other essays.

What many members found unbearable was the feeling that they were under pressure to subordinate themselves to an inscrutable authority. No one disputed Frau Dr. Wegman's right to communicate her knowledge and opinions, but people did object to having to accept them as revelation or dogma. There were leading members within the Society who demanded that the new Leading Thoughts, like those of Dr. Steiner, should be carefully studied in group meetings. And Dr. Kolisko spread it about everywhere that these "Leading Thoughts" came from the *Vorstand*. He knew very well that this was not the case. On a later occasion Frau Dr. Steiner asked him how he had come to assert things that he knew not to be true. His answer, that he had not considered it his task to "pass the *Vorstand*'s conflicts on to the members," seemed to him a sufficient reply. This is the first, crass example of how Dr. Kolisko felt himself justified, for tactical reasons, in reporting things as he would have liked them to be.

※

How did Frau Dr. Steiner behave during this period? For twenty-three years she had worked alongside Rudolf Steiner as his trusted, close colleague, bearing his name and leading the Anthroposophical Society for so long a time.

In the first days after Rudolf Steiner's death she experienced a severe mental and emotional shock from maneuvers that attempted to sideline and intimidate her at a time when she expected sincerity and honest, straightforward truth.[7] Because of this she felt the right thing to do was to withdraw and confine herself to her section work, rather than getting in the way of those who had made it clear to her that she was not wanted, and that if she did not passively subordinate herself she would have failed to understand the real sense of the Christmas Foundation Meeting. Yet since the new course began with things that were contrary to what Dr. Steiner would have viewed as right, her conscience compelled her to distance herself from a state of affairs that tried only to retain the outer appearance of what should have been inner truth. She had a different view of the Christmas Foundation Meeting from those who were now determined to set the agenda, and to whom she was a hindrance. She therefore decided it was better for someone to take her place who would be better able to accept what was going on, and wrote to Dr. Kolisko, already a prime mover in the German executive council. Another person who could be considered was Fräulein Dr. Röschl, the leader of the Youth Section. Both people were determined to take a leading role, and already occupied important positions. At that time, however, she did not have any idea that those two people were both working intently on the new course, and that

---

7   Section 4 gives some indication of the things that happened, which are so painful that they cannot be described in detail.

this had already been fully considered and discussed. She still believed that Dr. Kolisko would take an open, unprejudiced view and would handle things fairly and tactfully.

But in a subsequent discussion in the *Vorstand* it turned out that no one wished to agree to the step that Frau Dr. Steiner had considered taking. When she saw that Herr Steffen would also leave the *Vorstand* if she did, she decided to stay. The group of people, too, who at the time were the secret movers behind much of what was happening, regarded the resignation of a *Vorstand* member as a threat to their plans. To carry out their "mystical" intentions, they needed to retain the outer form of the appointments made by Dr. Steiner.

Yet the extensive work that Frau Dr. Steiner had taken on in managing Rudolf Steiner's literary estate, and the many tasks she already had to fulfill, made it impossible for her to respond to the wish of many older members and take an active part in the leadership of the Society. She wrote to this effect on May 19, 1925, in a "Private Announcement," which she published in the *Mitteilungsblatt,* no. 22, May 31. Part of it ran as follows:

> It is not my intention to take a direct and active part at present in leading the Society. Younger people are there to do that. If I listened to the wishes of various friends, and undertook this, I would have to neglect what I regard as my immediate task: the work in my section and the enormous task of working on Dr. Steiner's literary estate. That is enough for the strength and years of life that still remain to me. I could not take on any more. So let me thank those who believe that intensive efforts on my part within the leadership would be desirable. In addition, let me express the hope that, once certain difficulties unavoidable in such a decisive transition have been overcome, the mighty life force in the work of Dr. Steiner will show all our inadequacies and weaknesses to be nothing worse than minor blemishes, mere sunspots. Such spots do not make the sun shine any less brightly or awaken any less life.

Yet it became increasingly clear that the attitude of whole groups of members was sowing more and more confusion. Herr Steffen had, it is true, demonstrated that there was agreement between the *Vorstand* and Frau Dr. Wegman about the School of Spiritual Science question, when he introduced the first Class Lessons. However, this had no effect because some members still sought a special position for Frau Dr. Wegman. This was compounded by the way the "new Leading Thoughts" were received. In Dornach itself, at a discussion of Dr. Steiner's "Leading Thoughts," the members had to sit there and listen as Fräulein Dr. Röschl asserted that Frau Dr. Wegman's "Leading Thoughts" had "expanded and enlarged upon" Rudolf Steiner's teachings.

One morning at nine o'clock, soon after the publication of these first [new] "Leading Thoughts," Frau Dr. Steiner was surprised to receive an unannounced visit from Stuttgart by Dr. Stein, Dr. Kolisko, and Frau Kolisko, who descended upon her like inquisitors. Dr. Stein started off by reproaching her bitterly, saying that he had barely managed to prevent a move to make Frau Dr. Steiner honorary president of the German Society. This initiative had come from Count Keyserlingk. Although Frau Dr. Steiner had known nothing of this matter, and could say with a clear conscience that she would not have accepted this honorary position anyway, Dr. Stein felt it necessary to continue to berate her for some time like an indignant judge. Then Dr. Kolisko felt called upon to express his outrage about the fact that Dr. Unger had failed to discuss Frau Dr. Wegman's "Leading Thoughts" at the last group meeting, although he, Dr. Kolisko, had talked about them enthusiastically for two hours. Dr. Kolisko demanded confirmation that the whole *Vorstand* was united in standing behind these new "Leading Thoughts." When Frau Dr. Steiner replied that she could not confirm this, since the first she had heard of them was through the *Mitteilungsblatt,* Dr. Stein once more tried to pressurize her into recognizing the authority of Frau Dr. Wegman by referring to her significant incarnation. This attempt to terrorize Frau Dr. Steiner lasted until two o'clock in the afternoon.

But the most painful thing for Frau Dr. Steiner was the deception practiced on members by the way Frau Dr. Wegman's articles had been published. The members must of necessity believe that the matter had been discussed and considered by the whole *Vorstand*. This misuse of trust had given rise to something that would inevitably have direct repercussions.

It gradually became apparent through the further course of events that energetic attempts were being made to prevent Frau Dr. Steiner's influence within the Society; and also to deprive her of everything to which she might assert a claim, as well as of all to which she had an indisputable right. People were attempting to dispute her rights by undermining her personal standing in the Society. This was considered the best means of opposing the view of Herr Steffen and many older members that Frau Dr. Steiner ought to take over as chair of the *Vorstand*. Above all people claimed that her esoteric development was insufficient, that she still belonged to the "Dark Ages" and that, therefore, she could not be expected to understand the real meaning of the Christmas Foundation Meeting. Such people were afraid of the great trust invested in her by the older members especially; but they believed that they could surmount this problem by deliberately ignoring her presence and turning the younger members in particular against her. They tried to use the Christmas Foundation Meeting to support their case, claiming that it had wiped the slate clean of all that had previously been justified. The group of members from whom these things proceeded was the same that also had such strange views about the meaning of the Christmas Foundation Meeting, and wished to find grounds for Frau Dr. Wegman's sole dominion.

Frau Dr. Steiner was both personally wounded and felt it to be shameful for the Society when it was claimed after Dr. Steiner died that he had made no provisions in the case of his death, and that—although the Atelier had been thoroughly searched—no one had thought to ask her before making such assertions and trying to implement unauthorized new measures.

A will and testament of Rudolf Steiner did in fact exist, in which he had made provision for his estate. This will was fully legal, and had been deposited at the Berlin administrative court, with several copies in Dornach. In this will Dr. Steiner transferred the copyright of all his works, as well as the rights of ownership and disposal of all his literary estate, documents, letters, lecture notes, etc., to Frau Dr. Steiner. She received these rights in order to "decide, as she sees fit, and in accordance with the intentions I made known to her, what should be done with the above-mentioned [documents]."

Although this will was indisputable, it was passionately contested for years by the group of members to which we have repeatedly referred, because it had been written *before* the 1923 Christmas Foundation Meeting. These members believed that the literary estate should be made over to Frau Dr. Wegman or the *Vorstand*, not Frau Dr. Steiner. Frau Dr. Wegman also held this view.

Immediately after Dr. Steiner's death people discussed how best and most fittingly to preserve the atelier in which he had worked so long, where he had lain during his whole illness, and in which he had closed his eyes for the last time. Frau Dr. Steiner at first wanted herself and the *Vorstand* to look through and order all the papers and manuscripts there. When Frau Dr. Wegman dismissed this idea out of hand, Frau Dr. Steiner declared that she would wait eight days before entering the atelier, so as to give Frau Dr. Wegman time to sort things out as she saw fit. It later turned out that almost all of Dr. Steiner's manuscripts and notebooks had been removed at this time. After strenuous efforts, Frau Dr. Steiner succeeded in at least getting back from Frau Dr. Wegman the items whose existence she knew of, and whose appearance she could describe. Only a few people in Frau Dr. Steiner's immediate circle ever knew about this. However, members' groups had already started holding discussions about how to manage the literary estate and the publishing house. These two separate issues were regarded as one, which led to further confusion. Names of people were even cited who, with Frau Dr. Wegman's agreement, were to get ready to take on the job of managing the publishing company.

Dr. Steiner had given quite specific instructions about the publishing company, and there was no reason why these should not be adhered to after his death. Frau Dr. Steiner's sole right of managing the Philosophical-Anthroposophical Publishing Company could no more be disputed than that of Frau Dr. Wegman to manage the Clinic and Therapeutic Institute, which had also become part of the General Society. It must be emphasized that the decision to incorporate the publishing company into the Society dated back to the 1923 Christmas Foundation Meeting, but Dr. Steiner had subsequently stated on repeated occasions that this did not affect existing rights and agreements, and that, in this respect, everything should "remain as it was," as he put it.[8]

The publishing house had been founded by Frau Dr. Steiner herself. She had always been its owner and had never required any material help; it had never been bought from her; had never been encumbered by a mortgage or debts; and represented an increasingly valuable asset. Yet it was simply to be taken out of her hands, although she had just safeguarded its future for the Society by means of it becoming part of the General Anthroposophical Society. By doing so she had also ensured that no relatives of hers could make personal inheritance claims on it after her death. Dr. Steiner had always—particularly after the 1923 Christmas Foundation Meeting—pointed to the publishing house as a model for a healthy business, and praised the able, exemplary way that Frau Dr. Steiner and Fräulein Mücke managed it.

People thought they could brush all this aside however. One crass example of how Frau Dr. Steiner was treated occurred in the summer of 1925, at the time the book *Fundamentals of Therapy*[9] was due to appear. Frau Dr. Steiner and Fräulein Mücke both learned about this book from an advertisement in the *Mitteilungsblatt*, no. 37, September 13, 1925. This advertisement announcing a new publication by the Philosophical-Anthroposophical publishing company had not been sent in by the latter but by Frau Dr. Wegman. Since it was a book written by Dr. Steiner, no objections could be raised of course. The publishing company paid the amounts billed in its name, for a book printed and bound without its

---

8 The adoption of the publishing house and the clinic into the structure of the Anthroposophical Society was not formally completed until March 1925. Frau Dr. Steiner remained the owner of the publishing house, as one can see from the records.

9 Published today as *Extending Practical Medicine: Fundamental Principles Based on the Science of the Spirit* by Rudolf Steiner Press.

knowledge, and also settled the royalty fees claimed by Frau Dr. Wegman as "coauthor." After the book had appeared, the attitude that colleagues of Frau Dr. Wegman showed toward it caused widespread indignation. Dr. Kolisko and Dr. Zeylmans made a habit of referring to it as the "medical book by Frau Dr. Wegman," even in public lectures. Yet those who invented this phrase were best placed to know that Frau Dr. Wegman had not even had a significant hand in the book.

Such attitudes show that in some quarters of the Society people were too eager to try to make up for the loss of Rudolf Steiner by finding a replacement. The consequences threatened to become dire. In the *Mitteilungsblatt,* no 41, of October 11, 1925, Frau Dr. Steiner wrote the following reflections on these first months:

> The mood of "jubilate" that rose in us so strongly from the bereavement of the first months, resounding like the cheerful shouts of children who want to banish the creeping fear of oncoming darkness, has given way to serious, sober reflection. There are indeed signs that we dare to become fully aware as a Society of what we have lost, which no mystical daydreams should deceive us about, however enticingly they spread their illusory wings. With the voice that fell silent on the evening of September 28, 1924, our Society lost its admoniser who warned us of every false step, whose penetrating gaze was enough to dispel the airy froth of our fantasies, who reminded us again and again, "If you would take one step on the path of esoteric development, you must first take three steps on the path toward moral perfection." This should be our shield against all efforts of the tempter to blind us and lead us astray—this and the oft-repeated warning to serve absolute truthfulness. Is this seemingly simple foundation (which is nevertheless far beyond us) one that we will continually turn to and keep before our eyes?

Frau Dr. Steiner continued by warning us of all the dangers that she felt were approaching, and that then indeed came about: false esotericism and the ensuing lust for power.

In those first months up to the founding of the World School Association, Herr Steffen was not yet aware how great the difficulties would become. Although he had concerns, he kept them to himself and waited to see how things would develop, for he did not want to intrude on anyone's freedom. He hoped that in the long-term earnest endeavor and real achievements would become the measure by which individuals would be judged within the Society. In addition, he believed that things were bound to be difficult to begin with, and that such difficulties would soon be overcome.

It was for these reasons that he made no protest against the letters and "Leading Thoughts" of Frau Dr. Wegman, despite the fact that in a very early meeting of the *Vorstand* he categorically rejected Frau Dr. Wegman's proposal to continue the "Leading Thoughts" series. It was his view that the "Leading Thoughts" given by Rudolf Steiner were already an inexhaustible resource, and that no one ought to presume to emulate this work of spirit, of the highest refinement and perfection, that Rudolf Steiner had created in spite of his illness. But the "new Leading Thoughts" and everything else appeared nevertheless. Herr Steffen still did not protest, even when Frau Wegman occasionally sent her manuscript to the printers without having shown it first to him, the editor of the *Mitteilungsblatt*. He resigned quietly from the editorship, however, on receiving a letter from Dr. Schickler in Stuttgart, in which the latter demanded that Frau Dr. Wegman's "Leading Thoughts" should appear under the heading "Leading Thoughts, issued by the Goetheanum for the Anthroposophical Society," as had been the case while Dr. Steiner was alive.

Neither had Herr Steffen complained when Frau Dr. Wegman completely failed to inform him of her intention to hold the Class Lessons in Paris once more. When she later started Class Lessons in Dornach he opened them himself, and introduced her as secretary of the *Vorstand*. He assumed that this had cleared up all misunderstandings, for his very presence had shown that the other *Vorstand* members—who, given this sad state of affairs, were afraid to involve themselves in such an activity—recognized Frau Wegman's right to read the Class Lessons. Current circumstances made anything other than repeating Rudolf Steiner's Class Lectures seem out of the question. Herr Steffen went to great lengths, at this time and even years later, to hold the *Vorstand* together.

In doing so he paid no heed to the treatment he personally received, which anyone would have wished to be different. Yet the *Vorstand*'s unity was threatened when, in a very disturbing attack, Dr. Kolisko and Dr. Stein severely reproved Herr Steffen for introducing Frau Dr. Wegman to the members as "secretary" instead of "Leader of the School of Spiritual Science." Such measures taken by certain members, as well as the rights claimed by Frau Dr. Wegman herself, eventually gave rise to quite unsustainable conditions.

The necessity of filling the position of the chair [of the *Vorstand*] eventually came about when the authorities required it, and cited legal stipulations.

Within the Society there was strong opposition to the naming of a new chair. The view of Frau Dr. Wegman, described above, was shared by many. In theory one can say that the wish to leave the division of roles within the *Vorstand* as it had been during Dr. Steiner's lifetime expressed a certain piety, even if not much realism. This may indeed have been the genuine view of some members. But we can also wonder whether a chair—even one limited to the smallest possible sphere of activity—might not have got in the way of certain members and hindered the sole regency of Frau Dr. Wegman. The facts themselves provided an answer to this question.

Let us first examine the actual state of affairs in the winter of 1925. Herr Steffen was the deputy chair, and it was therefore the most obvious thing to entrust him with the chair. Frau Dr. Steiner had, in the previously mentioned article of May 19, stated clearly the capacity in which she wished to be active in the Society, yet there were groups of members who remembered that she had previously led the Society for many long years. That is why they thought that she should at least be considered for the position of chair. However, in other circles this idea gave rise to the greatest anxiety.

At the Annual General Meeting of December 29, 1925, after some unpleasant initial discussions, the office of chair was transferred to Herr Steffen, who only accepted it reluctantly. In certain circles people hoped that they could get round the "poet" as they wished. But after no more than a few days conflict had become unavoidable.

One must look back to this time to understand why Herr Steffen, all through the following years, was unable to get an answer about what the rights of the chair were. It is hard to answer such a question when one has no conception of what such rights might be, or rather cannot conceive of a chair who is in fact nothing, since he is only there to retrospectively approve things that have been done by others without his knowledge and against his will. The fact that certain groups demanded this from the outset gave rise, in January 1926, to the first major conflict.

Frau Dr. Steiner had not become chair, but some still felt a danger and threat inherent in the possibility that she might take on the position of deputy chair. Those who feared this wished to get rid of the position altogether, which would have needed a change in the statutes. On one occasion, in the presence of Frau Dr. Steiner, an intended change to the statutes was indeed mentioned, but no one said that this was in order to abolish the role of deputy chair. When, in a gathering of functionaries, she quite unexpectedly learned that this was what lay behind the change, she saw that she had been maneuvered into a *fait accompli,* and, feeling this to be degrading and dishonorable, raised objections to such a way of proceeding. It did not occur to her to claim the office for herself, and a year later, when this was proposed to her, she turned it down. But she did not want to be caught out unawares in this way, and could not agree to the apparent "reasons" that were presented, because she did not feel they were honest. But now the storm against her broke in earnest, and the most malicious things were invented and spread about—by people such as General Secretary Dr. Zeylmans, by Waldorf teachers like Dr. Stein and Dr. Kolisico, and by other members for whom the suggestion that a "change to the statutes" had been mentioned was proof enough. They blissfully disregarded the fact that this phrase in itself does not indicate what is going to be changed.

Herr Steffen had to intervene at this point, but also for a different reason.

The Crisis in January and February 1926

On Sunday, January 24, 1926, Herr Steffen announced to members who had gathered for a lecture in the Goetheanum carpentry workshop that two factors compelled him to address all members of the Anthroposophical Society. The first was the increasing scope of agitation against Frau Dr. Steiner. The other was that, against the will of the *Vorstand*, a World School Association had been founded without the founders even telling the *Vorstand* afterward. It was being claimed nevertheless that the *Vorstand*, represented by Fräulein Dr. Vreede, had been responsible for this founding. Frau Dr. Steiner had initially wished to withdraw from the *Vorstand* because of these renewed insults, and Herr Steffen also wanted to resign as chair. Instead, though, he had decided to make a positive attempt at healing the conflict. He suggested to the members that they might dedicate themselves to earnest endeavors as part of a Rudolf Steiner Association, which he wished to ask Frau Dr. Steiner to become the patron of, so as to protect Rudolf Steiner's life work and sustain truth and freedom within the Society. On the following day all *Vorstand* members recognized this Association as a legal body within the Anthroposophical Society.

On January 27, Herr Steffen once more discussed the two factors mentioned above in a gathering of members. It became apparent that open disrespect for the *Vorstand* displayed by the founders of the World School Association had not met the resistance that might have been expected; and that in the teachers' college of the Waldorf School, where Dr. Stein and Dr. Kolisko exercised decisive influence, malicious gossip about Frau Dr. Steiner had assumed dire proportions. To justify himself, Dr. Stein then read the draft of a letter of apology that he had just written to Frau Dr. Steiner. He considered that this was an end to the matter. However, Frau Dr. Steiner vehemently dismissed the flippant apology and said that

Dr. Stein and Dr. Kolisko were deliberately spreading lies. She was able to say this because Dr. Stein had himself had to admit this in many instances. It was also known that Dr. Stein had gone on and on with his agitation against Frau Dr. Steiner, even after he himself had accepted from Dr. Unger that Frau Dr. Steiner had not been given sufficient information in the matter of alteration to the statutes. After sending his letter of apology to Frau Dr. Steiner, he had announced in Stuttgart that he had not really meant it, and had only written it for the sake of peace. After the World School Association had been founded, Dr. Kolisko continued to spread the lie that the *Vorstand* had been involved in its founding, in just the same way as he had previously intentionally misled members with his false statements about the relationship of the *Vorstand* to the "Leading Thoughts" of Frau Dr. Wegman.

Then Guenther Schubert took the floor and pointed out that members were obliged to take Herr Steffen's call seriously, and themselves make efforts to counteract the dangers that had arisen. In quite general terms he mentioned that he had gathered from conversations with Dutch members that they were stirring up things against Frau Dr. Steiner, and that they had strange views about the way the Society was being led. This was also seen as an explanation of the peculiar way that the World School Association had been founded.

The decision was made to wait for the arrival of Dr. Zeylmans, who was expected the following day. He was the chief founder of the World School Association, and had briefly gone to London to consult with a few members involved in it about the difficulties that had now arisen. Dr. Zeylmans arrived in Dornach on January 28, but refused to speak in front of all the members. He wanted to do this instead in a smaller circle, which the *Vorstand* had invited to gather in the evening. Nevertheless, Dr. Zeylmans demanded that the invitation already issued to Herr Schubert be withdrawn. Although Herr Schubert was a good friend of Dr. Zeylmans, the latter had been told that Herr Schubert had insulted him, the Dutch General Secretary, and thus the Dutch Society as a whole. Dr. Zeylmans refused to have a personal conversation—with Herr Schubert. Herr Steffen

The "Memorandum"

censured Dr. Zeylmans' conduct and left the decision with Herr Schubert, who then voluntarily withdrew. Since Herr Steffen had himself turned to the members to hear their opinion, the attitude of Dr. Zeylmans was also an attack on Herr Steffen, who as always left himself completely open to every view and criticism.

In the smaller circle, Dr. Zeylmans declared that, as the person appointed by Dr. Steiner to be General Secretary, he could not tolerate accusations from the members, but only from the *Vorstand* or another General Secretary. Frau Dr. Steiner remarked that she had not refused to sit down and talk with Dr. Stein and Dr. Kolisko, even though she felt their attacks on her had been of a quite different order.

On January 12, Dr. Zeylmans had written a report on the founding of the World School Association, but had never sent it to the *Vorstand*, so Herr Steffen did not receive it until January 25, from a third party. This report was written in a way that clearly suggested the *Vorstand* had been closely involved. Dr. Zeylmans now explained his position, expressly citing the fact that Fräulein Dr. Vreede had not opposed the founding of the Association, and had thus been understood to give her agreement. Dr. Zeylmans also claimed that the *Vorstand* had suggested he use his own personal initiative. It turned out, however, that the *Vorstand* as a whole had not said this, but that Dr. Zeylmans was referring to nothing more than initial discussions with individual *Vorstand* members. On the contrary, at a meeting on January 3, at the express wish of Dr. Zeylmans, the *Vorstand* had given Fräulein Dr. Vreede the task of acting as its "intermediary" in preliminary negotiations, on the condition that under no circumstances whatsoever could a founding take place without further and direct agreement with the *Vorstand*. Dr. Zeylmans, however, had gone ahead and founded the Association on the following day, January 4.

The *Vorstand* wanted to wait before founding a World School Association because, although Dr. Zeylmans had on January 1 read out a list of names of certain individuals suggested as founders, there was no provision made for legal representation of the Waldorf School and the

Waldorf School Association. The official representatives of the Waldorf School Association were Herr Molt and Herr Leinhas, and Herr Steffen was chair of this Association. On the evening of January 3 a conversation took place between Dr. Zeylmans, Herr Molt, and Herr Leinhas, in the presence of Dr. Kolisko and several Waldorf teachers. Nevertheless, when no agreement could be reached, Dr. Zeylmans said he would just go ahead and found the Association without the Waldorf School or the Waldorf School Association, for he was not leaving Dornach until he had done so. Dr. Kolisko said that one should just go ahead and found the Association, and afterward ask who wanted to be part of it. It had been clear to Herr Leinhas from the beginning that binding agreements had already been made long since in Holland and England. The list of names was in fact not really a suggestion but consisted of those who had already been chosen to run the Association, for which only retrospective confirmation was sought in Dornach. Herr Leinhas also became aware of a link originally planned between the future World School Association and the Waldorf School, which he feared could represent the gravest danger to the latter. A particular group of members clearly wanted to realize its own aims. This circle was even said to have held a "founding" celebration already.

At the meeting of January 28, Herr Leinhas described this murky background as "the ambition for power of certain circles." Dr. Zeylmans had in the meantime seriously insulted Herr Leinhas, and though he retracted immediately, this did not dispel mistrust about his own intentions.

In this same meeting, something stated by a Dutch member (Herr Stibbe) was passed on, to the effect that Holland should be regarded as a kind of reincarnation of Macedonia, from which Alexander was now to lead his troops to the West, rather than to the East. This showed who really stood behind the planned World School Association, and explained why the initiative had come from Holland and England. Dr. Zeylmans apparently brushed the remark of this "young man" aside, but had to admit that he was one of the members of the founding committee as well as one of his own most intimate friends.

Herr Steffen felt that the last chance of mutual understanding had been lost when the Waldorf School college of teachers, after hearing from Frau Fels that the *Vorstand* knew nothing of the founding of the Association, still continued its negotiations with Dr. Zeylmans. The latter had likewise accepted an invitation to conduct negotiations on January 22 in Stuttgart, without first informing the *Vorstand* in Dornach. In the course of these negotiations they even decided to ask the *Vorstand* to celebrate belatedly the founding of January 4 on February 27, Rudolf Steiner's birthday.

The way that Herr Steffen addressed the members has already been described. He wanted the Society to form its own opinion, and the opportunity for this was now to be offered in the form of a members' meeting, scheduled for February 6. Herr Steffen also commissioned two people from opposite camps, Dr. Unger and Dr. Stein, to review everything thoroughly once more and present the members with a report on what had occurred.

On February 6, the members' meeting took place and Dr. Unger read out a written report containing a precise description of events. (The preceding account was taken from this report, partly using Dr. Unger's own words.)

Dr. Stein, on the other hand, found a way round the uncomfortable truth by playing the—for him very strange—role of "knowing nothing" rather than making any reference at all to the course of events.

The position of Fräulein Dr. Vreede was also discussed at length. The unclarity of her role consisted in the fact that, although the *Vorstand*'s "intermediary," she had viewed Dr. Zeylmans' private initiative as legitimate, and had therefore not protested at the founding meeting of January 4. At this founding she had expressly referred to herself only as the "intermediary" of the *Vorstand*, and on receiving Dr. Zeylmans' report of January 12 had raised objections both by telegram and letter to the incorrect formulations contained in it. But it remained an open question why she had altogether failed to pass on any news to the *Vorstand*. It must be remembered, however, that Herr Steffen did not reproach her at all, and when someone demanded that Fräulein Dr. Vreede should resign from the *Vorstand*, he dismissed this idea as absurd.

Frau Dr. Wegman had known of the founding—not, as she emphasized, in her capacity as *Vorstand* member, but as a private individual. What this really meant only became clear in 1930, when the World School Association's strange finance plan was discovered.[10]

But now the consequences of an ideology that declared that the Society did not need a chair became glaringly obvious. When the proponents of this view made efforts to ensure that Herr Steffen and not someone else should take on the chair, they did not omit to point out that the Society was merely fulfilling a legal requirement, a formality, and nothing more. Herr Steffen had taken up his post on December 29. A mere six days later (on January 4), without the agreement of the chair and the *Vorstand*, although claiming that this agreement existed, an anthroposophicly oriented, worldwide pedagogical movement was founded. Herr Steffen was also kept in the dark as chair of the Waldorf School Association, as was the association's deputy chair, Herr Molt, and the treasurer, Herr Leinhas. In addition, the Waldorf School Association was at the time the only competent, publicly representative body for anthroposophic pedagogy. The Waldorf School was thus also excluded. The attempt to divert important streams of anthroposophic life away from Dornach and all places where Herr Steffen and Frau Dr. Steiner had an influence, and redirect them into the hands of a certain clique, now became apparent for the first time.

Who were the founders of the World School Association and their helpers? They turned out to be those members who had so energetically spearheaded views about the meaning and purpose of the 1923 Christmas Foundation Meeting, and Frau Dr. Wegman's dominance in the leadership of the Society—views that had brought about such difficulties the previous year. The high profile founding of the World School Association exposed their intentions, aims, and methods for all to see. These were more or less the same people who later, in 1934, initiated the so-called Statement of Intent and founded the so-called association of free

---

10 See page 175f.

anthroposophic groups. In the whole intervening period they were also the ones who attempted to exercise the sort of influence on the life of the Society that, from 1926 onward, earned them the title—though not used by themselves—of *"Übervorstand."* They were the following: Dr. Kolisko, von Grone, Dunlop, Kaufmann, Dr. Zeylmans, de Haan, several doctors, and in the decisive early years especially Dr. Stein, who in those days had not yet retreated into the background. Since these individuals played a significant and sometimes leading role in the executive committees of the German, English, and Dutch Societies, and in the college of teachers of the Waldorf School, and also exercised a powerful authority in the Free Society led by Dr. Lehrs, it is hardly surprising that their influence was far-reaching. The following account will show how this group of leading members repeatedly tried to realize their own particular aims with the help of Frau Dr. Wegman or Fräulein Dr. Vreede. Likewise, these two *Vorstand* members repeatedly drew support from this *Übervorstand* to assert their own intentions even against the will of the other *Vorstand* members. This circle of members linked themselves more closely with Frau Dr. Wegman in the early years, and later more with Fräulein Dr. Vreede. In the beginning their struggles were mainly directed against Frau Dr. Steiner, while in later years they turned increasingly against Herr Steffen. Relations between Frau Dr. Wegman and Fräulein Dr. Vreede changed greatly over the course of time. In the following account, therefore, the names of these two people will only be mentioned together where there is objective justification for this.

In general, the gentlemen of the *Übervorstand* tried to subject the Anthroposophical Society to their will, and later, when it turned out that they could not do this, to claim a special position for themselves within the Society. Not only the events themselves showed this, but they also made no absolute secret of their ambitions. "We wanted to take hold of the reins of the Society, but we did not succeed." This phrase of Dr. Stein's is still remembered by many, as is the other: "We must have our way."

When Herr Steffen showed that, in the matter of the World School Association, he was not prepared to grant retrospective approval for things that should never have happened, his opponents adopted an attitude that they resorted to on subsequent similar occasions as well, of seeming to view the whole thing as harmless misunderstanding. They explained that it was just commendable over-enthusiasm that had led them to act in the way they did. No serious problems could possibly have arisen, they felt, if all members were as faithful to the esoteric *Vorstand* as those who believed that they had so deeply grasped the meaning of the Christmas Foundation Meeting. Dr. Kolisko protested in the meeting of February 6, 1926, against "heartless efforts to ascertain facts that were no longer relevant." It was, he said, not a court of law, and he objected to questions that could have been posed only in a mood of mistrust. He did not find fault with himself and his friends for harboring ambitions of power, but accused his critics of being in danger of provoking a split in the Society.

At the very beginning of the discussion, Dr. Zeylmans had demanded restrictions on freedom of speech, and Herr Steffen had repeatedly defended the right of each person to complete freedom of speech. Herr Schubert had already been deprived of the possibility of speaking by his exclusion from the smaller group meeting, which Dr. Zeylmans engineered. Since then Dr. Zeylmans had commissioned a written protest by the Dutch members, which raised objections to the supposed insult to the Dutch Society. Dr. Zeylmans had however omitted to ask Herr Schubert for his account of things, of which there was also a shorthand copy. Dr. Zeylmans read out the protest to the meeting, but it made little impression because most of those present were aware that the Dutch Society had not been insulted in any way. Herr Schubert dismissed the protest in a few words, and expressed the hope that inadequate information would never again allow Dr. Zeylmans to lead the members in Holland to senseless acts of this kind. He also said that the two factors that had compelled Herr Steffen to intervene—agitation against Frau Dr. Steiner, and blatant disrespect shown to the *Vorstand*, not to mention what had happened with the World School Association—would not be resolved until the group of members that had revealed itself in such an unmistakable light should change its attitude. At the same time he referred to results of supposed karmic research as the cause of the problems, and quite openly discussed the role Frau Dr. Wegman had been assigned in this context. He also mentioned the foolish view about Macedonia, which he himself had heard being loudly trumpeted abroad by the member in question.

Looking back on all the confusion that had unsettled the members for months, Herr Schubert put a number of questions to Herr Steffen, in the hope that his answers would provide a clear indication of the best way forward for the Anthroposophical Society. These questions concerned Rudolf Steiner's successor, leadership of the School of Spiritual Science, the finances, the false reports by Dr. Wegman in the *Mitteilungsblatt*, and the danger of forming sects.

Herr Steffen replied by saying that he did not believe there was any personal successor to Rudolf Steiner, and that the *Vorstand* had the task of leading both the Society and the School. Further details concerning the School were due to be discussed at a meeting of Class members scheduled for the following day.

Herr Steffen referred the financial questions to the Goetheanum's administrators. Dr. Grosheintz eventually gave a report on this. He spoke of large-scale expansion, already partly realized or at the planning stage, mortgages taken out, and securities given—all things that had been initiated by the Clinic and Therapeutic Institute, but that had been concealed from the *Vorstand*, even though the Anthroposophical Society was legal guarantor for these financial obligations. Some of these plans were canceled, but the funds later used to start many ventures in other countries.

Herr Steffen did not wish to comment on the articles in the *Mitteilungsblatt*, but left this to Frau Dr. Wegman, who subsequently declared that she could not reply to this question.

Herr Steffen addressed the danger of sectarianism, saying that it could only arise through people who did not take the science of the spirit seriously. Instead of seeing that the concrete effects of karma were unfolding in our actual situation and present capacities, such people immerse themselves in unreal illusions, dreaming up past causes for effects that they do not wish to come to terms with. Referring to the Alexander legend, Herr Steffen expressed the opinion that anyone who accepted views about reincarnation presented in this way—whether based on truth or not—either had a blind, dogmatic trust in authority, or was simply a gossip, for Dr. Steiner had clearly stated that anyone really able to know his former incarnations also knows he must keep quiet about them. Airing such truths about people still alive robs them of all possibility of fulfilling their present tasks.

Further discussions contributed little to reconciliation or agreement. Even after all that had passed, Dr. Kolisko rose in indignation once more and compared Herr Schubert's behavior with the act of Herostrates, who set fire to the temple of Ephesus in the hour of Alexander's birth!

There was huge commotion, finally, when Herr Steffen ended the meeting by urging that the reasons be made known for Fräulein Hoffmann leaving the Waldorf School's college of teachers.

The next day, February 7, 1926, the members of the School of Spiritual Science met. It was decided that a thorough report of this meeting for all members should not only be allowed but be required.

The meeting began with Frau Dr. Wegman reading out a written declaration, whose most important point was THAT SHE DID NOT IN ANY WAY REGARD HERSELF AS RUDOLF STEINER'S SUCCESSOR, THAT SHE MADE NO CLAIMS TO LEADING THE SCHOOL OF SPIRITUAL SCIENCE, BUT WOULD LIKE HERR STEFFEN TO TAKE THIS ON. In addition, she thought that the other *Vorstand* members ought to read the Class Lessons as well, which they had already discussed doing.

Herr Steffen replied that he did NOT want to take on leadership of the School, and would only be able to accept responsibility, as chair, for the various sections, when proof was offered that the situation in the Society had really improved. It was agreed that in future Herr Steffen and Frau Dr. Steiner would hold the Class Lesson readings, and that Frau Dr. Wegman would continue the Lessons with those who wished to receive such spiritual instruction from her.

Herr Steffen emphasized that misunderstandings that had previously arisen from the way that Frau Dr. Wegman had established herself amongst members outside Switzerland, could now be regarded as resolved.

Frau Dr. Steiner spoke of how the most important thing was to develop a sense for truthfulness, to distinguish whether words, which anyone can use for any purpose, actually issue from truth. She went on to say that, for her, the worst aspect of the situation had been caused by younger members thinking they could judge and decide esoteric matters without possessing the maturity necessary for this, which the laws of human nature dictate can only develop after one's thirty-fifth year.

Questions connected with Rudolf Steiner's literary estate and the Philosophical-Anthroposophical Publishing Company were now aired, and this gave Frau Dr. Steiner her first chance to speak about these things to the members. Since she wished to read out the exact wording of the relevant documents, she left the meeting to collect them from her house. Those waiting experienced the strange mood of tense expectation, mingled with a sense of shame, that only now, and in such sad circumstances, the Society was going to hear Rudolf Steiner's will and testament. Some of the members present, however, adopted a dismissive attitude. Frau Dr. Steiner then read out various documents whose content is already familiar to the reader from the account of 1925. Frau Dr. Steiner did not make known these things in her own defense, but because the assertion that Dr. Steiner's will had been revoked by the 1923 Christmas Foundation Meeting not only led the Society astray, but even made it seem as if Dr. Steiner—who had retained clearest consciousness to the end—had been unaware of why he had not cancelled those documents. Because of the view amongst certain groups within the Society that Frau Dr. Steiner had not understood what Rudolf Steiner intended with the 1923 Christmas Foundation Meeting—a view that led them to wish for a particular kind of leadership—she also read out parts of a letter that Dr. Steiner had written to her on February 27, 1925. It ran as follows: "It is only with you that I can share judgments of thought and feeling." And: "It is only your judgment that has inner authority for me." In an older letter Dr. Steiner had written that Frau Dr. Steiner *"always understood him to such an extent that what is done by her after my death can be regarded as being done in my name."*

The reasons for Fräulein Hoffmann's resignation from the college of teachers of the Waldorf School were that she could no longer endure the enmity against Frau Dr. Steiner that held sway there. She also condemned the binding agreements made with some young people from the "inner circle," in preparation for the World School Association. These things were astonishing given the fact that this "inner circle" had formed and continued to develop after a conversation with Dr. Steiner, who eventually came to the point of giving the few who were present a shared meditation. Frau Dr. Steiner had also been present on this occasion, and had thus also received this verse, regarded by the others as an indissoluble link with one another. In general, the attitude of many youth leaders in those years was in complete contrast to the repeatedly expressed wishes of Dr. Steiner, who regarded Frau Dr. Steiner as the most suitable person to negotiate with young people, and expected—there is written proof of this—that these youth leaders would always turn first to Frau Dr. Steiner with their questions. In certain youth circles people simply disregarded the fact that Frau Dr. Steiner had for years been achieving outstanding things with numerous young people in her section.

It is of some historical interest that at the end of the meeting of February 7, 1926, Herr Munch was able to sum up accurately the whole situation by reading the final sentences of the *Autobiography* by Rudolf Steiner. What is even more telling, though, is that when Herr Englert read this out again in 1934, those people in the Society to whom it referred were still more or less the same ones: "But most people placed greatest importance on the absurdities that have formed and developed within the Theosophical Society, and that have led to endless squabbling."

The "Memorandum"

Necessary Clarifications

In the context of these events we must now mention something that only a few members have known about until now. It is impossible to keep this secret forever. Speaking of it is the last and only means of preventing an ineradicable shame from deepening still further.

In the *Mitteilungsblatt,* no. 16, April 19, 1925, Frau Dr. Wegman wrote the following sentence on "The sickbed, the last days and hours of Dr. Steiner": "At four in the afternoon, the pains came back, and my inner unrest would not be calmed. I insisted on letting Frau Dr. Steiner know, who was in Stuttgart at the time."[11] Since everyone knew that Frau Dr. Steiner was still at an evening of recitation of poems by Dr. Piper[12] at eight o'clock and did not return to Dornach until the following morning, these words could be interpreted—and were by numerous members—only as meaning the following: that Frau Dr. Steiner had been informed shortly after 4 p.m., but had remained in Stuttgart, because she apparently thought her poetry evening more important, and thus put off her departure until the next morning.

We must now give another quote:

> The truth is that Frau Dr. Steiner was not told until 10.30 at night, and was informed that although things had taken a turn for the worse there was no need to set off immediately, and that someone would contact her the next morning. When she was contacted SHORTLY BEFORE SIX IN THE MORNING, she set off without delay.

These words are by Herr Leinhas, who helped Frau Dr. Steiner with her departure, and accompanied her to Dornach. He dictated them to Herr [Gunther] Schubert, in the presence of Frau Dr. Steiner and Herr Dr. Unger. Herr Schubert added them to the manuscript that he wished to use

---

11 Even though Frau Dr. Wegman did not herself telephone, it was she who arranged it, and the Mitteilungsblatt report, with its catastrophic consequences, was authored by her.

12 Dr. Steiner had himself wished for this evening of recitation to take place, because he was glad to see Dr. Piper being supported.

in the members' meeting of February 6, 1926. Herr Dr. Unger also wished to discuss this matter.

Why did this not happen? Because Frau Dr. Steiner did not wish it. A quarter of an hour before the meeting, she asked Herr Leinhas to pass this message to Herr Schubert. The latter crossed the words out with pencil, and they are still there in the files. Frau Dr. Steiner later repeated that she did not wish these things to be mentioned simply to protect her against smear campaigns. At that time she also still hoped that the fanaticism in certain circles would calm down, and that people would soon relate to each other more humanly again. However, in 1934, it could still be discerned that Goetheanum colleagues thought Frau Dr. Steiner's behavior strange and inexplicable, because former members of the Free Society, in which these things went the rounds, had simply taken this calumny at face value. Frau Dr. Steiner, it was said, had the "karma" of coming too late, even to Dr. Steiner's death.

Herr Steffen, who did not dream for a moment that he was being told lies in this holiest of matters, passed on the news that others had thought fit to tell him. In the account he immediately wrote, entitled "In memoriam Rudolf Steiner," he reported that Frau Dr. Steiner was told at eleven o'clock at night "that Dr. Steiner had taken a turn for the worse," and that "a car could not be laid on until between seven and eight the next morning."

The opponents of Frau Dr. Steiner thus not only managed to keep her at a distance as Rudolf Steiner was dying, but also used the fact of her supposedly intentional absence as an accusation or a fateful indication that she did not wholly belong to Rudolf Steiner and Anthroposophy. She herself remained silent, and continually forbade her friends from speaking on her behalf.

Now, though, it is high time to speak out, so that rigorous self-reflection can give the Society a solid ground of truth upon which to stand.

Another ill-willed fabrication about these events is the claim that Frau Dr. Steiner took the urn containing Rudolf Steiner's ashes into her personal possession, and that Frau Dr. Wegman had to step in to "save the urn for the Society." Frau Dr. Wegman, it was said, had here acted so commendably that this outweighed other possible misdemeanors, if indeed any had ever taken place.

Characteristic of these nonsensical assertions is their very manner of drawing conclusions, which was also apparent in regard to [Dr. Steiner's] literary estate, and on other occasions. It assumes that everything that remained in Frau Dr. Steiner's hands was necessarily lost to the Society. Frau Dr. Wegman, on the other hand, is supposed to have had no personal investment in these things, but must always have represented the good of the whole Society. And since it was impossible to prove any actual personal ambitions on the part of Frau Dr. Steiner, people dreamed them up, and then portrayed them as something that must be prevented.

Frau Dr. Steiner was surprised and shocked to become aware of this, even while the urn was being taken from Basel to Dornach, in the behavior of Frau Dr. Wegman.

It wounded her deeply to see that they ascribed intentions to her that she did not have; and in this instance, that they wanted to prevent the urn being placed in the atelier. Frau Dr. Steiner had never contemplated placing the urn in Haus Hansi while waiting for a suitable room to be available in the new Goetheanum. At that time, though, it would have occurred to many that Dr. Steiner had kept the urns of a number of members in his house, among them that containing the ashes of Christian Morgenstern. Herr Steffen and Dr. Noll also thought that Dr. Steiner's ashes might be placed beside these others. It would therefore have been quite understandable if Frau Dr. Steiner had expressed a wish for this to happen, yet she did not, because of the whole situation.

When the behavior of Frau Dr. Wegman and Fräulein Dr. Vreede clearly showed that they ascribed these intentions to her, a bitter remark forced itself from her, to the effect that it really was not necessary to use maneuvering tactics to prevent her taking the urn to Dr. Steiner's room, for she had never considered doing so. At this the two others responded with a torrent of violent and insulting words.

Much that might be said about the events of those days must, for understandable reasons, be left unspoken. It is sufficiently clear from the examples just cited that, in the battle against Frau Dr. Steiner, all human kindness was pushed ruthlessly to one side.

Where ill-willed distortions can be denied their power, we have a duty to speak out. However, where we are confronted with wrongs that cannot be put right, even by plain and truthful speaking, may the unspoken truth still exercise its influence.

If there should ever be reasons for speaking of these things, there are a number of members extremely well placed to shed true light on them.

1926 and 1927

At the end of the meetings in February 1926, Herr Steffen expressed the hope that the difficulties would now be resolved, and that a thorough, conscientious report on the situation would allow peace and confidence to be reestablished throughout the whole Society. Following those stormy February days, apparent calm did set in. However, in reality nothing at all had changed in people's opinions and convictions. It immediately became clear that the assurances and promised given by Frau Dr. Wegman *were the opposite of her true beliefs and intentions,* and had been nothing more than a way of gaining time in order to consolidate her position.

There was increasing divisiveness between members, mainly because of the very way that recent events were reported. Alongside the open opportunism of the *Übervorstand*, there was much talk of the "martyrs" who, for the sake of peace, had refrained from defending themselves. The easy view—that all the difficulties could be explained by Frau Dr. Steiner's jealousy, by her inability to reconcile herself with Frau Dr. Wegman's privileged position—was not only put forward by Dr. Zeylmans and Frau Dr. Steiner's other opponents, but was also accepted by members quite far-removed from these events, who knew little or nothing of the people involved.

To begin with, people behaved as though nothing had happened. The only difference was that they took care to be more circumspect and restrained. The Alexander legend continued to be promoted, no longer so loudly and insistently as before, but more secretly and "in confidence."

That had the advantage of a more "esoteric" appearance, and of allowing people to deny these things as mendacious rumors and distortions. The impossible kinds of situation this sort of behavior led to will become apparent in the crass examples of the 1930 Annual General Meeting.

For the time being, though, people sensed the onset of renewed difficulties. Frau Dr. Wegman soon departed for Paris and London again, where she continued to be regarded as the leader of the School of Spiritual Science, and Dr. Steiner's successor. A new occasion for using passion and agitation to try to tackle questions of principle came in October 1928. The tragic thing was that the whole commotion, which lasted until the spring of 1927, was not caused by real circumstances but by outright delusions.

Back before Christmas 1925, Frau Dr. Wegman had approached Frau Dr. Steiner to urge her to take up the "old esotericism" again. Frau Dr. Steiner refused. Frau Dr. Wegman later asked Herr Steffen to put this request to Frau Dr. Steiner once more. Frau Dr. Steiner again refused.

At roughly the same time a public periodical with an anthroposophic board of editors, the Austrian *Blatterfurfreies Geistesleben,* spread the erroneous view that it was only with the new founding of the Anthroposophical Society and the Classes of the School of Spiritual Science in 1923 that Rudolf Steiner had "created an objective esoteric path of schooling." Previous to that, it said, he had only given personal instructions to individuals.

Ten months went by and no one had contradicted this error. Therefore, in October 1926, Herr Arenson wrote an open letter disproving the false report with a simple reference to chapter 68 of the *Autobiography,* in which Rudolf Steiner himself describes the esoteric lessons given during 1904 to 1914. While he was on this subject, Herr Arenson also took the opportunity to say something further about it, which he felt it was high time to mention. He wrote, "And here, let me just mention in passing an experience of which I regard it my duty to speak, given my advanced age. There are, after all, only a few people still alive who witnessed this scene."

It was a memory, therefore. At a celebration Rudolf Steiner had once said that Frau Dr. Steiner's collaboration with him (in those days she was still Fräulein Von Sivers) should be regarded as full in every sense, not just symbolic—as was the case with all the others involved at that time. Herr Arenson went on to draw a parallel between work on the "Leading Thoughts" (which, according to Dr. Steiner's own words in the *Mitteilungsblatt*, no. 31, 1924, should be studied with the help of the lecture cycles) and esoteric work, where he felt intensification and deepening to be as important as repetition. Herr Arenson expressed himself thus:

> I recommend a careful reading of this address in *Newssheet* no 31. One cannot avoid concluding that it is impossible to plumb the depths of the "Leading Thoughts" without the spiritual wealth that preceded it. SHOULD THIS NOT APPLY LIKEWISE TO THE ESOTERIC REALM?

That is all—a question. No denial of the status quo, but a stimulus to deepen and intensify it.

But Herr von Grone read into this "a peal of bells heralding a storm." To make sure his prophecy was fulfilled, he then set the storm going himself. Suddenly there resounded senseless calls of indignation on all sides, that "Frau Dr. Steiner wants to bring back an older esotericism—a flagrant attack on the Christmas Foundation Meeting that must be hindered at all costs." At this a storm of letters was unleashed, and a whirlwind of frenetic activity: people set off in all directions, open letters went the rounds, etc., until a written Declaration was drafted and presented to the Dornach *Vorstand* at the beginning of December 1926.

The thing that was hardest to understand about the whole situation was that Frau Dr. Wegman made no mention of her request to Frau Dr. Steiner. That would have calmed things down. Frau Dr. Steiner and Herr Steffen were unable to breathe a word of this without fanning the flames still more, and making the accusing fingers point instead at Frau Dr. Wegman. But the attacks on Frau Dr. Steiner continued for months on end. Not until things had calmed down somewhat, in February 1927, did Frau Dr. Steiner speak about them in an open letter—of which hardly anyone took any notice. "Nothing had happened" yet again.

Frau Dr. Steiner wrote the following on February 1925, under the title "DELUSIONS." The series of open letters that followed Herr Arenson's article has, perhaps, now come to an end, and I believe the time is right for me to make a few remarks about it. They can best be formulated as questions.

1. Why did people read so much into Herr Arenson's letter, and completely overlook the real reason it was written? Why did people attribute so little significance to this real reason, and continually overlook it as though it did not exist? In our Society, should we not feel obliged to correct something mistaken published through lack of knowledge of the actual facts? And is it not astonishing that this took so long, as there was no other way of informing members that an anthroposophic periodical had wholly misrepresented the facts? To say that Rudolf Steiner only gave us personal esoteric instruction up until the Christmas Foundation Meeting was indeed a misrepresentation. False information, not contradicted, forms people's opinions, affecting the future in a fateful, destructive way. How is it that people fail to notice the good service done to the Society by those who ascertain the truth? Or have we lost a sense for such things?

2. Are those who insinuate that Herr Arenson has all kinds of secondary motives, who let their fantasy run riot in such an extravagant fashion, aware to what degree they are deluding themselves? The fears that such people tried to awaken centered on the notion that I was re-introducing an old form of esotericism. ARE PEOPLE SUFFICIENTLY AWARE THAT I WAS PERSONALLY ASKED BY FRAU DR. WEGMAN TO RE-ADOPT "OLD ESOTERICISM," ALREADY BEFORE CHRISTMAS 1925, AND THAT SHE ALSO ASKED HERR ALBERT STEFFEN TO REQUEST THE SAME THING OF ME? AND THAT I DISMISSED THIS REQUEST, THAT I ANSWERED HER WITH A MOST DEFINITE "NO"? After all that has happened people may realize that there were good reasons for doing so. But if one cares to, one might also see that I would not have needed underhand means to achieve such a thing, as they have been so easily led to believe by storm-stirring Herr von Grone and those who inspired him, and that such a move would even have had a certain official sanction, which I chose to disregard. Herr von Grone set

his campaign of misinformation in motion with an extraordinary, deluded letter, which he also copied and circulated and then stirred up opinion against me. This had a powerful effect. Proof of this is a letter from the circle of priests, which is in my possession and whose flights of fancy are almost novelistic in conception. Herr von Grone closes his vicious circle with a grand gesture. He tries to justify his overzealousness with the following view:

> After all, from the time of the founding of the School of Spiritual Science onward, in fact since the re-founding of the Society altogether, did Dr. Steiner not make the School leaders on the Dornach *Vorstand* strictly and solely responsible for every initiative, even for mere suggestions to members relating to esoteric matters?

But he is forgetting a few very important points. He is forgetting, for instance, that two gentlemen of the German executive council tried very energetically to influence Herr Steffen in esoteric matters[13] and tried to exert this sort of influence within the Society. He is forgetting that there was an OPEN LETTER that suggested EXCLUDING THOSE MEMBERS FROM THE FIRST CLASS WHO DID NOT HAVE THE ATTITUDE TOWARD THE "LEADING THOUGHTS" OF MAY TO AUGUST 1925 THAT CERTAIN CIRCLES CONSIDERED DESIRABLE. This gesture of his is therefore lacking in any real substance. He was able to forget such things so easily because those circles, which it is comfortable to refer to as "the other camp" (although this phrase, too, was not originally based on any reality), did not care to use such things as ammunition. But he interprets Herr Arenson's article as "Taking the initiative and exerting influence on the most important, esoteric matters," and thus as something that is of "central concern to the Society," against which one must go on the offensive. He overlooks the fact that an error was corrected that, if it had not been, would have rendered the esoteric *Vorstand* guilty of a sin of omission.

---

13 Dr. Kolisko and Dr. Stein [see page 82f].

The course of events has shown what occurs when one gathers one's strength to tackle this sort of thing, and it would be no bad idea to reflect a little on what happened. Herr Arenson gives a few ideas about the way he sees our work continuing and developing as Dr. Steiner might have wished; and this is called "an initiative, an attempt to restructure the School of Spiritual Science"! To call it that is highly tendentious and objectively untrue. Someone who is seventy-two, and is thinking only of how best to fulfill his tasks on earth before he goes to meet his teacher and guide in the world of spirit, may well consider it necessary to express his views about the mistakes and childishness of other younger and less experienced people... That is his right and even his duty, especially when a great deal of harmful gossip has been going on, and various bits of nonsense. It was this nonsense that drove him to share a memory that would no doubt otherwise have remained concealed deep within his soul, but is important to him because it testifies to the continuity between old and new. He presents it as a contrast to all the tendentious gossip that has been so eagerly spread about, even sees it as his duty since he may well not live much longer and will then be called to account before Rudolf Steiner. Even so, however, this is no restructuring of the School of Spiritual Science. The best answer is provided by the fact I presented before: that I, the one whom others feared this of (and there is proof available of such a claim), was myself urged by the chair and secretary of the esoteric *Vorstand* to take up the old form of esotericism once again; and that I was very careful not do this because of the great immaturity I observed all around me.

But Herr von Grone writes: "This event (the article by Arenson) affected me like a peal of bells heralding a storm. This was the first move to act without consulting the *Vorstand* in Dornach..." O *saint simplicitas!* SURELY ALL THE FEBRUARY EVENTS CAME ABOUT PRECISELY BECAUSE OF CONTINUAL, ENERGETIC, AND EXTREME ATTEMPTS TO ACT WITHOUT CONSULTING THE DORNACH VORSTAND!

Satire is the only possible means of treating further of these things. Pathos does not suit them—it becomes untrue and hypocritical, as was the "honest citizen" tone and "utter conviction" of the latest Clarification [title of an open letter], a tone that can be poured out at random over everything to confuse the issues and dress them up in whatever way one pleases. One has to resort to gallows humor to do justice to these things. The "Declaration" however can be accused of trying to create an appearance that is at odds with the facts underlying it. It awakens false ideas, and is itself based on delusions, on things that have no reality. But the "clarifications" and "admonitions" use a large number of words to try to twist a large number of facts. They insinuate and tempt, they even dare to sully Dr. Steiner himself, which is rather distasteful. They have been written in blindness, and can only be excused, if at all, perhaps, as a well-meaning attempt to intervene where accusations are loudest by someone unfamiliar with the actual facts and their origin, who has been subject to a certain influence. The untruth has been spreading that Herr Arenson's letter had the kind of secondary motives described above, and therefore I felt compelled to give this explanation. The priests above all should consider whether it is befitting for their office to spread views based on hypotheses that amount to lies, and to show no understanding for the duty that Herr Arenson felt obliged to fulfill.

I close by turning to the members and asking this question: Would it have been possible to keep silent about all this?

❦

This was what Frau Dr. Steiner wrote at the time, without particular emphasis on the "Declaration." This Declaration is still interesting today, for it represents the first and relatively harmless form of the subsequent "Statement of Intent"; and the way that it came about can be seen as the first chapter, as it were, of the psychology underlying that later document.

Details of the origin and writing of the Declaration have never been fully cleared up, since they were shrouded in darkness and secrecy in a way very similar to that surrounding the earlier founding of the World School Association, and the subsequent writing of the "Statement of Intent." But what could not be denied is that a part of the German executive council of the time was responsible for writing and disseminating it. Herr von Grone, Dr. Rittelmeyer, and Dr. Stein admitted this in statements that, though somewhat different from each other, were the same in essence. Only Dr. Kolisko reported in a group meeting that the Declaration had come from several "members," and from various countries. Herr Leinhas, who as we will see had weighty reasons for examining these things closely, wrote in an open letter, "I acknowledge the justification of each of these statements, apart from the one given publicly by Dr. Kolisko, in which I see an attempt to avoid speaking the truth before the anthroposophic public."

The fact that something was wrong in the whole affair became clear when it turned out that the Declaration, set in motion by five members of the German executive council, was carefully kept secret from the German executive council's other four members. These heard nothing of the active publicity for it in many countries, of the gathering of ninety-eight signatures and of the document being handed to the Dornach *Vorstand*. But when they did learn of the whole business by chance, shortly before the Declaration arrived in Dornach, people spoke of "betrayal." Dr. Rittelmeyer had also known nothing about the fact that Dr. Unger and the three other *Vorstand* members were not supposed to hear about the Declaration.

The four members of the German executive council who had been kept in the dark were Herr Dr. Unger, Herr Leinhas, Herr Dr. Palmer, and Fräulein Mücke.[14] They were excluded by their other colleagues, because it was assumed that they would not sign the Declaration. If their refusal had become known this would have acted as a warning sign, making many examine the apparently harmless document more carefully for its underlying tendency. Nothing would then have come of the whole effort. By keeping it quiet, on the other hand, the people involved had succeeded

---

14   At the last moment, in Dornach, Herr von Grone urged Fräulein Mücke to sign the Declaration. She refused, in particular because the signatures of a part of the German *Vorstand* were missing. Herr von Grone replied that Dr. Unger had not wished to sign; yet, in another instance, Herr von Grone received someone's signature on replying "Yes" when asked whether Dr. Unger was in agreement.

in putting out a declaration of "faithfulness and will to work together" from which certain names were very obviously lacking. The bearers of these names were now forced to defend themselves, which led to still more conflicts.

This is a clear example of how the early stages of certain occurrences are almost more important than their final outcome. The content of the Declaration was a statement of faithfulness to the Dornach *Vorstand*, but at the same time took it upon itself to express an admonition to this *Vorstand* to be united, since Rudolf Steiner's spirit would only be able to continue working within the Society if all five worked together. This sweet-sounding dogma was an attempt to force the Dornach *Vorstand* in a particular direction. In the very first sentence the Arenson letter was cited as a threat to this unity, through the insincere and general assertion that "views about Dr. Steiner's continuing life and work have been propounded," whereas in fact such views had only surfaced in the authors' own circle. The whole thing was nothing other than an attack on the supposed power-lust of Frau Dr. Steiner, and on Herr Dr. Steffen who put up with it. Led astray by wording that concealed its real thrust, even Michael Bauer signed the Declaration, and afterward became painfully aware that he had unwittingly supported a campaign against individuals he deeply respected. The document runs as follows:

Declaration

Views about Dr. Steiner's continuing life and work have recently come to expression within the Society, but many members cannot share such views. In order to help clarify this situation, we would like to formulate how we understand Dr. Steiner's continued work in the Society.

1. When he died, Dr. Steiner left behind a *Vorstand* that he had repeatedly emphasized was, in its work with him, an esoteric one. We are convinced that a possibility exists in the Society for a living continuation of Dr. Steiner's work, if this *Vorstand* as a whole leads and guides the Society. We are also of the opinion that a *Vorstand* that still works in this way with Dr. Steiner must continue to be regarded as esoteric, even if the greatest

contrasts and differences are united within it. We cannot believe that Dr. Steiner's living work is served when anything of a partisan nature destroys this unified working of the *Vorstand*. We affirm the *Vorstand* in its totality and acknowledge it with all the authority that Dr. Steiner invested in it. *Even if we ourselves have given rise to something that is in opposition to the view presented here, we must condemn it.* We ask all members of the Society, in full consciousness of the serious situation in the Anthroposophical Society, and also the grave times in which we live, to be clear about this first condition of Dr. Steiner's continued effectiveness, and to avoid everything that might destroy it.

2. Dr. Rudolf Steiner left us an organism of social life that he hoped could become the bearer of living spirit. We are convinced that the Society will best work toward the future and open itself to the living continuation of Dr. Steiner's work when it retains these institutions in freedom, and through them tries to receive Dr. Steiner's further guidance. We are aware that life often necessitates change, but only this developing life itself, and the will of the whole *Vorstand*, can convince us that what already exists needs to be altered.

3. Following the departure of Dr. Steiner from the physical plane, we view the situation of the Anthroposophical Society and the large numbers of its determined opponents as cause for grave concern. Only the greatest sense of responsibility on the part of all members—particularly in avoiding partisan "camps," overcoming personal distrust, and everywhere seeking for what we all share—can, we believe, sustain the Society, give Dr. Steiner's spiritual work an organ imbued with humanity, and allow him the possibility of leading us forward strongly.

But we also know it is absolutely real and valid to remember, as Dr. Steiner once said, that "when, after my death, even just two people continue to work quite selflessly for the good of our undertakings, then I will be able to work with them."

"Even if we ourselves have given rise to something that is in opposition to the view presented here, we must condemn it." This sentence makes a particularly strong impression when one considers that the "Declaration" was itself such an act to be condemned, both because of its content, based on untrue premises, and especially because of the highly questionable way that it came about. It is also striking that, although we are told the *Vorstand* ought to lead the Society, no mention is made about leadership of the School of Spiritual Science. Yet the whole Declaration had actually arisen from "esoteric" indignation, and was intended to give Frau Dr. Steiner a shock that would keep her away from esotericism. But that is all less of a mystery when one considers that the names of those signatories, who were not unaware of what they were signing, were in fact Dr. Kolisko, Herr von Grone, Dr. Zeylmans, Mr. Kaufmann, et al. This was a declaration with a purely "Alexandrian" slant.

And these months of commotion had no real basis in reality! But the vagaries indulged in by Frau Dr. Wegman and the *Übervorstand* were meant to leave Frau Dr. Steiner in disgrace. People misused esotericism as a weapon in this battle and pretended to be defending the integrity of the Christmas Foundation Meeting. If Frau Dr. Steiner had accepted Frau Dr. Wegman's suggestion, it would have been said: "You see, we will have to leave those people to carry on in the old ways, for they cannot understand the new." Yet although she did not have this intention, people nevertheless ascribed it to her, and still declared: "See, those are the ones who always hark back to the past, to prevent what is new from flourishing!"

At the end of winter, on March 6, 1927, the Annual General Meeting took place. This time only business matters were discussed. But the question was raised as to why Frau Dr. Wegman had not prevented the whole senseless commotion of past months, which she could so easily have done with a few words. Frau Dr. Wegman replied:

> I was not expecting this question, naturally, but I very much welcome this request to speak to you. It was never my intention to attack Frau Dr. Steiner in any way. It could never have been, for Dr. Steiner would never have worked with me in the way he did if

I had not had the attitude that I did toward the one who was close to him.

So you can certainly assume, *of Dr. Steiner (!) as well*—that the work we undertook together would never have been so fruitful and productive if I had harbored resentment of any kind against Frau Dr. Steiner.

Then, after some general remarks, she says about recent events:

I would truly like to know what esoteric-related things I am supposed to have done against Frau Dr. Steiner or other *Vorstand* members. I do not know what they are. We have spoken a good deal about Class Lesson matters, and I believe we have reached complete clarity on that. When Frau Dr. Steiner said I was the one who had asked her whether she might give all of us, or at least those able to receive it, the old esotericism she knew from the past, THIS WAS ALSO TRUE. I did this because I have the highest regard for knowledge of this kind possessed by Herr Dr. Steiner. Moreover, I have the very greatest respect for the section for art, eurythmy, and speech formation. I am certainly among those who take enormous pleasure in the wonderful things that are now being presented to the world.

The same attitude reappears here that Frau Dr. Wegman had assumed when defending her "Leading Thoughts" and that in the future would become ever-more pronounced—an attitude that recognizes no real facts, no reality, no mistakes, no responsibility. Instead, the memory of Rudolf Steiner and the trust he had in Frau Dr. Wegman are supposed to be a guarantee, once and for all, that whatever results from her attitude, whatever effects are unleashed by her, are done in the name of Rudolf Steiner, and that anyone who judges her according to her deeds is attacking Dr. Steiner, as well. In addition, in this instance Frau Dr. Wegman also apparently deems it necessary to confirm that Frau Dr. Steiner had spoken the truth! Then she goes on to praise eurythmy, just in case Frau Dr. Steiner is still a little unhappy. The fact that the Class Lesson matter was still far from being settled had better be left on one side.

The German Society was in the throes of a severe crisis. An extraordinary General Meeting, which took place in Stuttgart on April 6, 1927, was preceded by numerous other meetings. About the Declaration Dr. Unger said, "I felt I was betrayed as never before in my life."

Herr Leinhas had closed his open letter (mentioned previously [page 104–105]), with these words:

> Instead let us take care that we can answer to Rudolf Steiner for what we undertake! Let us finally give up gossiping on every street corner about things that ought to be too holy for us to even touch upon in our thoughts. Instead let us take care that freedom of thought holds sway in our Society instead of dispute about doctrine; heartfelt, yes, heart-filled openness and truthfulness instead of an atmosphere of stuffy "diplomacy"; strict objectivity in matters of inner experience, instead of shouting like a street vendor about our own "results of research." Then we will have no need to fear for the state of the Anthroposophical Society.
>
> The guarantee of freedom of spiritual work, and of wholly neutral management by Dr. Unger, once more overcame the crisis. Dr. Unger, whom Dr. Steiner had in 1924 entrusted with special administrative responsibility for initiatives of the Anthroposophical Society in Germany, expressly refused to rely on using Dr. Steiner's name. Following the crisis in February 1926, Dr. Unger had made strenuous efforts to stop the German executive council falling apart. His opponents in the *Vorstand* claimed that he had only been entrusted with the management "because no one else had the time to do it." At this, Dr. Unger gave up all responsibility for anything that would in future be issued without his authority and personal signature. In April 1927, even this role was narrowed down to "wholly neutral management." Dr. Unger's task, to refrain from hindering the further aims of those people who had betrayed him, was a foretaste of the similar and increasingly insistent demands placed upon Herr Steffen.

1928 and 1929

The differences of opinion that led to such severe conflict about the leadership of the Society were so intimately related to individual members' whole approach to life that they found expression in every action, and surfaced in every realm of anthroposophic endeavor. Sharp criticisms were voiced on different sides, and this mutual disapproval affected almost everything that was said and done. Herr Steffen therefore decided to make a new attempt to sustain both the unified quality and the freedom of further work. In the Annual General Meeting of February 25, 1928, he informed the members that he had decided, as chair, to take over responsibility for everything done in the name of the Society and in the separate sections. He reminded people that Rudolf Steiner had also declared himself responsible, as chair, for all that might happen in the context and name of Anthroposophy. He had taken this so far that, in a court case about an anthroposophic publication, he allowed judgment to be passed on him instead of the author of the book.

In the *Mitteilungsblatt,* no. 11, March 11, 1928, Herr Steffen reported on the step he had taken and wrote:

> Circumstances within the Society, which have already been sufficiently aired both verbally and in writing, in meetings and resolutions, subsequently led me to make a statement on the occasion of the first Christmas Meeting after Rudolf Steiner's death. This statement, which I made on being promoted from deputy chair to chair, was to the effect that the sections of different *Vorstand* members must be responsible themselves for everything that they undertook. Given the present situation, I said, the chair could only take responsibility for his own actions. This statement was one necessitated by the facts themselves. It corresponded with reality, as was proved by the conflicts that broke out during February 1926.
>
> At that time I tried to maintain the unity of the *Vorstand* at all costs, by saying that I regarded it as a unity—even though the sections bore full responsibility for their actions. At the same time

I stated that I would respond to the resignation of a single member with my own resignation as chair.

This statement about the self-accountability of the different sections had to be most strictly adhered to, so that I would be unable to take sides when various attacks were made on the activities of their leaders. It became apparent, however, that this made our work more and more difficult. Members who could see all the implications remarked that the sections' autonomy required external form and documentation. Yet I considered that this would lead to a high degree of fragmentation of the life of our Society, which is exactly what my statement had aimed to avoid. A more or less official division of this kind would gradually have a negative effect on general anthroposophic work at the Goetheanum, and within the whole Society, particularly where lecture courses were concerned.

During the last few weeks, therefore, I have taken the decision to declare myself responsible, as chair, for everything in future undertaken by the Goetheanum in Dornach. *I first stated this in the* Vorstand *and then before the plenary session of the General Meeting.* THIS DECLARATION MAKES VOID THOSE EARLIER STATEMENTS MADE AT THE TIME OF THE CHRISTMAS CONFERENCE AND THE EVENTS OF FEBRUARY, WHICH I HAVE BRIEFLY SUMMARIZED HERE.

THIS CERTAINLY DOES NOT IMPLY THAT I WILL ALWAYS BE IN AGREEMENT WITH WHAT I BEAR RESPONSIBILITY FOR IN FUTURE. THE MULTIFACETED NATURE OF ACTIVITIES AT THE GOETHEANUM WOULD MAKE THIS IMPOSSIBLE. ONE CANNOT ALWAYS GAIN AN OVERVIEW OF THE WORK THAT IS DONE HERE, LET ALONE TEST AND EXAMINE IT. HOWEVER, THIS WILL AT LEAST ENSURE THAT CRITICISM IS DIRECTED IN ONE CHANNEL, SO THE WORK THAT IS NOW BEING SEVERELY UPSET AND DISTURBED CAN CONTINUE WITH AS LITTLE HINDRANCE AS POSSIBLE. Productive activity is impossible without some degree of peace and quiet. And if we are unproductive we will not advance. So we may perhaps hope that, given self-reflection and inner activity on the part of members, this necessary decision will lead to a deepening and strengthening of the Society.

Herr Steffen felt his decision to be a drastic "leap of faith." The members were grateful that his deed had created new possibilities and new hope. This step struck Dr. Unger in particular as full of promise. Only those who had the most reason to be grateful accused him of interference and presumption. It was clear to everyone that Herr Steffen was hoping he could in future prevent, or divert upon himself, such attacks as Dr. Zbinden, for example, had unleashed against Frau Dr. Wegman's medical work—an attack that had been violent in nature even though its content was wholly objective. Following his criticism Frau Dr. Wegman had dismissed Dr. Zbinden from the medical section in the fall of 1927, which many considered to be an illegal step. Other unsustainable circumstances had also arisen.

At the same Annual General Meeting it became clear how Herr Steffen intended carrying out his decision, when discussion arose about the "World Conference" planned to take place in London the following summer. Severe reservations were expressed about this plan. People distrusted the organizers and their assistants because they were the same individuals who had already wreaked such havoc as founders of the World School Association, adherents of the "Declaration," and as the *"Übervorstand."* People feared another attempt to divert the anthroposophic movement away from the Goetheanum. True, Herr Steffen had, on this occasion, been officially informed, and been shown a printed draft of the program. But the *Vorstand* was not consulted when plans were drawn up, even though this was intended to be a large-scale, "global" undertaking, involving enormous costs. The only proper consultation had been with Frau Dr. Wegman, regarded by the organizers as the only authoritative personality left after Dr. Steiner's death. People were also very unhappy that this World Conference was to take place roughly six weeks before the festive opening of the Goetheanum, and asked whether it would not be better to put energy, time, and money into this. The English organizers referred to a wish Dr. Steiner had indeed expressed, during his last stay in England in the summer of 1924, for a large event to take place. But it remained questionable whether Dr. Steiner would have welcomed a large-scale convention at the same time as preparations for the opening of the Goetheanum. What Dr. Steiner had said also took on a rather different character if one knew, as many did, that he had asked for a larger and above all better-prepared conference, saying he would not come back to England if future events were so inadequately prepared, poorly attended, and dully received as the Torquay summer course of August 1924.

Because of his concerns about the hard work still needed to prepare for the opening of the Goetheanum, Herr Steffen was not all that happy about the World Conference. Yet he gave this initiative the go-ahead, and the Goetheanum's official sanction and cooperation. The Annual General Meeting had the effect of getting the organizers to make some changes to their program, so that it had a less partisan flavor.

The World Conference took place from July 20 to August 1, 1928. Herr Steffen sent an official letter of greeting that was read out at its opening. Frau Dr. Steiner had the eurythmy group perform there. Dr. Wachsmuth gave a lecture, as did Dr. Unger, who took the lead from Herr Steffen and agreed to go, having also passed invitations to the German members on behalf of the German executive council. The conference's main speakers were Dr. Stein, who was still waging a campaign against Dr. Steiner's will, Dr. Kolisko, and Dr. Zeylmans.

The "World Conference" was held in a medium-sized hall in the Friends' House in London. About six hundred of the one thousand seats were filled, mainly by members, some of whom had come from other countries. It could hardly have been called a public success, and the financial short-fall was considerable.

Frau Dr. Wegman, who had promoted this World Conference as if it were her own, also wrote the official report on it, which one can read in the *Mitteilungsblatt*, no. 34, August 19, 1928.

Subsequently, the attitude of Herr Steffen and Frau Dr. Steiner was of course severely criticized. At the same time it was claimed that the

Vorstand had known all the details of the program from the beginning, and had been closely consulted. Even two years later, at a meeting of General Secretaries in April 1920, the following was said:

> Mr. Kaufmann: "Mrs. Merry (the secretary of the World Conference) passed the plans to the whole *Vorstand*."
>
> Frau Dr. Steiner: "I, for example, never had prior sight of such plans. It is nonsense to suggest this. I returned from a journey and learned that the World Conference was a fait accompli, and was to take place that same year. You may say what you like, but please leave your moral indignation on one side."

⁕

At the same time, as he assumed responsibility for the sections, Herr Steffen also took over as editor of the *Mitteilungsblatt* again. He now published his report on the Annual General Meeting, and also reported in detail on the activity of all the sections, as well as writing some essays on community building. He urged the members to intensify their spiritual work, gave guidelines for real artistic and scientific activity, and offered advice for developing a good writing style. He exhorted the members to ponder three questions: 1) How can work within an anthroposophic group have significance for contemporary cultural life? 2) The effects of agitation. 3) Esotericism in art and science, and dallying with esotericism (*Mitteilungsblatt*, no. 12, March 18, 1928).

In the *Mitteilungsblatt*, July 15, 1928, Herr Steffen published an invitation to all Society speakers and lecturers, which he had already discussed in the Annual General Meeting, to apply to take part in the conference celebrating the opening of the Goetheanum. It is important to quote the precise words of this invitation:

> At the Annual General Meeting of the General Anthroposophical Society on February 25, 1928, we were able to announce that the Goetheanum will open in the fall of this year, at Michaelmas. We announced a nine-day conference of artistic offerings (mystery plays, choir and eurythmy performances, etc.) and lectures. As

chair of the Anthroposophical Society, I believe I may say that we are seeking lecturers who have developed something new through inner work out of the wealth that Anthroposophy offers, and who have not yet presented this anywhere else. In making this stipulation I have been guided by something Rudolf Steiner said, "The Goetheanum wants to hear something new."

We are thus calling on members' inner, creative activity.

Colleagues are therefore invited to submit short proposals describing the theme and content of their lectures, so that the conference program can be drawn up as soon as possible. Our aim will be to create a program in which all lectures together form a whole.

It is unlikely that the *Vorstand* will be able to include all the proposals submitted. The number of members is thankfully large, while the conference itself is unfortunately short.

(If there are too many proposals, the lectures will be held over for later conferences.)

Herr Steffen also spent weeks drawing up a plan for lecture activity at the Goetheanum, for instructing speakers, etc., and wished to present this to the *Vorstand*.

However, Fräulein Dr. Vreede immediately protested at all this, because, in her opinion, every initiative should proceed from the *Vorstand*, and the chair ought not to make independent proposals. As soon as early summer these attacks began on Herr Steffen, as chair. She also protested against him taking over responsibility for the sections—not because she was against it in principal, but because she felt she had to reject the way that Herr Steffen had done this.

Herr Steffen withdrew his invitation and replaced it with one couched in general, formal terms, and issued by the *Vorstand*. Before the conference even began he had come to see how impossible it was to bear overall responsibility any longer, given the nature of the circumstances and the degree of mistrust about his intentions.

So although the opening conference went well, at least outwardly, it was not what Herr Steffen would have achieved if he had been allowed

The "Memorandum"

to carry out his suggestions. It did become apparent, however, that Herr Steffen's generosity would enable lecturing activity to run smoothly, even if speakers held very extreme points of view about Society matters. This at least had been demonstrated by the opening conference.

But at the end of the conference, at the General Secretaries meeting of October 8, 1928, Herr Steffen felt compelled by the continuous attacks of Fräulein Dr. Vreede to divest himself completely of the responsibility that he had so earnestly taken upon himself. Fräulein Dr. Vreede had summarized her complaints about Herr Steffen in a three-point letter: 1) Disregarding the *Vorstand*. 2) Betrayal of the Christmas Foundation Meeting. 3) Violation of the free life of the spirit.

To throw light on the real state of affairs we must now refer to a later statement explaining her behavior, which Dr. Vreede did not make until November 29, 1930.

In the passage quoted earlier Herr Steffen had written of how he had made the decision to take overall responsibility: "I first said this in the *Vorstand* and then before the plenary session of the Annual General Meeting." Fräulein Dr. Vreede held the view that this was incorrect, and that Herr Steffen had not declared his decision in the *Vorstand*. As a *Vorstand* member she felt herself "disregarded." But for two and a half further years, during which time she continued as *Vorstand* member, she never attempted to question either Herr Steffen or another *Vorstand* member about these lines in the *Mitteilungsblatt*. Instead she waited until November 29, 1930, and then read out the relevant passage to the General Secretaries[15] to use her error at a highly critical moment as a weapon against Herr Steffen. At the same time she turned for support to Frau Dr. Wegman, who backed her up by suddenly announcing that she too had known nothing of Herr Steffen's decision being discussed in the *Vorstand*. She also declared that Herr Steffen was altogether incapable of bearing such responsibility. Herr Stef-

---

15 She explained her point of view in this meeting in the following words: "This document, in which Herr Steffen took over this responsibility, amounts to a statement that I do not belong to the *Vorstand*."

fen was not able to leap to his own defense at that moment, since he could not always carry the minutes of all meetings around with him in his pockets. He said only that he did not make a habit of writing things that were untrue, which of course made little impression on the *"Übervorstand."* However, a few days later Herr Steffen read to members gathered in the carpentry workshop a detailed report on the *Vorstand* meeting of February 18, 1928, where the whole question had been discussed in full. The report expressly mentioned the presence of Frau Dr. Wegman, as well as that of Dr. Unger who had attended by invitation. It turned out, however, that Fräulein Vreede had not attended this meeting. It still remains a mystery why she did not immediately protest at the Annual General Meeting, or even at the preceding General Secretaries meeting, instead of waiting two and a half years—and in the meantime making unjustified accusations that rendered unified work at the Goetheanum impossible. Fräulein Dr. Vreede plunged the Society into the most desperate situation, preferring to assume that Herr Steffen had lied, rather than that she herself could have made a mistake.

In a talk given in April 1930 (before Fräulein Dr. Vreede had made her far worse accusations in the fall of 1930), Herr Steffen looked back on 1928 with the following words:

> If I had insisted on having my way, the Society would have been divided down the middle.... I was quite alone in this situation. I had intended to unite freely creative people—that was my "rallying call"; and then to present my plan to the *VORSTAND*, after which nothing further would be MY OWN SOLE DECISION. Although I stated this at the time, I did not have the full confidence of Fräulein Dr. Vreede; and very many members were of the same opinion. Now ALTHOUGH I AM A POET, I AM ACTUALLY MORE PRACTICAL THAN PEOPLE REALIZE. I AM ALSO SOMEONE WHO HAS ALWAYS HEARKENED TO THE PROMPTS OF DESTINY. I very quickly saw that Fräulein Dr. Vreede's objection was a sign directing me back to my real work as a writer. You know that I have in the meantime written two novels,

The "Memorandum"

as well as various other pieces, whereas I had done nothing of this sort for nearly a decade previously.

❦

At the Annual General Meeting of that year, 1928, Rudolf Steiner's will was once more under discussion. The French General Secretary, Mademoiselle Sauerwein, made claims for SOLE and EXCLUSIVE rights for all translations into French of works by Rudolf Steiner. This matter, which in the following years gave rise to continually renewed confusion and commotion, will here be followed to its conclusion.

Mlle. Sauerwein possessed a document in Rudolf Steiner's handwriting, which acknowledged that she had the right to translate works by him. She now claimed that she therefore had EXCLUSIVE rights, but initially refused to show the document. She went to the French courts. During a eurythmy performance, at her instigation, a bailiff appeared in order to demand payment of a fine for infringement of authors' rights, since a verse by Rudolf Steiner, translated into French, appeared on the program. Mlle. Rihouet, who had received permission from Frau Dr. Steiner to translate and publish a work by Rudolf Steiner, was summoned to appear in court. Frau Dr. Steiner had to give a written witness statement. The hearings went on for months, and notaries and lawyers had to be involved. Expert opinion finally concluded that Mlle. Sauerwein certainly did not have exclusive rights, but rather that Rudolf Steiner's will allowed Frau Dr. Steiner, as his heiress, to decide whom to allocate translation rights to apart from Mlle. Sauerwein. *Mlle. Rihouet had anyway received personal permission from Dr. Steiner to translate his works, for he wanted to support her periodical* "La Science Spirituelle."

During all these years, Frau Dr. Wegman and Fräulein Dr. Vreede supported Mlle. Sauerwein in her battle against Frau Dr. Steiner and Mlle. Rihouet. By visiting her and giving her ostentatious signs of friendship, they made their position clear. The organizers of the "World Conference" also celebrated the presence of the French General Secretary, with the clear aim of backing her in her battle against Frau Dr. Steiner. This led to violent clashes in the meeting of General Secretaries already referred to, of October 8, 1928.

⁙

In Germany, too, people had continued the battle against Rudolf Steiner's testament. Dr. W. J. Stein, in particular, won further accolades for himself as the savior of the Christmas Foundation Meeting, believing that his dialectics had infallibly proven the incompatibility of the will with Dr. Steiner's intentions after the Christmas Foundation Meeting. The rather less sharp-thinking group of young members around Dr. Lehrs was fed a fairy tale that also found ready credence: during his illness, apparently, Dr. Steiner had wished to go from the atelier into his house in order to destroy the will, but was hindered by weakness from doing so. Those who believed this did not stop to consider the fact that a statement in one's own handwriting is by law fully sufficient to cancel one's own previous will, and replace it with another. Dr. Steiner was writing right up to the end, and would have known very well how to make new arrangements if he had so wished. A word or a note from him, such as he often wrote for this purpose, would have been enough to bring him whatever he wanted. This happened on a nearly daily basis, and often in regard to the most important matters. The best proof of the falsity of this invention, however, is the fact that Dr. Steiner had himself deposited a copy of the will with the authorities in Berlin, and that it could only have been canceled by one written later.

As a result of the meeting of October 8, 1928, Dr. Stein felt it necessary to temporarily withdraw from the German executive council. But letters from Herr von Grone started the whole testament debate off again within this council. At a meeting on January 1, 1929, in Dornach, Dr. Unger addressed the underlying principles of the question once more. He asked the German executive council to give a clear statement to the effect that Dr. Stein and anyone sharing his view of Rudolf Steiner's testament was unsuited to occupy the office of German executive council member, and should be urged to resign permanently from this council. But since

Dr. Unger's motion was not accepted at this meeting, HE NOT ONLY RESIGNED FROM THE GERMAN EXECUTIVE COUNCIL, BUT ALSO FROM THE ANTHROPOSOPHICAL SOCIETY IN GERMANY, and from then on affiliated himself with Dornach. On the following day, Dr. Stein announced via Herr von Grone that he was withdrawing permanently from the executive council.

On January 4, 1929, as he entered a lecture hall in Nuremberg to give a lecture on the theme "What is Anthroposophy?" Dr. Unger was shot and killed by a mentally ill person.

There was great shock at Carl Unger's sudden and tragic death, and many people reflected on his services to the anthroposophic movement. Yet others did not cease their hatred against the man who, for example, had written in his report on the World School Association:

> I would like to protect the Anthroposophical Society from burdening Rudolf Steiner's karma lectures with our present difficulties. Each of the two sides from whom we have heard accounts this evening [by Dr. Unger and Dr. Stein; see page 87], surely number among them representatives from both the streams Dr. Steiner was referring to. If we are to speak of two "will directions" that are expressed in these divergences, it can only be of FREE and UNFREE THINKING. What we must protect ourselves from are repeated attempts to fetter thought, to impose particular points of view. This includes the continued efforts made to silence others.

Dr. Unger was also convinced that "I WILL NEVER BE ABLE TO GAIN MORE INFLUENCE THAN MY ANTHROPOSOPHIC WORK IS WORTH."

In the Stuttgart circles of the Free Society, it was possible to say things such as what Dr. Unger had, as though by the grace of God, been prevented by his death from becoming an opponent of Anthroposophy. In his latter days he had supposedly shown signs of such a thing. Elsewhere it was said that Dr. Unger had, after all, caused Dr. Stein's resignation by his demand that Rudolf Steiner's will should be acknowledged, and the world of spirit had been unable to tolerate this.

Because of this sort of posthumous attack, Frau Dr. Steiner published some of the very last letters of Rudolf Steiner, in which he complains bitterly about opposition toward Dr. Unger, in the *Mitteilungsblatt*, no. 14, March 31, 1929. This opposition, which clouded Dr. Steiner's last days, was embodied in Dr. W. J. Stein and his friends. We would like to print some excerpts from these letters.

On March 13, 1925, Dr. Steiner wrote to Frau Dr. Steiner:

> In Stuttgart it seems that something is rearing its head again against Unger. It will affect you too, but you will find the right way of dealing with it. It is quite clear that now, when I am ill, circles such as the Waldorf School must try out things for themselves. It is already happening with the conference arrangements. Unger was going to give a lecture during the conference, but the administrative council of the Waldorf School is making this impossible. Unger is not supposed to give a lecture during the Waldorf School conference (since it is for the Anthroposophical Society and not for the conference). So at this point the Stuttgart executive council writes to tell the Dornach *Vorstand* what ought to be done. It is quite impossible for us here in Dornach to intervene, at such a late stage, in a matter that belongs to one of the most disastrous Stuttgart scenarios. Therefore, I can only send a message to the Stuttgart executive council that we cannot intervene. That, of course, does not prevent you from doing whatever you think is right in Stuttgart, if people should approach you about it.

On March 20 1925, Dr. Steiner wrote:

> ...Unger ought to be supported in the future within the Anthroposophical Society. However, what will happen if this tendency to make his position in the Society untenable keeps coming to the fore?

The LAST letter ever written by Rudolf Steiner, on March 23, contains this request: "It might be good if you could find the time to talk with Unger's opponents. I have already written about the way things are going."

As late as 1934 Herr von Grone disseminated an open letter, prefaced with the phrase "Trusting in the community-building power of the enclosed contents," in which the most foolish idiocies were expressed about Dr. Unger. This letter was by Dr. Lehrs, and saying anything about it is a waste of breath.

After Dr. Unger died the German executive council issued an official statement in the *Mitteilungsblatt*, no. 6, February 3, 1929. The statement is dated January 20, 1929, and signed by Herr Leinhas. It begins as follows:

> Dr. Walter Johannes Stein resigned from the German executive council on January 2, 1929. On January 13, the Stuttgart administrative council (Dr. Kolisko, Leinhas, Dr. Palmer, and Dr. Rittelmeyer) met to consult about RESTRUCTURING THE GERMAN EXECUTIVE COUNCIL, WHICH THE DEATH OF DR. UNGER HAD MADE NECESSARY. Circumstances necessitated that the undersigned take over financial administration. He regards this as a provisional measure only. Dr. Kolisko, Dr. Palmer and Dr. Rittelmeyer declared themselves willing to continue as administrative members of the executive council. The decision was made to reapply for recognition by the Dornach *Vorstand*, as the German executive council members are its functionaries according to the "Principles," and then to obtain the endorsement of the members of the German Society. Recognition by the Dornach *Vorstand* occurred in its meeting of January 18, 1929.

What effect could Dr. Unger's death have had on the composition of the German executive council, since he had even resigned from the German Society? The fact was that Dr. Unger's resignation, which cast such a poor light on the German executive council, had initially been kept fairly quiet; and then, after the shock of Dr. Unger's death, was sidelined and disregarded. Apart from this, Dr. Unger had also agreed that his resignation would only be fully valid from January 15, both because there was some business still left to sort out, and because, above all, publicity had already gone out in the name of the German Society for the lecture program planned by him. But he had actually already provisionally handed over business management to Herr Leinhas on January 1. His sudden death, though, provided a pretext for speaking of the need for "restructuring the German executive council."

This reorganization consisted only, initially, in no longer having to take account of the views represented by Dr. Unger, giving free rein instead to the influence of Dr. Kolisko. The fact that Herr Leinhas no longer kept this influence at bay was seen by many members as an inexplicable and regrettable change in attitude. But since Herr Leinhas never tired of demonstrating the complete consistency of his own behavior, we cannot give any reasons for this change, but only ascertain its actual consequences. The direction subsequent events were to take became apparent soon after the above-quoted inaugural manifesto was published.

Herr Leinhas who had previously taken the World School Association and the "Declaration" as a warning sign, and kept as great a distance as possible between himself and Dr. Kolisko, now began to close ranks with him on more and more issues, even though Dr. Kolisko never ceased from "trying not to speak the truth to the wider anthroposophic membership." Herr Leinhas was increasingly caught up in the "atmosphere of stuffy diplomacy" he so abhorred. Just two years later he was to emerge as the liquidator of the small residue of funds that still remained from the former German Society.

1930

The events of 1930 deserve a full and detailed analysis. They were of decisive significance BECAUSE THEY CAUSED THE LAST HOPE OF RECONCILIATION TO FADE. Looking back on the extraordinary General meeting of December, the Society's situation was one that made inevitable the decisions of following years.

The General Meeting on April 26, 1930, was of far less significance than the meeting of General Secretaries that preceded it. We will describe this now, based on the short-hand minutes taken at the time.

Herr Steffen read out a letter by five Goetheanum colleagues requesting permission to attend the meeting. Herr Steffen wanted those assembled, rather than himself, to decide on this, and after a one-and-a-half hour discussion, a vote was taken. Twenty-four voted in favor, eleven against, while twelve abstentions came about through refusal to engage in any consultation process on the matter. When the Dornach members waiting nearby were informed of the results of this vote, they decided not to make use of a permission granted with such reluctance and mistrust.

Seen as a symptom, this event highlights the unpleasant way that agreement in all matters of importance was intentionally made impossible. What was really going on here? Dr. Steiner had set up the so-called General Secretaries' meetings as a way of consulting with relevant members about the Society's affairs. He referred to it as an "expanded *Vorstand*." Nothing more precise was imposed concerning its composition, rights, and duties, and in the short period preceding Dr. Steiner's death it played no particular role. But in later years it exerted influence upon how the Society was led in a way that aroused members' indignation.

While it was not possible to dispute its composition as such, it was used in an arbitrary and unjust manner. The Society in each country naturally had the right to elect an executive council with as many members as it wanted. Yet this resulted in the English and Dutch Societies, which each had about six hundred members, in sending as many representatives to Dornach as the German Society with its eight thousand members. Over the course of time the English Society had doubled the number of its executive council members. This and other disparities enabled Frau Dr. Wegman's supporters to be in a majority in the meeting of General Secretaries, which was as they wanted it. The lack of Dornach members was particularly evident. Frau Dr. Wegman herself protested against their admission with the words: "Of course it's no good if five more come when votes depend on a majority. *Then five people can completely change the way things are actually meant to go.* We can't work like that."

Herr Steffen said, "It is quite clear to me that Dornach also ought to have a few people in this meeting. If I look about me I don't see many Dornach people." Frau Dr. Wegman spoke of "those few people" [outside], and he replied: "They're not just a few people! They are Herr Aisenpreis, the architect who built the Goetheanum..." and so on, and he pointed out that these were people who had taken an active part in the life of the Society for a long time, even for decades. (They were: Herr Aisenpreis, Frau Waller-Pyle, Herr Staten, Frau de Jaager, and Herr Schubert.) Dr. Wachsmuth drew attention to the fact that some of those present, by contrast, had only joined the Society a short while back.

This lopsided sort of justice was also apparent in the next meeting of the year, when Mlle. Sauerwein, who could not be present because of illness, suddenly got four people to replace her, without anyone raising an objection. The *Vorstand* had naturally not been asked about this.

Characteristic of the efforts to use moral phrases to cover up actual sabotage was the claim, also repeated on this occasion, that people were basically in agreement but that the way something arose must be rejected. Fräulein Dr. Vreede had already practiced something similar when she made it impossible for Herr Steffen to take responsibility for the sections. It was supposedly better that the Society should go under altogether than that anything should deviate from the way that Fräulein Dr. Vreede or others expected. This was Fräulein Dr. Vreede's attitude again on this occasion, and Mrs. Merry, on behalf of the English representatives present, said that "in principle they agreed with admitting the Dornach members, but had voted against because they could not agree with the manner of their admission."

The way some people spoke of the "expanded *Vorstand*" revealed that they were not against extending the "esoteric positions" occupied by the *Vorstand* members to themselves as part of this expansion. As really practical people, Dr. Zeylmans and others suggested that, alongside *Vorstand*, General Secretaries, and General Meeting, there should be a fourth body. If this had ever come about it would have been neither "esoteric" nor "exoteric" but quite simply pointless. Luckily nothing came of it.

The following is also of symptomatic importance. Dr. Kolisko had heard that Herr Steffen, Frau Dr. Steiner, and Dr. Wachsmuth were in favor of admitting the Dornach people, while Frau Dr. Wegman and Fräulein Dr. Vreede were against it. In spite of this he then demanded that the

The "Memorandum"

meeting itself should not continue discussing it, but that the *Vorstand* ought to make the decision based on a unanimous vote. "The *Vorstand* has not made a decision on this. This is precisely what contributes to the very greatest difficulties."

When others likewise demanded unanimity for esoteric reasons, Dr. Wachsmuth said:

> Would you think it esoteric if I said that I would change my opinion just so that we get unanimity? Giving up one's own opinion like that would actually be unesoteric. This is a problem that has been occupying and paining some people for years already! But sooner than demand unanimity from the *Vorstand* in such things, we would do better to decide here and now that the Anthroposophical Society should never have a *Vorstand* at all. Such a thing is impossible; you will not find such a *Vorstand* anywhere. And I also do not think that Dr. Steiner was so removed from ordinary life as to think that the five people he had called upon would always be of the same opinion. This interpretation will get us nowhere.

And before this, when consultation within the meeting had been rejected, he had said:

> Are we going to work together here, or should the *Vorstand* always decree what is to happen? If everything is decided in advance there is not much point in sitting here at all. If the *Vorstand* is meant to have a united response about everything.... I would like to ask you whether you are quite sure that, when the *Vorstand* decides something unanimously, there are none who reject such a unanimous decision? But I do think that this is really a question of truthfulness, which is well worth discussing.
>
> The second point on the agenda was the so-called Nordic petition, which we will come back to later, since no decision was made about it until December.

The last point must be examined at length, for it was because of this that VORSTAND MEETINGS COULD NO LONGER TAKE PLACE IN THE SAME WAY AS BEFORE.

It was to do with the following: At the beginning of 1930 the *Vorstand* had received several letters asking why Frau Kolisko had not read Class Lessons in Stuttgart for the past two years, and whether she might soon begin with them again. In a meeting of the *Vorstand* Frau Dr. Wegman had been adamant that this should not happen and that the right to read the Class Lessons should be restricted to three *Vorstand* members. Herr Steffen, Frau Dr. Steiner, and Dr. Wachsmuth, on the other hand, were in favor of allowing this right to certain other trusted persons. Dr. Wachsmuth was therefore directed by the *Vorstand* to reply to the most recent of these requests from a Stuttgart member by saying that the present situation had not changed, and asking for patience until a final decision had been reached. The matter thus seemed to have been settled for the time being.

But at the next *Vorstand* meeting, Herr Steffen had to read out another letter, which contained a request from ninety Stuttgart members for Herr Arenson to read the Class Lessons. At the same time the letter recalled that Dr. Steiner himself had acknowledged that Herr Arenson was suited to do this. Before any further discussion, Frau Dr. Steiner said that on her travels recently she had heard that Frau Kolisko had announced she would begin again with her Class Lesson readings on February 27. All *Vorstand* members, including Frau Dr. Wegman, expressed their astonishment that Frau Kolisko had confronted the *Vorstand* with a *fait accompli*, without request or communication. Since Frau Dr. Wegman had insisted that Class Lessons might in future only be read by three *Vorstand* members, it was agreed to inform Frau Kolisko and others that UNTIL FURTHER NOTICE (and these words were emphasized), only these same *Vorstand* members would read the Class Lessons. On receiving the *Vorstand*'s decision Frau Kolisko protested vehemently in writing, but in no easily understandable manner. She declared that she could not accept the *Vorstand*'s decision, and would come to Dornach in person to justify her point of view. Frau Kolisko then met with the *Vorstand* in Dornach, but the whole matter was not cleared up. What arose was wholly unexpected. It turned out that Frau Kolisko had informed Frau Dr. Wegman of her intention, once in person during the agriculture conference the previous January, and the second time in a letter, and believed that she was acting "with the agreement of Frau Dr. Wegman."

What had happened was discussed in the General Secretaries meeting of April 25, 1930, and it was shown that Frau Dr. Wegman had received Frau Kolisko's letter some days BEFORE the *Vorstand* session during which she had expressed such astonishment. It also turned out that Frau Dr. Wegman had caused the words "until further notice" to be *omitted* from the *Vorstand* letter to Frau Kolisko and others, which had given the message a *quite different sense*. It had been left to Frau Dr. Wegman to add a few extra friendly lines to the letter, since people knew how close Frau Kolisko felt to Frau Dr. Wegman. The other *Vorstand* members signed the letters, along with other post that was being sent, without checking the exact wording again, for they had no reason to think that the content would be incorrect.

When asked why she had not mentioned receiving Frau Kolisko's letter at the *Vorstand* meeting, Frau Dr. Wegman replied, "We were not discussing that at all! This is a misunderstanding. I am very sorry. If I had known that a catastrophe could occur, then I might perhaps have said other things. I don't know." She also said that Frau Kolisko's letter had not been addressed to her as a *Vorstand* member and secretary. "This letter had no reality for me." She asserted that it was not the expression of intent that mattered but the accomplished fact. "I was very astonished at this accomplished fact. *It wasn't the notice of intent, but the accomplished fact that surprised me."* YET THE ACCOMPLISHED FACT WAS ALREADY CONTAINED IN THE NOTICE OF INTENT. This contradiction was as incomprehensible as the view she now expressed, that "Frau Kolisko has the absolute right to hold Class Lessons," even though she herself had omitted the words "until further notice," and thus canceled that same right. She justified leaving out these words by saying:

> It was like this for me, in fact: I was not keen on an expansion of the Class. I actually wanted to limit the Class again to the

Vorstand. And so I also thought that the letters sent to these various people who were holding Class Lessons, *Kolisko*, Graf Polzer and Collison, should make this clear; and that, because we (!) were against expansion, we should ask people not to hold the Class any longer, and give the Class back to *Vorstand* members. *This is what I wanted to express.*

At the end she said, "Now we have a situation where people think I had bad intentions..."

Herr Steffen: "I did not accuse you of that."

Frau Dr. Steiner: "It could have been an oversight. At any rate it is highly embarrassing."

Then the subject was dropped, and Herr Steffen went as far as simply falling silent at the next General Meeting when an explanation of Frau Dr. Wegman's position on this matter was requested.

This had to be recounted in some detail, for it is the reason why *Vorstand* meetings became senseless and impossible from that time on. Frau Dr. Steiner said, *"The real misfortune is that we have no solid ground beneath our feet when discussing important things: reality lies somehow somewhere else, and we learn about it only afterward. That is our problem and tragedy, which can drive one to despair."*

For the time being things were managed by Dr. Wachsmuth discussing current business in several meetings, with Herr Steffen and Frau Dr. Steiner on the one hand, and on the other with Frau Dr. Wegman and Fräulein Dr. Vreede. This arrangement came about after Frau Dr. Steiner, who did not want to burden Herr Steffen with individual meetings, wrote to him to say that she would take part in whole *Vorstand* meetings again once an honest basis for agreement and understanding had been created. Since this could not be achieved, the multi-meeting approach was tried.[16] The large number of journeys undertaken meant, however, that several *Vorstand* members were always away at any one time. Moreover, when

---

16 Dr. Vreede used this to reproach Herr Steffen with creating a clique in the *Vorstand*.

summer came, with its increase in conference activity, it was difficult to continue even with this arrangement. Matters were then settled by letter or telephone, and it was not only Frau Dr. Wegman or Fräulein Dr. Vreede who were contacted in this way. On all occasions, though—and we will come back to this—all *Vorstand* members were consulted. Talk of being "passed over in matters of the greatest importance" is really not admissible.

Thus, a situation was created that might have been improved only through honest and open judgment. Yet there was little desire for this. Things were hushed up instead, and kept from the members as far as possible. As though nothing at all had happened, Fräulein Dr. Vreede and Dr. Zeylmans raised objections to things that they themselves had brought about, but for which they made Herr Steffen responsible. This was mainly to do with conferences in Dornach and Holland.

In the summer of 1930 a large-scale youth conference took place in Holland, the so-called "Kamp de Stakenberg." From the beginning it had been planned as an international, "worldwide" undertaking, and lectures were given in German, English, and Dutch. The Dutch Society, or rather its executive council, was the organizer, and Dr. Zeylmans was Camp Leader. Herr Steffen had been informed about these plans at the start of the year and had left everything in Dr. Zeylmans' hands. But there was dismay in the Society when people got to see the printed and disseminated publicity material. Many members felt that the touting way that Anthroposophy was advertised in a "Camp newspaper" was an affront to the dignity of the Anthroposophical Society. The actual course of the conference confirmed people's fears. Dr. Stein was the main speaker, while Dr. Zeylmans, Dr. Kolisko, and Mr. Kaufmann represented Anthroposophy in their own manner. The whole thing had a partisan character from beginning to end. It seemed we were back once more in the days of the World School Association and the World Conference.

The presence of Dr. Wachsmuth prevented the worst excesses. Besides disputes that arose about the strange lectures of Dr. Stein, the main difficulty was the following: there were plans to turn the "Camp newspaper" into a big, international youth magazine. When Dr. Wachsmuth demanded that this should not happen without prior discussion and permission from the Dornach *Vorstand*, Dr. Stein replied. "We already have the magazine, and it already has a name." Once again, therefore, we were confronted with a *fait accompli*.

All these facts, and the background to them that he knew so well, were disregarded by Dr. Zeylmans when, soon after, he began to complain about the state of the Society. At the same time Fräulein Dr. Vreede protested against a new attempt by Herr Steffen to make some improvements to the Dornach conferences. All these complex, interrelated questions gave rise to an exchange of letters in which the various points of view became clearly apparent. We would like to reprint the letters here—which were published once before, in 1930.

Letter from Fräulein Dr. Vreede to the General Secretaries and Executive Councils

Dornach, October 8, 1930
To: General Secretaries and Executive Councils of the Society in each country

Regretfully I am obliged to draw your attention to the following matter, which relates to the forthcoming Christmas conference. In doing so I must also refer to the previous Michaelmas conference.

This Michaelmas conference—not to mention previous ones—came about under particular circumstances, about which the program printed in the *Mitteilungsblatt* of September 7 gave some inkling. The following exchange of letters provides further details of this. On the afternoon of August 28 I received the following letter from the secretaries' office, on whose envelope was written "extremely urgent":

August 28, 1930
Dear Frau Dr. Wegman
Dear Fräulein Dr. Vreede

The program for the Michaelmas conference has to be passed to the *Mitteilungsblatt* by Sunday. Since no further meeting is possible before next week, because of all the lectures and performances, and because Frau Dr. Steiner is away, we would like to ask you to give us your suggestions for Michaelmas conference lectures as soon as possible, so that we can draw up a program. Frau Dr. Steiner has told us that she will present two Mystery Dramas; and the two eurythmy performances, and Saturday evening events, are booked in as usual, as well as a Class Lesson. In addition the following gentlemen have, based on certain collaborative work, decided to work together along particular lines to produce a unified theme for this Michaelmas conference. Precise details are noted at the bottom of the enclosed draft program, where the number of lecture hours required for this is also marked with crosses. This leaves available two whole days, and 4 to 5 lectures, and bearing in mind the short time left, we would ask you to name 4 to 5 speakers.

I would be very grateful if you could supply these names by this evening, since I may have to telegraph the speakers still for exact details of their themes, and receive their replies before the end of the week, so as to meet the *Mitteilungsblatt* deadline.

> Yours truly
> on behalf of the *Vorstand* at the Goetheanum
> signed: Dr. Guenther Wachsmuth

This draft program was more or less identical with the one printed in the *Mitteilungsblatt* of September 7, but of course did not mention my lecture and those of October 4. The draft also announced a lecture by Professor Eymann, which was then replaced in the actual program by "Reading of a lecture by Dr. Steiner." However, Professor Eymann is also listed with the other gentlemen who, as it says in the above letter, had "decided to work together along particular lines to produce a unified theme for this Michaelmas conference." Professor Eymann, who has done much service to the anthroposophic cause and is highly valued by it, is not, as far as I am aware, a member of the Anthroposophical Society, even to this day.

I responded to this letter on the following day—after being asked twice by the secretariat when my answer was arriving:

Herr Albert Steffen, chair of the Gen. Anthroposophical Society
August 29, 1930
Dear Herr Steffen

Yesterday I received a letter from the secretaries' office marked "extremely urgent," which I assume you know something about. The letter is addressed to Frau Dr. Wegman and myself, but refers to matters that concern the whole *Vorstand*. I have often said that I will not contemplate any partition of the *Vorstand*, and I therefore cannot accept a letter couched in this way, for it would amount to my countenancing such partition. If I were to carry out what is asked of me in this letter, I would have to hold a separate meeting with Frau Dr. Wegman, so as to settle on the 4 or 5 speakers assigned between us. I reject such a procedure, since it would compel me, against my will, to contribute to forming cliques within the *Vorstand*.[17]

It is clear from the planned program for the Michaelmas conference, which was enclosed with Dr. Wachsmuth's letter, that preparations for this program are already far advanced. Yet there is no clear reason why discussions that the eight gentlemen held with Herr Wachsmuth and yourself should not have included the other *Vorstand* members as well. As far as I myself am concerned, I would always make time to participate in *Vorstand* consultations, also involving other members. I believe that very good things can proceed, particularly for conferences, from the work of a group united by objective viewpoints, a "college" or such like; and that it can be nothing but beneficial if groups of this kind meet with the *Vorstand*. It is precisely for this reason that I very much regret that the present draft-program did not come about in this way.

In this context I must remind you of our rules of procedure,[18] which have unfortunately not been adhered to as far as the regularity of *Vorstand* meetings is concerned. The absence of one or even two *Vorstand* members does not need to be a reason for failing to convene the meeting. It will be necessary to hold one to discuss the Michaelmas conference, and I ask you to call one, or arrange for one to be held.

With respectful greetings
signed: E. Vreede, Ph.D.

---

17 This refers to the previously mentioned difficulties [see page 131].

18 Accepted by the *Vorstand* in January 1930, these made provision for meetings of the *Vorstand* "every 14 days." At the Annual General Meeting, Fräulein Dr. Vreede declared that she had never accepted these rules of procedure. However, Dr. Wachsmuth then mentioned that the rules stated that three votes could decide matters. In reality, the rules of procedure were not as relevant as the actual state of affairs. Nevertheless, Fräulein Dr. Vreede used them when it suited her, and then denied their validity again when she so wished.

A copy of this letter is going to each *Vorstand* member. Herr Steffen replied:

August 30, 1930
Dear Fräulein Dr. Vreede

I have once more read through the letter to you and Frau Dr. Wegman, a copy of which Herr Dr. Wachsmuth sent me, and still find it in accordance with the rules of procedure.

The program has to be ready on Sunday to meet the *Mitteilungsblatt* deadline. It was not possible to hold a meeting during this time. Frau Dr. Steiner was away and Herr Dr. Wachsmuth is more than spoken for at present by the conference and the obligations it involves. I would also have found it difficult to attend a meeting. You may, as you say, always be able to find the time for a meeting, but the other three people involved could not.

In your letter you write that it is clear from Dr. Wachsmuth's plan for the conference "that preparations for this program are already far advanced." This is not the case. I have not had any discussion about it with either Frau Dr. Steiner or Dr. Wachsmuth. Frau Dr. Steiner was asked about the artistic events by telephone shortly before her departure. The plan for the program was sent to her. She knew nothing about the decision of the gentlemen concerned to "work together along particular lines to produce a unified theme." This was not decided until the evening of August 27, after a presentation of Goethe's fairy tale. It is a good decision, and the manner of its communication to *Vorstand* members is correct in every way. We should actually be grateful for what they have offered.

Our attempt to produce unified work causes you to speak of a partition of the *Vorstand*. There is no talk of such a thing among us. This problem does not in the least belong here. I must tell you that your use of such expressions is an impermissible attempt to stir up conflict.

It appears almost as if you wish to try once more to undermine and destroy necessary work. This alienates me all the more because I thought that you had seen how destructive this was two years ago, when you wrecked my attempt to establish lecture activity at the Goetheanum.

I very much hope that you will in future direct your critical sense at the bad things occurring within the Society, rather than at what is good!

With anthroposophic greetings signed: Albert Steffen

On the following day Dr. Wachsmuth asked me whom I wanted to suggest as speaker at the conference. I replied that I had no suggestions, but that I would speak myself. As always I left it up to Dr. Wachsmuth to enter this lecture in the program as he saw fit. When the program appeared in the *Mitteilungsblatt* I saw that my lecture and those suggested by Frau Dr. Wegman were separated off from the other lectures in a striking way.

In the final program for the Michaelmas conference, after the lectures marked with a cross were over, an open forum discussion was planned on Thursday, October 2. This was introduced by a long talk by Herr Steffen, of which, unfortunately, I do not have a transcript. It was given in a way that inevitably gave rise to the impression that the conference as such only included the lectures given by the newly formed "working group," and the artistic performances that were also mentioned. The other lectures (mine of Saturday, September 27, which was purely anthroposophic in content, and I then continued on the Sunday, as well as the medical lectures of October 4) were passed over in complete silence. A corresponding echo of this conference can be found in the *Mitteilungsblatt* of October 12.

On October 9 I departed, initially for Stuttgart, and on October 16 wrote from Munich:

Munich, October 16, 1930
Dear Herr Steffen

Please accept for publication in the *Mitteilungsblatt* the enclosed announcement from the mathematical-astronomical section.

Since I am likely to be away until about October 27—I am planning to take part in the Berlin conference on nutrition, and probably also the opening of the Hamburg branch offices—I would like to ask you now to make no decision yet on the next Christmas conference, so as to avoid any repetition of the Michaelmas conference situation. I would be wholly unable to approve such a thing.

> With respectful greetings
> Signed: E. Vreede, Ph.D.

In Hamburg I learned from Herr Dr. Poppelbaum that he had received a written communication on October 11—he thought from the *Vorstand*—asking him to give a lecture at the Christmas conference. The letter stated that the theme had already been announced by Herr Steffen, and that it involved an expansion of the Goetheanum "working group" so warmly welcomed by members. The letter was issued by the secretariat at the Goetheanum and signed by Dr. Wachsmuth, without the usual addition of: "on behalf of the *Vorstand* at the Goetheanum." (I am recalling the letter from memory; I do not have it before me.)

I must now assume that other leading members of the Society have received a similar invitation to participate at the Christmas conference, and that they too are under the impression that it comes from the *Vorstand*. As one can see from the above this is not the case. What this means is that the forthcoming Christmas conference, which marks the seventh anniversary of the Christmas Foundation Meeting held by Dr. Steiner, is being arranged by a part of the *Vorstand* only. It means that only some other members are involved, representing only a portion of the sections, and a portion of members who lecture at the Goetheanum.

Since things have reached such a pass I am left with no alternative but to turn to the General Secretaries and executive councils of each country (including the executive committee of the "Free Anthroposophical Society"). Dr. Steiner, after all, described them as functionaries of the General Anthroposophical Society, and in a certain sense as an "extended *Vorstand*." I hope that they will express their views to the *Vorstand* as soon as possible.

> With anthroposophic greetings signed: E. Vreede, Ph.D.

The "Memorandum"

LETTER FROM HERR DR. WACHSMUTH TO THE GENERAL SECRETARIES AND EXECUTIVE COUNCILS

Dornach, October 30, 1930
To: the General Secretaries and executive councils of each country

The letter that Fräulein Dr. Vreede addressed to the General Secretaries and executive councils on October 29 1930, casts a light on the circumstances it describes that is incorrect in important respects. The picture it gives therefore needs to be corrected. At the same time, it must be mentioned that the *Vorstand* members themselves, and members of the Society, have for a long time found it unsatisfactory that conference programs could be arranged only by individual *Vorstand* members suggesting speakers of whom they approved. This led to programs that were composed naturally of a more-or-less unconnected "mosaic." In spite of this, many lovely Dornach conferences have been held, whose value was in their individual events and lectures. However, a unified approach and theme was missing.

As is known, Herr Steffen made the attempt some time ago to work toward a more unified lecture activity by appealing to speakers and by proposing interrelated themes—an attempt that failed at the time because of opposition from Fräulein Dr. Vreede. Some of the most active conference lecturers, from the most varied spheres of activity, were still concerned to improve this unsatisfactory state of affairs. Instead of simply standing by and complaining, they thought it better to get down to positive, objective work themselves. In August 1930, with a view to the approaching Michaelmas conference, they held open, unprejudiced discussions about this. They did this without partisan allegiance of any kind, without involvement of any sort of "clique," but simply as free human beings from the most varied spheres of work who live full-time in Dornach. It was their concern to create a better structure for conferences, and they were convinced that such a problem could not be solved either by complaints or denial, but by positive work alone, and by actually getting down to it and making a start. They therefore decided:

1. To ask Herr Steffen for a unified theme for their lectures, and then to hold open discussions about how each of them would approach the theme, as far as possible relating and adding to one another's perspectives, helping one another and working in such a way that members and audience could also experience this collaboration.

2. Anything that could have impinged on the freedom of others, or could have had any negative or exclusive character was expressly avoided. The *Vorstand* members were asked, as before, to suggest speakers, and at the same time the other *Vorstand* members were informed of the proposed theme of this group. Thus all sides had complete freedom to suggest speakers, themes, etc. The draft was presented and announced in the name of all *Vorstand* members, and the whole conference—including the lecturers of this group and also all others—was accepted and convened by the whole *Vorstand*. Thus everything was done in an exemplary and correct way, observing and expressly safeguarding the rights and obligations of *Vorstand* and lecturers, and above all people's personal freedom and capacity for initiative. This group did nothing in the whole conference that was negative, dismissive, polemical, or infringed upon others' freedom. Those who accuse us of this do so because of their own agenda, not ours. Why should some of the speakers not work together on a common theme for a School of Spiritual Science conference? Or others work together on another theme? Moreover, why should such groupings not be open and fluid? Must all speakers always have to choose a theme different from one another? Or all speak on one single theme? Could they possibly do this anyway? Surely it is a great step forward to have groupings according to theme rather than a random potluck? The group that made a beginning at this—an initiative that it would be nice to acknowledge, and was indeed acknowledged by very many listeners—was fully and happily aware of the unending variety and future potential of their impulse. Looking toward the Christmas

conference this group was also planning to suggest involving some external speakers, who had freely chosen to accept a theme from Herr Steffen (see letter to Dr. Poppelbaum, etc.).

Just as before, this was going to be proposed to the *Vorstand* and integrated into the conference program. In the relevant *Vorstand* meeting, Herr Steffen proposed a fine theme relating to the theme of the Christmas Foundation Meeting seven years before, one expressly for all Christmas conference speakers proposed by the *Vorstand*. Therefore, what happens is this: a few people are asked if they would like, and be able, to talk on a certain theme. Then this is proposed to the *Vorstand*, at which point any *Vorstand* member is free to make additional suggestions, with the final decision resting with the whole *Vorstand*. Isn't that permissible? Could one proceed more soberly and correctly? Is there anywhere in the world a responsible, official body (or individual) that, when it wishes to make proposals for some specific work or other, does not have the right and duty to hold nonbinding consultations with colleagues or employees? Should *Vorstand* members and section leaders, or also General Secretaries and members of executive councils of other countries—all those who have authority in their own sphere—never in future have the right to consult and share information with their colleagues before they discuss specific issues?

These are important questions! If we judge things objectively, should we not rather welcome an initiative that aims to prepare thoroughly such discussion? Especially when, in the process, all scope for development, change, and decision is left completely open? If the mere fact of a few people coming together of their own free will to work together to the best of their ability is seen as negative and exclusive, then this would also apply to every working group within our Society that did not involve some 17,000 members—which is of course completely ridiculous and would prevent any worthwhile or specialized work of any kind being done. One could then also make the same reproach in all cases where, as has happened in the past, particular days are given over at conferences to specialized lectures for certain sections. Rejection, exclusion and restriction of freedom was not inherent in the way this group worked together for the good of the conference, but is inherent, rather, in those who try to prevent such serious work from occurring. This group, which never regarded itself as something fixed and unchanging, but simply wanted to provide a stimulus for something necessary to come about, did not infringe freedom of speech in any way, and cannot expect its own freedom of speech to be restricted.

In her letter Fräulein de Vreede also mentions the short amount of time that was available for organizing the conference. Any such reproach can only apply to those who were either late in making suggestions or did not address the question at all, and failed to contribute positive proposals. On this, as on many other occasions, the letter from Dr. Wachsmuth quoted by Fräulein Dr. Vreede signified nothing other than urgent notice that it was high time to settle the matter. It would be strange if those who failed to involve themselves in a timely initiative also reproached those who took it. All the wishes expressed on all sides were nevertheless taken account of and carried out.

The whole manner of Fräulein Dr. Vreede's approach is surely based on a fundamental misunderstanding. She behaves as if shared work can be achieved by means of formal measures, controls or prescriptive statutes and regulations. That is a futile aim and shows a failure to recognize spiritual and human realities. It surely has nothing to do with the Christmas Foundation Meeting, to which she so often refers. Others, who sometimes believe that there is another, better way than that of Fräulein Dr. Vreede, love and honor the Christmas Foundation Meeting and its spiritual impulses no less than she does. They believe, for instance, that the real, positive work of this group is at least as true to the spirit of the Christmas Foundation Meeting as any formal interpretation or outpouring of documents. Nothing was or is further from our aim than to hinder Dr. Vreede's own freedom of thought and work. It can also be proved that this freedom was never infringed.

May Fräulein Dr. Vreede likewise leave us free to pursue positive work, in the way Rudolf Steiner and the Society would wish, even if this way differs somewhat from her own. It ought to be possible to carry out such work for the good of our Society, soberly, without anxiety, with mutual respect for every real achievement. Then these birth pains, so clearly necessary at the present, will give way in the future to much that is beautiful and increasingly good.

With anthroposophic greetings, signed: Dr. Guenther Wachsmuth

⁕

Letter from Dr. Zeylmans to the Dornach *Vorstand*

The Hague
October 22, 1930
Dear *Vorstand*

After thinking about this for a long time, and with a heavy heart, I feel obliged to address a few questions to you. The answers I receive will be of decisive importance for the nature of my further work within the Society.

Various occurrences, especially in recent times, make it impossible for me to perceive the underlying direction in which the General Anthroposophical Society is being led. As a result, I have also failed to understand the relationship between the actions of the Dornach *Vorstand* and what was inaugurated by Dr. Steiner at the Christmas Foundation Meeting of 1923/4. As you know, I have a quite particular, dual connection with the Christmas Foundation Meeting. First as General Secretary of the Dutch Society, and second as a doctor who has close contact with the medical section. I have repeatedly failed to understand the relationship of the Dornach *Vorstand*, and in particular its chair, to either the national Societies or the sections.

I know that I am not alone in having such problems. A number of leading individuals in the Societies of various countries are also gravely concerned about this lack of clarity.

I will try to explain what I mean with a few examples. At the same time I must emphasize that it is not these examples themselves that I consider so important, but the underlying issue I believe they indicate.

The first example is to do with the [*Vorstand*'s] relationship to the Dutch Society. Things have occurred, particularly in respect to the Kamp de Stakenberg, which, with the best will in the world, seem to indicate that the *Vorstand* does not really take the Dutch Society seriously in certain respects or me in particular as General Secretary.

I hope that I am mistaken. If I am, though, it will be possible to explain the following things to me.

Around February 1930, I wrote to the Dornach *Vorstand* (via Dr. Wachsmuth) to say that the Dutch executive council had decided to take up Herr Grelinger's initiative. The Dutch Society planned to organize and lead the camp. I had intended to act as camp leader. I enclosed an invitation to all *Vorstand* members to attend the camp. Yet I received no answer to this communication and invitation, although Dr. Wachsmuth did answer a question I had put to him in the same letter.

At the Annual General Meeting soon after, it turned out that this letter had not, or had only fleetingly, been discussed in the *Vorstand*. Herr Steffen and Frau Dr. Steiner knew nothing of this letter. Frau Dr. Wegman and Fräulein Dr. Vreede had only a vague recollection of it.

This small matter alone would not have led me to pursue the matter. However, speaking about the camp at the same General Meeting, Herr Steffen said that the fact that Dr. Wachsmuth would attend was at least a guarantee to him that a certain standard would be maintained. Such a statement was of importance to those who had discussed the question of "standard" at some length. I had to stand by and hear that the fact that the Dutch executive council and myself as general camp leader were organizing the camp was no guarantee of high standards to Herr Steffen. (I only mention this now because I have since overcome all the pain that such a hurtful statement caused me. I am not motivated by any personal feelings.)

The "Memorandum"

In August, when I reported to Herr Steffen on how the camp had gone, he said, more or less, that he had also had good reports from Dr. Wachsmuth, and there "was no need to worry about the camp."

Nevertheless, none of the five reports and several newspaper notices about the camp were printed in the *Mitteilungsblatt*. A newssheet, entitled "What is Happening in the Anthroposophical Society," publishes nothing about a large-scale youth conference organized by the executive council of a national Society. Now I am sure that there are explanations for all that I have described. However, such explanations will need to be convincing to dispel the impression that the leadership of the Dutch Society has been treated in a way that it cannot possibly continue to accept.

A less than satisfactory answer will therefore oblige me to draw my own conclusions.

I hope with all my heart that it will be possible to explain what happened in a way that enables me to recognize and accept the underlying perspectives.

For it is this and this alone, rather than particular instances, that is ultimately important. I could mention a number of similar examples from the past, but that is not my intention at all. I consider it perfectly possible, for example, that the chair bases his decisions on views that are difficult for me to understand. Then I must really ask for help in doing so.

The second example relates to the [*Vorstand*'s] meetings with the General Secretaries and executive councils.

It was previously agreed that these meetings should be held four times a year. We last met at Easter, and before that at Michaelmas. Why? Moreover, why are we not informed in advance if the meetings are not going to take place? Why must we learn of it by chance? It is possible that *Vorstand* members feel that the meetings are not really necessary—or that other and larger numbers of people should attend? On the last occasion, Herr Steffen suggested several individuals because, he said, there were so few from Dornach present. Various people disagreed, saying that if the whole character of this gathering was to be changed it ought to be discussed first. I must say that I am still of this opinion.

It may be necessary to alter radically these meetings, and perhaps quite different people should participate. I myself have often thought this. Then it should be discussed in some way or other. One cannot be part of a council and then suddenly discover that one actually belongs to a quite differently composed body. Either this is a meeting of General Secretaries and national executive councils with the Dornach *Vorstand*, an "expanded *Vorstand*" as Dr. Rudolf Steiner once said, or it is something else. I will happily welcome this something else, but first I must be able to see what it is [see page 125].

The third example concerns the relationship between the chair of the Society and the sections, as this was apparent at the last Michaelmas conference in Dornach.

You will remember how keen I was at the General Secretaries meeting of Michaelmas 1929 to introduce a different way of holding conferences, and how outspoken I was against "mosaic-type" programs. It therefore goes without saying that I would very much welcome any initiative designed to bring about a more cohesive form of conference.

Yet the Michaelmas conference program made a very embarrassing impression on me. This impression was exacerbated by the way that Herr Steffen spoke at the open forum evening. He talked there at great length about what the collaborating "group" had intended and achieved, but made no mention at all of the previous item on the program (Fräulein Dr. Vreede's lecture), and what was still to come (the medical section).

Given that Herr Steffen is the chair of the Society, this amounted to an exclusion from the Michaelmas conference of those not mentioned by him.

The only reason I still delivered my own lecture was that I felt I owed it to the attending members.

Once again, though, I must allow the possibility that I have failed to understand Herr Steffen's guiding principles. He referred to the fact that this group of speakers was brought together by their striving for freedom. It is all the more strange, then, that someone who for years has been striving for a really free position within the Society felt so excluded by such efforts.

Something is surely not quite right with this "freedom." The conference was structured to focus on a group of speakers representing one section (Dr. Wachsmuth and his colleagues) and two working groups. Since the chair associated himself only with this group of speakers, two sections (those of Dr. Vreede and Dr. Wegman) were excluded as a matter of course. Even if the intention exists, as I was unofficially told, to expand this group (by involving a few doctors), this does not alter the fact. I very much hope that the program for the Christmas conference 1930 comes about in a different way. Many members are looking toward Christmas 1930 as a significant moment. It would be infinitely sad if a conference were to be held that a number of members felt themselves excluded from. I hope this will not be the case.

Finally I would like to ask you not to take this letter in the wrong way. It is truly not intended to increase the number of difficulties, but rather to help resolve all the existing ones.

Many in our Society are in the grip of a mood of crisis, while many others feel despair. The finest conferences and the most positive work cannot conceal this fact. Above all, very many people are extremely confused about the leadership of our Society. To clarify this confusion would perhaps be a significant step at this point.

>Very much hoping for an answer, I remain
>yours faithfully
>signed: Dr. W. Zeylmans

Herr Albert Steffen's response to Herr Dr. Zeylmans:
Dornach, October 29, 1930
Dear Herr Dr. Zeylmans von Emmichoven

Your letter to the *Vorstand* of the General Anthroposophical Society was forwarded to me in Hamburg. Since it is not addressed to me personally but to the whole *Vorstand*, a reply should come from all the *Vorstand* members rather than from me alone. Since some of them are either on their travels or are about to set off on them, an answer may be somewhat delayed. Therefore I would like to give you my response in the meantime, as far as I am able. This will of course not render a reply from the other *Vorstand* members unnecessary. In fact, I will myself urgently demand such a reply, which will be of great importance to me as well as to you.

In responding to your questions in general first of all, I may say that it has always been my aim to lead the Society in a way that is faithful to the Christmas Foundation Meeting. You know, however, that responsibility for this leadership does not lie with me alone, and that present circumstances are extraordinarily complicated. Your questions compel me to remind you that they became so because, immediately after Rudolf Steiner's death, many things were done in the Society without my knowledge and against my will; and further that I was not supported, even hindered, in carrying out what I regarded as right (and also expressed in no uncertain terms). I refer you to the shorthand transcripts of various General Meetings and gatherings of General Secretaries and executive councils.

You write, "I have repeatedly failed to understand the relationship of the Dornach *Vorstand*, and in particular its chair, to either the national Societies or the sections. I know that I am not alone in having such problems. A number of leading individuals in the Societies of various countries are also gravely concerned about this lack of clarity."

Although it is the task of the whole *Vorstand*, to whom your letter is addressed, to explain this situation to you, I must point out that I myself have already spoken about it. Can I remind you that, at that time (spring 1928), I assumed overall responsibility for introducing a more unified leadership into the Society? Also that this was my aim in preparing the opening of the Goetheanum at Michaelmas 1928, but that I was prevented by Fräulein Dr. Vreede from organizing the conference as I intended, and in consequence, to my great sorrow, was forced to relinquish this overall responsibility once more, and hand it back to the separate sections. I myself never questioned the "relationship of the Dornach *Vorstand*, particularly that of its chair" to the national Societies. But I would like to hear what I am reproached with, and therefore request that you name these "leading individuals" so that I can learn what I ought to be doing.

Perhaps I can also present certain things connected with the behavior of such individuals toward the Dornach *Vorstand* and myself in particular, which seem to me to need explaining.

Your first example concerns the Stakenberg camp, a matter to which, as editor of the *Newssheet,* I can respond without reference to the *Vorstand.* When Herr Grelinger talked to me on this subject last Christmas, I immediately asked him whether he had communicated about it with the executive council of the Dutch Society and you. He replied that he had, and I therefore felt that everything was in order. I myself raised absolutely no objections to the camp. I had no reason to be concerned until I was accused after publication of the camp newspaper. Before I had even read it myself, I was besieged from all sides by demands, both verbal and written, to explain how an anthroposophic journal could be written and disseminated in this way. In some quarters of the Society its content was regarded as superficial and inflammatory. Nevertheless, I had known nothing of its founding, let alone the articles printed in it. People pointed out that the Society's chair ought to be informed of such undertakings, and they asked whether the newspaper would carry on after the camp was over. The fact that you, as camp leader, had no say in this issue of the paper surely raised some justified concerns. Dr. Wachsmuth, as member of the *Vorstand* of the General Anthroposophical Society, was also able to keep his eye on groups that were not part of the Dutch Society.

It is true that when you reported back to me on how the camp had gone, I said something to the effect that "there was no need to worry about it." But I meant NOW THAT THE CAMP WAS OVER. I must tell you that I learned afterward of various things that I would have preferred to have heard from you. For example, that there were plans afoot to carry on with the camp journal, once more without my knowledge, and that Dr. Wachsmuth had opposed this. I would like to ask you whether you do not consider such a proposal an intrusion on the sphere of responsibility of the Society's chair.

All these things meant that the camp affair became a matter for the *Vorstand.* It is quite natural that I passed the reports about it to the

Vorstand, apart from a few naive reports and letters that it was left to me to publish or not, and that, if they had appeared, would have just raised some smiles amongst readers. Then Fräulein Dr. Röschl, of her own accord, withdrew the reports that she had sent to me.[19] The newspaper items, though they spoke of great successes, were without real substance.

I very much regretted that you as camp leader did not supply me with an official report for the *Newssheet*—one written by yourself—that I could have accepted without first showing it to the *Vorstand*. (I could not do this with the reports from Dr. Röschl, Pache, Marti, etc., but had to present them to the *Vorstand* first.)

The second example you mentioned concerns our meetings with the General Secretaries and executive councils. I have to say that too much offense was done to the chair's honor on the last occasion to enable me to take the initiative myself in calling a meeting of General Secretaries and executive councils again. Naturally I am prepared to bring up the question within the Dornach *Vorstand* about whether such a meeting should take place, and would also be happy to participate in it. I would also find it acceptable if a participant at previous meetings makes this proposal. I myself, though, can no longer suggest it, for I believe I would once more be exposed to insults. On the last occasion I made a suggestion. This was surely my right as chair. It was opposed and I let it drop. The matter is therefore decided, and I will not bring it up again. What I suggested was open to free decision, and everyone had the opportunity to express a view. I dealt with things in a perfectly correct manner. I therefore wholly fail to understand the following sentence that you wrote: "One cannot be part of a council and then suddenly discover that one actually belongs to a quite differently composed body."

My suggestion was open for free discussion by all executive council members of the General Anthroposophical Society, and all General

---

19 Quite of her own accord, as it turned out, and without expecting any response from the *Vorstand*.

Secretaries or their representatives. The majority was actually in favor, but when I saw that this would give rise to dissatisfaction, I withdrew it, with the agreement of the artists who had waited outside for more than an hour. It naturally offends me greatly that you censure the chair in this way to the whole *Vorstand*. Censure would be much more fitting wherever proposals are made that do not involve the chair of the General Anthroposophical Society!

Your third example: the relationship between the chair and the sections as it appeared at the Michaelmas conference at Dornach. I can respond to this only after the other members of the *Vorstand* of the General Anthroposophical Society have expressed their own opinions and I have read their replies. The whole affair has a history that needs to be taken into account. After Fräulein Dr. Vreede's attitude had made it impossible for me to structure conferences in a coherent way, I passed this task to the whole *Vorstand*. Conferences assumed, as you say, a mosaic-like character, and would have retained this if the working group that came together for the first time for the Michaelmas 1930 conference had not formed. If this had not happened, nothing at all would have been done to create a unified program. These three groups, representing scientific, cultural, and social initiatives, asked me for a theme. I offered this in real hope, and was not disappointed. For the first time in a long time there was a mood of confidence. However, instead of gratitude comes blame, even though nothing wrong was done. No one's freedom was restricted, and for my part I will not restrict anyone's freedom in future. Nevertheless, I will also protect my own freedom.

As I said already, this is not yet a conclusive reply to your third example. Yours sincerely

signed: Albert Steffen

On November 29, a meeting of General Secretaries took place, at which various participants presented reports. The following account by Herr Joseph Geith gives such a clear picture of events that we would like to reproduce it in full. Careful comparison with the shorthand minutes has shown it to be reliable and complete, and it is printed here with only minor alterations and additions.

❧

Report by Herr Geith on the Meeting of November 29, 1930

10 a.m. Herr Steffen greets those present and welcomes them to Dornach. He emphasizes that this meeting has been called at the request of Fräulein Dr. Vreede. He mentions that on the previous day, November 28, 1930, a preliminary meeting of General Secretaries had been held, to which, without his knowledge, the German executive council had sent out invitations on November 17. On November 25, five copies of the announcement of this preliminary meeting had been received by the Dornach *Vorstand*, along with the request that the *Vorstand* itself should not attend but should make a room available. This was the first time that a members' discussion had been held at the Goetheanum without the *Vorstand* being invited. Herr Steffen himself was not even invited, although he is the Swiss General Secretary. On November 20, Herr Grosheintz had been urged to take part as Swiss representative, but he rejected this, saying that Herr Steffen, not he, was Swiss General Secretary.

Herr Steffen protests, both as Swiss General Secretary and as a human being. He would like to ask, he says, whether he should chair today's proceedings, since it seems he is no longer recognized as chair of the Society.

Herr Leinhas declares that the *Vorstand* could certainly have attended this preliminary meeting, for nothing had been discussed that it should not have heard.

Those calling the meeting had just wanted to avoid inviting all the other individuals who usually participate in these gatherings but who are not General Secretaries.

The "Memorandum"

Herr Dr. Wachsmuth states that this was nevertheless the first time a meeting had taken place at the Goetheanum at which all he was expected to do was get the room cleaned and the chairs set out.

Herr Leinhas asks that the minutes of this meeting remain in the *Vorstand*'s possession. Herr Dr. Kolisko, Dr. Zeylmans and Frau Dr. Wegman do not approve of the minutes of the last General Secretaries meeting being issued to members, since people had assumed that what they said would remain confidential.

Herr Dr. Wachsmuth protests about Dr. Kolisko describing his passing on of the minutes as a "grotesque" action, which has led to "mischief." Dr. Wachsmuth only complied with instructions he received to pass on the agreed minutes.

Various friends declare that they will not be able to speak as freely as they wish if they do not get an assurance that today's minutes will remain confidential. Herr Steffen replies that he retains the right to repeat to anybody else what he says here today. Herr Rector Bartsch agrees with this point of view, and suggests postponing a decision on this question to the end of the meeting. This is accepted by a majority.

3 *p.m.* Herr Dr. Lauer states that Fräulein Dr. Vreede's request for people to put forward their views on what has occurred is no doubt a symptom of the fact that the *Vorstand* is no longer managing to cope with its tasks, and is looking to the General Secretaries for help. He proposes a thoroughgoing reform of the *Vorstand*'s structure.

Herr Steffen does not agree that the *Vorstand* has summoned the General Secretaries because it is not coping with its tasks. It was not he who turned to the General Secretaries, but Fräulein Dr. Vreede who summoned them without asking him. Nor did Frau Dr. Steiner or Dr. Wachsmuth summon them. He asks that people get to the point and state their views about the real issue, the letters that Dr. Vreede and Dr. Zeylmans have written attacking him. He emphasizes that the letter from Dr. Zeylmans is addressed to the *Vorstand* and not to the chair, and he therefore awaits Frau Dr. Wegman's answer to it, for the other *Vorstand* members have already passed their replies to Herr Steffen.

Herr Dr. Zeylmans states that his letter was not intended as an attack on Herr Steffen, but that he was asking for clarification, since there are various occurrences that he does not know how to explain. At the request of Herr Steffen he reads out his letter. He then says that he had not wished to accuse Herr Steffen of anything, and that he was just expressing the concerns of the members.

Herr Steffen replies that even if Herr Zeylmans did not consciously intend to attack him, the letter is nevertheless an attack.

Frau Dr. Wegman does not see any attack in the letter, but only a statement. She herself, however, refuses to express a view about the camp and the Michaelmas conference.

Herr Geith puts forward the point of view that Dr. Zeylmans' letter did indeed become an attack when he later sent a copy of it to all General Secretaries.

Herr Steffen asks those present to state their views about his behavior at Michaelmas.

Herr Geith says that a large proportion of German members fully endorse Herr Steffen's behavior, and gladly welcome his initiative.

Several speakers express regret about Herr Steffen's attitude over the camp issue, and in the preparation of the Michaelmas conference.

Herr Dr. Boos speaks of thousands of members in Germany who have full trust in Herr Steffen.

Dr. Zeylmans replies that there are also thousands who have grave concerns about the way Herr Steffen is leading the Society.

Herr Gentilli declares that the Italian members are full of admiration for the way Herr Steffen embodies Anthroposophy, and that this gives them the greatest trust in him. He regards it as an offense to human dignity to intervene in the free actions of such an individual.

Representatives from the North wish Herr Steffen to have complete freedom and independence, and say that he should be able to choose his own colleagues.

Fräulein Dr. Vreede says that the chair has duties as well as rights. The Society has a history. Dr. Steiner himself clearly showed the way he

The "Memorandum"

wanted things to be handled. Now the Societies of whole countries are being denied their say.

Frau Dr. Wegman states that Herr Steffen, as chair, must also consult with the other *Vorstand* members. Should two members of the *Vorstand* not retain the position that they ought to have?

Mr. Dunlop compares the *Vorstand* to the human hand whose five fingers work together. The chair should not be distinct from the others.

Herr Steffen thinks that the chair actually should occupy a higher position, otherwise there would be no need for a chair at all.

Herr Steffen and also Dr. Wachsmuth ask participants at the meeting to say how they view the chair's position.

Frau Dr. Wegman protests against the idea that Herr Steffen should ever take over responsibility for the sections.

Herr Leinhas is of the opinion that the chair ought to take the initiative, but that he should involve the other *Vorstand* members in this.

Herr Steffen states that he had wanted to take the initiative in 1928 already, to organize lecture activity in preparation for the opening of the Goetheanum. At that time Fräulein Dr. Vreede had accused him of denying the Christmas Foundation Meeting, of harming the free life of the spirit, and of diminishing the importance of the *Vorstand*. These are three absolute untruths. Now Dr. Vreede is on the attack again. The Christmas conference is fast approaching and we have not been able to arrange anything. The consequence of this attack by Dr. Vreede is that he cannot speak at Christmas, since he no longer has sufficient preparation time left.

Herr Dr. Wachsmuth suggests giving Herr Steffen complete freedom for a certain period, for half a year or so. The more freedom Herr Steffen has, the more he will assure the rights of the other *Vorstand* members, and the more freedom he will guarantee for others.

Herr Rector Bartsch enthusiastically supports this suggestion.

Herr Dr. Kolisko is in favor of a unified *Vorstand*. He thinks that the Society will be split by adopting the proposal put forward by our friends in the North.

Fräulein Dr. Vreede returns to the subject of preparing the Michaelmas conference, and complains about being invited so late to contribute suggestions. The program was already more or less complete when she was consulted.

Dr. Wachsmuth says that he cannot understand why Dr. Vreede did not make her wishes known at an earlier point. She has known for years that the Michaelmas conference takes place at the end of September. The group of speakers that worked together at this conference first formed itself and then turned to Herr Steffen to ask for a common theme.

To illustrate this, Herr Steffen reads the minutes of the *Vorstand* meeting at which the forthcoming Christmas conference was discussed. It is clear from this that Herr Steffen made suggestions and asked the other *Vorstand* members to make their suggestions too. Fräulein Dr. Vreede at the time rejected discussion about these suggestions, because of her letter of October 19, 1930. Herr Steffen had therefore been compelled to withdraw his own suggestion.

Herr Dr. Grosheintz thanks Herr Steffen for reading out the minutes, since they clearly show that he acted in a wholly correct, impeccable way.

Fräulein Dr. Vreede says it is not enough to quote these minutes, for all that led up to them also needs to be taken into account. She did not reject Herr Steffen's suggestion, but just the discussion about it.

Dr. Boos accuses Dr. Zeylmans of using as a smoke screen his statement that the composition of the *Vorstand* must not be altered, but that the seed that Rudolf Steiner planted at the Christmas Foundation Meeting should be allowed to grow. Dr. Boos calls Dr. Kolisko a blackmailer and deserter for always using the threat of a split in the Society. When the curative eurythmy course appeared Dr. Kolisko had said this was the beginning of the split. The root of all the difficulties in the *Vorstand*, says Dr. Boos, was Frau Dr. Wegman's theft of esotericism in 1925. This was also Anthroposophy, but a negative Anthroposophy that has become destiny, and that we must transform into something positive through shared work.

The "Memorandum"

Herr Dr. Zeylmans objects to Dr. Boos' impossible manner of speaking. If he, Dr. Zeylmans, were chair of the meeting he would censure his mode of expression.

Dr. Wachsmuth, who at Herr Steffen's request has taken over as chair of the meeting, censures Dr. Boos' manner of speaking.

Herr Leinhas asks Herr Steffen whether he can put up with participants at this meeting being called blackmailers and deserters.

Herr Steffen regrets that he is being called upon to issue reprimands, whereas no one was reprimanded when he himself was under attack, and when the dignity of the chair was violated on several occasions. He rejects the manner and mode in which Dr. Boos speaks, but not the content.

Frau Dr. Wegman immediately protests and demands an explanation from Herr Steffen.

Dr. Boos does not wish to place Herr Steffen in the position of having to issue reprimands, retracts his statements and rephrases them.

At further urging from various participants, Herr Steffen says that after the death of Dr. Steiner the "Leading Thoughts" by Frau Dr. Wegman appeared without his consent. One such "Letter to Members" was even sent direct to the printers in Basel without being shown first to him, the editor. Herr Dr. Schickler had severely reproved him for not prefacing Frau Dr. Wegman's "Leading Thoughts" with the phrase: "Issued by the Goetheanum," as had been the case with Dr. Steiner's "Leading Thoughts."

Frau Dr. Wegman replies that at the *Vorstand* meeting following Dr. Steiner's death, when she had asked Herr Steffen what he wished to do, he had said he wanted to do nothing. This was why she felt obliged to do something herself. She only wanted to indicate important points.

Herr Steffen states that one only has to read his essays of the time to know that it is nonsense to say he wanted to do nothing. However, it was his opinion that Dr. Steiner's "Leading Thoughts," which contained such spiritual riches, were sufficient. He wanted to carry on the *Mitteilungsblatt* in the same form in which he had produced the first issues after Dr. Steiner's death. He also stated that Frau Dr. Wegman had no right to hold a Class Lesson in Paris at that time. He does not wish to give any further reasons, for then he can no longer remain in the *Vorstand*. He does not wish to offend other people and therefore PREFERS TO WITHDRAW. From now on he will hold no further lectures in the Goetheanum, unless he is invited to do so. He will retain leadership of his section and editorship of *Das Goetheanum*. This will free him to put all his energies into the Society.

At this point, Herr Steffen is urged by several members, particularly Frau Dr. Wegman, to talk everything through. He refuses, saying the reason he has withdrawn is to avoid having to do so. The members should have no worry about the Society, for he will work on its behalf with all his strength. Herr Steffen continues to be pressured, so that he is finally forced to state that Frau Dr. Wegman had failed as esotericist, that she had not attained a certain level. Frau Dr. Wegman had no other rights than that of secretary, but in Paris had presented herself as if she did. Herr Dr. Stein and Dr. Kolisko had reproved him (Herr Steffen) in the gravest terms, saying that he had introduced Frau Dr. Wegman as secretary and not as leader of the School of Spiritual Science. Although Herr Steffen said that if people compelled him to further elaboration he might come to the point of having to leave the Society, he was still urged to give further explanations. Frau Dr. Wegman cited the fact that she had felt herself appointed by Rudolf Steiner as co-leader of the School.

Finally, Herr Steffen stated that he naturally acknowledged everything that Dr. Steiner had said about Frau Dr. Wegman, including a fact to which Frau Dr. Wegman had often referred. Nevertheless, after Dr. Steiner's death, there had been no spiritual succession, and it was only this that he could acknowledge. This is his personal opinion, he is not imposing it on anyone, and he regrets that he was forced to say it. He did not want to say it.

At this many friends asked Herr Steffen to accept the office of chair once more. However he insisted on his resignation. Then Dr. Wachsmuth declared that he also could not remain in a *Vorstand* to which Herr Steffen did not belong. He expressed the fear that Frau Dr. Steiner, who had not been able to attend the meeting, would also step down. He was expressing his deep, honest concern, he said, in asking Herr Steffen to consider what will happen to the Goetheanum if the Society breaks up. He emphasized the difficult situation the Society would find itself in regard to the world at large if Herr Steffen does indeed withdraw.

Herr Leinhas held Herr Steffen responsible for all that will happen to the Society if he does not accept the chair once more.

Herr Steffen then stated that, since Herr Leinhas was "holding a pistol to his head" he would accept the role of chair once more in regard to the world at large and the authorities, but on condition that he no longer has to take part in any meeting of the *Vorstand*, must no longer organize conferences, and does not oversee any further meetings.

He added that it would have been better if people had not forced him into it, but they simply had no trust in his assurance that things would go well if he was not part of the *Vorstand*.

Herr Dr. Wachsmuth then asked Herr Steffen whether he had now robbed him of his freedom. Herr Steffen replied that this was not the case, and that he himself would have said the same in his position. He thanked him.

With this, the meeting came to an end. It was three in the morning.

❦

To give a different angle from Herr Geith's report, we print below the report written by the executive council of the Anthroposophical Society in Great Britain.

Report

The following report is issued for the information of the members of the Anthroposophical Society in Great Britain by the Executive Council. It is signed by those who attended the meeting on November 29.

On November 29, as previously announced in the weekly *Newssheet*, the *Vorstand* met the General Secretaries and members of the Councils of National Societies and Groups of the Anthroposophical Society. The occasion of the meeting was a letter that had been circulated to the Executives of the National Societies by Dr. Vreede, together with Dr. Wachsmuth's reply, and a letter from Dr. Zeylmans as General Secretary of the Dutch National Society to the *Vorstand*. Dr. Vreede complained in her letter that Herr Steffen and Dr. Wachsmuth had made arrangements for the Michaelmas Conference at the Goetheanum after insufficient consultation with the other members of the *Vorstand*. Nor could she approve of the way they had begun to arrange the Christmas Conference, which she regarded as of especial importance since it marked the seventh Christmas since the Foundation Meeting. In his reply Dr. Wachsmuth urged that Dr. Vreede was as free as Herr Steffen to make any proposals she wished. Dr. Zeylmans in his letter asked for an explanation of the one-sided way that the Michaelmas Conference had been carried through and expressed his difficulty in understanding the attitude of the President [chair] to activities of the Dutch Society, particularly in connection with the Stakenberg Camp, of which no report had appeared in the Weekly News of the Society.

A preliminary meeting of the various General Secretaries and Executives was convened for the previous day by Herr Leinhas on behalf of the Executive of the German Society. To this meeting Herr Steffen, who besides being President of the General Society is Secretary General of the Swiss Anthroposophical Society, had not been invited, but the invitation had been sent to another leading member of the Swiss Executive who had, however, declined to accept it. The Swiss Society was therefore not represented at this preliminary meeting.

At the meeting with the *Vorstand* on Saturday, November 29, it became evident that the issues to be raised were wider than those defined in the letters circulated. The representatives of the Societies in Norway, Sweden, and Denmark proposed that Herr Steffen should be president of the Society with the fullest powers, the members of the *Vorstand* remaining merely as heads of their sections; and it transpired that the main division of the opinion was between those who supported this proposal and those who wished the *Vorstand* as such to remain the leader of the Society as indicated by Dr. Steiner at the Foundation Meeting at Christmas 1923. The difference of opinion became critical when Dr. Roman Boos, in a violent and abusive speech (for which, at the insistence of Mr. Dunlop and others, he was called to order by the President), accused Dr. Wegman of having been the principal cause of the dissensions in the Society. In calling Dr. Boos to order, however, the President indicated that he agreed with the substance of Dr. Boos' remarks, and a few minutes later he resigned the Presidency, saying that, if he retained that position, he would be obliged to reveal matters concerning Dr. Wegman about which he would much prefer to remain silent. Herr Steffen was thereupon pressed (especially by the Scandinavian representatives) to accept the leadership of the Society without the *Vorstand*, which they declared was no longer in existence. But he replied repeatedly that the *Vorstand* would continue to exist in spite of his absence from its meetings.

On being pressed by Dr. Wegman herself and others to reveal the precise nature of his complaints against her, Herr Steffen referred to her continuing the "Leading Thoughts" after Dr. Steiner's death, and to her conduct in regard to the First Class of the School for Spiritual Science in 1925. To this Dr. Wegman replied that she had been entrusted with a special responsibility by Dr. Steiner and moreover that she had shared this responsibility with the *Vorstand* as a whole.

In the exchange of opinions that ensued, Herr Leinhas and Dr. Wachsmuth warned the members present that it must be disastrous for the Society if no way were found of preventing the division that now seemed imminent. With great earnestness Dr. Wachsmuth placed before the members the picture that has never been absent from the minds of many—the Goetheanum—the needs of the Goetheanum on the physical plane and the liability of the Society for its maintenance. Finally the President said that he would withdraw his resignation but that in future he did not wish to take an active part in the arrangement of conferences, nor would he attend the *Vorstand* meetings.

The meeting then concluded with the decision to call a Special General Meeting for all members of the Society on December 27, 1930.

(In a statement delivered a few days later at a meeting attended by two of the signatories to this report, Herr Steffen briefly confirmed the decision as to his own future activities that he had taken at the meeting on November 29.)

Signed by Mr. Dunlop, Mr. Kaufmann, and by six others

There is no point in refuting this document word for word, but it demonstrates extraordinarily well how, without actually lying, responsible leaders can mislead those who depend for their information on such a report. One could consider it an insult to the English members that they were not thought adult enough to know the truth about a battle of the severest kind, which decided matters of great importance for the destiny of the Society, and in which people experienced some of the most shocking things of their lives. Instead they were fed, like young children, a fairy tale.

The most important points can be printed on two sides of paper. Nevertheless, when half of the space is taken up with long-winded formulations, not much remains for anything else—although nothing would have stopped people from adding a couple more pages. What, then, did the English members learn from this? Fräulein Dr. Vreede's complaints and an unimportant remark by Dr. Wachsmuth, rendered laughable by the way it was formulated here. The complaints by Dr. Zeylmans, which appear justified since no mention is made of the vital fact that Herr Steffen rejected them. Then the strange observation that the Swiss Society was not represented "because" of Dr. Grosheintz' refusal to attend. This is followed by a comparatively full description of Dr. Boos' behavior, during which Mr. Dunlop supposedly conducted himself so well. (In fact, Herr Leinhas was the one who took the initiative here, while Mr. Dunlop just joined in the protest afterward.)

Then we have Herr Steffen's resignation, and an account that makes the repetition of the request by northern members seem the only important thing. The worst is still to come, though; instead of a description of the earthshaking event that it was, it is made to seem as if Herr Steffen had resigned simply to make a few remarks, the content of which has long

The "Memorandum"

been known, and that sound childish in the way they are reproduced. Frau Dr. Wegman, it appears, refutes these easily, with a reply that presents indisputable facts. Actually, Frau Dr. Wegman had not only spoken about "responsibility" but also laid claim to high esoteric status; and it could have been, at most, nothing but her own view that she wished to share responsibility with the whole *Vorstand*. Indeed, she laid claim to sole rights, and asserted only that she had always informed the *Vorstand* in advance, which was hotly disputed by Herr Steffen. Then, in this English report, Herr Leinhas makes his appearance—without his "pistol," and as a person of the same mind as Dr. Wachsmuth. This is followed by a strange example of Mr. Kaufmann's sentimental style.

Finally, Herr Steffen supposedly asks to be left in peace, rather than his wishes being portrayed as conditions. Two Englishmen, one of whom is Mr. Kaufmann, at least manage to hear Herr Steffen speaking, two days later, of a "decision." What they do not hear, strangely, is Herr Steffen reading out the report of a meeting, from which it is clear that Frau Wegman took part in an important *Vorstand* meeting on February 18, 1928, that she stated on November 29, 1930, had not occurred. This report shows that the serious accusations made by Fräulein Dr. Vreede, whose consequences were so disastrous for the Society, were based on, if not caused by, an error on her part [see page 118f].

Herr Steffen also read out his reply to Dr. Zeylman's letter, and said that he only wanted to make clear that Dr. Zeylmans had sent his letter to all the General Secretaries in spite of, and without taking account of, the substantial objections contained in Herr Steffen's reply. And further, that this letter was then made the basis of preliminary negotiations on November 28, without any mention being made of the existence of Herr Steffen's reply; and that then, when Dr. Zeylmans appeared at the meeting of November 29, Herr Steffen had to ask him whether he had ever received the reply. Finally, Herr Steffen repeated what he had already told the General Secretaries, which is of some interest given later accusations that were made. Herr Steffen said that, for all the weeks still remaining until the

Annual General Meeting, he would not communicate with anyone, either verbally or in writing, about the affairs of the Society.

The fact that Mr. Kaufmann showed no interest in either the words or the inner torment of Herr Steffen is his own affair. That he thought it superfluous for English members to hear more precise information about Herr Steffen' situation is up to English members themselves to judge. One should really not expect Mr. Kaufmann to report on such unimportant details as the following:

The English representatives had arranged for the discussions of November 29 to be translated, and Mr. Kaufmann was officially designated translator. He did this job admirably. Then, however, Herr Gentilli started his talk, in which he described Herr Steffen as a free spirit who also leaves others free, a creative person indispensable to the Society because he also stimulates others to be creative. Mr. Kaufmann refused to translate this. Herr Steffen responded that he did not care whether it was translated or not, but found this strange behavior from an anthroposophist. At this Mr. Kaufmann declared he would translate it after all. However, Herr Steffen then said that perhaps Herr Gentilli's words had given the impression that only he, Herr Steffen, was free and creative. Herr Gentilli replied that this was not what he had meant, but Herr Steffen insisted that it should not be translated because the English representatives might misunderstand it. At this Mr. Kaufmann suddenly became very keen to translate. Herr Steffen reflected a little, thanked Herr Gentilli for his understanding, and then described how, although it was only for "official reasons" that many now present elected him to chair of the Society in December 1925, he had nevertheless put all his energy into the task; at the same time he had never prevented any *Vorstand* member from doing what he or she thought right, and "if some believe this is not true, let them give me an example." He emphasized that he had never wanted to hold the first and foremost position, and recalled the saying that the "first shall be last." This speech by Herr Steffen was then translated.

The "Memorandum"

A little later, when Fräulein Dr. Vreede launched a long tirade against Herr Steffen, Mr. Kaufmann asked to be allowed to translate immediately. He himself subsequently held the floor and said that it was not acceptable to speak of Herr Steffen as a free and creative person, for this was insulting to Fräulein Dr. Vreede and all the many other creative people in the Society.

It should be remembered that this all took place in the fall of 1930. These were the very same General Secretaries who took part in the April meeting, with the whole drama involving Frau Kolisko's Class Lessons, and Fräulein Dr. Vreede, and who were not exactly overjoyed at Frau Dr. Wegman's behavior, who also all knew about the Stakenberg Camp problems, some of them even having participated themselves. These same people arrive in the fall as though nothing had happened and talk about a "lack of consultation in the *Vorstand*," of the "negation of whole national Societies," and so on. However, reality nevertheless broke through this hard crust of delusion, and it became absolutely clear that we were faced with a parting of the ways, which did indeed take place during the next few years, in spite of all attempts to plaster over the cracks.

How did Herr Steffen assess his own position? The following becomes clear from his statements:

First of all, letters containing unjustified and sometimes untrue claims about him make the rounds of the Society. Without taking further account of the *Vorstand*, Fräulein Dr. Vreede turns directly to the General Secretaries. The Society's functionaries meet together at the Goetheanum, without Herr Steffen and the *Vorstand*. Though he is Swiss General Secretary, Herr Steffen is excluded, and is not even allowed to send a delegate. Dr. Zeylmans, who is the accusing party, is even proposed as chair of the meeting. The letter from Dr. Zeylmans is used as basis of the discussion without the functionaries hearing that Herr Steffen has long since made serious objections to it. Then comes the meeting of November 29. Herr Steffen asks in vain throughout a whole morning for a discussion about the letters and the forthcoming Christmas conference. When this finally happens, a torrent of new accusations is unleashed. He finds it particularly painful that, once again, such forceful emphasis is placed on the leadership of the Society being separate from the leadership of the School of Spiritual Science. This is the reason that Dr. Kolisko, in particular, speaks repeatedly of the distrust so many members supposedly have toward Herr Steffen. Herr Steffen's former attempts to bear responsibility for everything, and to organize lecture activities, are described as intervention, and also rejected for the future. He reads out the minutes of a *Vorstand* meeting, in which Fräulein Dr. Vreede actually refuses to discuss preparations for the Christmas conference. It is noted in the minutes that the chair's dignity was violated. Younger people, such as Pache, Stibbe, and Lehrs give him a dressing down. No one ever protests about any of this. Finally Herr Steffen is compelled to say to Herr Stibbe:

> Herr Stibbe, one cannot, as you do, give cursory moral sermons to people who are (to give you my age) forty-five or forty-six, who have some proven experience in life, and who have earned a certain name for themselves. This is enough to make anyone blush with shame for you. Just think for a moment how things have been all these years. Have we not poured out our hearts' blood? The matter must be pondered earnestly, not grossly glossed over as you have done, no matter how "refined" your words may sound.

Then Mr. Kaufmann then refuses to translate Herr Gentilli's speech. Then comes Dr. Zeylmans and lists the concerns he already expressed in his letter about Herr Steffen's administration of the Society, and complains that the Dutch Society cannot establish any real connection with the "whole *Vorstand*." It is this, he says, which leads to Dutch members—and there are "many examples" of this—coming to Dornach full of enthusiasm and there being "poisoned" by certain individuals, being told things about the state of the Society in such a way that they have to conclude that he (Dr. Zeylmans) has always given quite false pictures. Fräulein Dr. Vreede also speaks of the negation of national Societies, particularly the Dutch. As if the Dutch members—even if guiltless themselves—represented by Dr. Zeylmans, Herr de Haan, and Herr Stibbe, had never negated the chair of the Society. As if there had never been a World School Association, or

The "Memorandum"

malicious gossip about Frau Dr. Steiner, or an "Alexander legend" complete with a North Sea Macedonia.[20]

After this, Fräulein Dr. Vreede reads to Herr Steffen from the *Mitteilungsblatt*, to prove that he had written a lie. Then, following renewed attacks from Dr. Zeylmans, and from Dr. Kolisko—who holds the threat of a division in the Society over Herr Steffen's head if he should have anything to do with the Nordic petition—Dr. Boos stands up and initially refutes many things in a straightforward way, but then gets carried away and uses offensive language. The meeting refuses to tolerate such a thing. Dr. Zeylmans, Dr. Kolisko, and Frau Dr. Wegman cannot be insulted! Dr. Zeylmans protests first of all, and even dares to say, "The fact remains that a great number of things have happened, some of which have not been fair on Herr Steffen, and it may be quite good *that these have been thrown into the ring. We may not all find this pleasant, but it was perhaps necessary.*"

Then comes the other protests, and Herr Steffen resigns, because he does not wish to discuss certain things connected with Fräulein Dr. Vreede's bodhisattva lectures and the founding of a Dutch limited partnership for the Einsingen factory (see the following). His words are twisted and the situation is turned on its head. He resigned as chair so that he would not have to speak about certain things, but people insist that he must now speak because he has resigned. He defends himself in vain against Frau Dr. Wegman, who says he has accused her and put her under suspicion. He does not wish to speak, is even ready to leave the Society altogether. But no—Frau Dr. Wegman must have her way. Herr Steffen first mentions the Leading Thoughts, and then recalls that Frau Dr. Wegman was, as *Vorstand* secretary, accorded full rights to read the Class Lessons. He is unable, he says, to acknowledge any other claims. Frau Dr. Wegman heatedly rejects the idea of being acknowledged as secretary only, citing a cross which Dr. Steiner had given her, and documents that

---

20 Herr Stibbe is the same co-founder of the World School Association whom Dr. Zeylmans so decidedly rejected at the time (see page 85f).

supposedly confirm her elevated esoteric stature, and states that because of these things she wishes to be recognized as leader of the School and successor to Rudolf Steiner. Only then does Herr Steffen voice his opinion—but not as chair, for he had resigned—that the only possible succession is of a spiritual nature, which must be demonstrated by actual achievements. Whatever Dr. Steiner may, quite rightly, once have said and done could lapse if one did not attain a certain level, and Frau Dr. Wegman had failed in this respect.

Frau Dr. Wegman replies that no one apart from Dr. Steiner could judge such a thing!

The parting of the ways became clear at this moment: free judgment based on actual achievements; or trusting in authority and renouncing one's own judgment—even about oneself. She refers to a golden cross, but this soon turned out to be a medical emblem that Dr. Steiner gave to other doctors as well; and to documents that the other *Vorstand* members were unable to interpret in the way she claimed. Yet it was not documents but achievements that were really at stake here.

⸙

The extraordinary General Meeting began on December 27, 1930, and lasted three whole days. The focus of discussion was the so-called Nordic Petition, of which various versions existed and that was continually revised so that Herr Steffen would approve it. He rejected it in no uncertain terms, however, after having also rejected the earlier versions presented at meetings in April and November. The aim of these Nordic petitions was to hand over to Herr Steffen the power of decision about leadership of the Society, because people trusted that he would not misuse this freedom, and would not infringe the freedom and rights of others either. Exactly how this would be carried out was left to Herr Steffen, although people made all sorts of suggestions in the hope that he would accept them. Dr. Wachsmuth also supported this plan, on both his own behalf and that of Frau Dr. Steiner, who was off sick at the time.

The "Memorandum"

Herr Steffen rejected the idea because he did not consider that changes in the *Vorstand* were possible, and because the mistrust of influential people had on past occasions robbed him of even the slightest freedom. This situation could not alter in the future, as long as circumstances in the Society remained as they were. Although the great majority of members trusted him, they were at least partly represented by functionaries who did not, and who for years already had caused him offense as both chair and human being. Herr Steffen drew consequences from the Nordic Petition in a way different from what some had expected; he made no attempt to violate the freedom and rights of his opponents. THIS DECISION MADE FURTHER HEALTHY DEVELOPMENT POSSIBLE. Most members were very disappointed when Herr Steffen kept to his decision to remain chair only on the three conditions he had already given. (Even after Easter 1934, he did not retract his refusal to organize conferences.) This stance of Herr Steffen allowed members to make use of their freedom, and to form their own relationship to Dornach without being imposed upon by certain officials. When these functionaries refused to heed even the clearest expression of mistrust by members, continuing instead to talk of "appointments" and "missions," the members did the only thing left to them. They broke through the barriers, disassociated themselves from their representatives, and forged their own direct channel to Dornach. Shortly before the General Meeting, the Stuttgart Branch withdrew from the German Society and affiliated itself directly with Dornach. Details of this will be given later.

But those who subsequently believed they were duty-bound to speak grimly of Herr Steffen's supposed "dictatorship" ambitions would do well to ponder what it means to be besieged for three days on end by a plea signed on behalf of thousands of members—and to resist it, when a single word would have sufficed to gain oneself every freedom, as well as power.

Goetheanum colleagues appeared together for the first time at this meeting, and handed over a statement to the effect that because of the events of the last few years they had decided to acknowledge the leadership of Herr Steffen, Frau Dr. Steiner, and Herr Dr. Wachsmuth in all matters connected with their work and the preparation of conferences, and to take no further account of the inevitable objections raised by Frau Dr. Wegman and Fräulein Dr. Vreede. These colleagues' opinion was not shared by everyone, but they expressed the direction in which things were going, which was acknowledged more universally at the Annual General Meeting of 1934.

At the General Meeting of December 1930, discussions were held about all the things that had been causing havoc again for months, and which had formed the murky background of recent meetings. These assume a far worse character if one compares the professed innocence of people's words with the actual, consciously concealed facts.

An inexplicable interest in bodhisattvas had recently awakened. Once again the circles of people surrounding Frau Dr. Wegman made the most impossible claims in this case through talk of the expected arrival of a bodhisattva. To counteract the crazy fantasies to which he had to listen time and time again, Herr Arenson looked up various passages in Dr. Steiner's works where the latter had spoken about the nature of bodhisattvas. It became clear from these passages that even a spiritual researcher cannot recognize an incarnated bodhisattva before the person concerned is at least thirty-three years old. Herr Arenson gave a lecture about these matters, and also had it copied. Fräulein Dr. Vreede then gave lectures in which she disputed Herr Arenson's points, and left open the possibility that a bodhisattva might be expected in the imminent future. At the same time she felt the need to express extremely odd and almost incomprehensible opinions, to the effect that particular circumstances had made it necessary for Dr. Steiner to overstep certain spiritual laws.

At any rate, people soon realized with horror that a new sensational theme was all the rage in those circles in which "karma research" had previously assumed such grotesque forms. It is not clear who was responsible for starting this. Frau Dr. Wegman did not prevent this nonsense going on in the circles close to her, though in the General Meeting she declared that she had only spoken of bodhisattva "forces."

There was another individual connected with these things, who had only recently joined the Society. Apart from the fact that this young lady, Fräulein Benthien, liked to list all sorts of wonderful incarnations for herself and other members, she had also apparently discovered where the bodhisattva was now living. Names of members were even mentioned at the General Meeting, though they had nothing to do with the matter themselves. A few days later one of them received a letter from Fräulein Benthien, in which she said that she herself had never mentioned his name in this context: "I have always strenuously denied this, for I have known since 1922 that this bodhisattva was still young, and not yet a member of the Anthroposophical Society." Then she speaks about her time at Arlesheim, saying, "In the clinic at the time people were making great efforts to find the bodhisattva. It never occurred to me to think you were the one, for I knew differently."

Sadly, Fräulein Benthien had a considerable influence among Frau Dr. Wegman's most extreme and devoted adherents. Leading members of these circles regarded Fräulein Benthien as an initiate, and even thought her messages from the spirit world came from Dr. Steiner and should be regarded as directives for the Society—so the whole business had gradually assumed serious proportions. Yet Frau Dr. Wegman did not feel obliged to do anything about it, neither as a *Vorstand* member nor as an esoteric leader. When asked about this at the General Meeting, she treated the whole affair as something she did not even wish to express an opinion about, since she regarded Fräulein Benthien merely as one of her former patients. Yet this was of little importance compared with the fact that younger members in particular were being led astray by her. Although attempts were naturally made in the General Meeting to deny everything and make it seem as if this was all malicious invention, it soon turned out that people's fears were very well founded. Fräulein Benthien not only wrote the above-mentioned letter, but in a whole pile of other letters written by her, and deposited on the *Vorstand*'s table, she presented fantastical findings about reincarnations she had "researched," and other such sensationalism.

The moment Fräulein Benthien heard what had been said at the General Meeting, she left the Anthroposophical Society and several prominent members followed suit.[21] They included one of the two leaders of the Free Society, Hen Wilhelm Rath. They became firm adherents of Fräulein Benthien. It was rumored that Herr Rath had also said that the Goetheanum was nothing but a lump of concrete, which it was not worth wasting any money on. This view—also shared by Fräulein Benthien—was mentioned at the General Meeting in the presence of its author and not retracted by him. In other similar "mystic" circles, it was likewise said that the "spiritual Goetheanum" was no longer in Dornach.

The idea that these things should not be spoken about, judged, or criticized was enough to drive one to despair. The worst instance of this was provided by Frau Dr. Wegman herself. She described how Fräulein Benthien had formerly been her patient for a long period, and had told her much that, as a doctor, she must retain confidentiality about. But this was completely beside the point: it was not so much what Fräulein Benthien had said as a patient, but what she had said subsequently—and not to doctors—that had been taken up by certain members. According to Dr. Wegman one should refrain from judging these things too, and even she herself did not wish to. Her very words were, "What else has been said about Fräulein Benthien? That she has a pathological clairvoyance. Now what does that mean? I myself cannot always easily judge whether something is pathological or not." In addition, on another occasion she said, "It is not so straightforward to judge a person in this way." Frau Dr. Wegman, a medical doctor, who a few weeks before had demanded to be acknowledged as co-leader of the School with Dr. Steiner, cannot "easily" judge whether someone's clairvoyance is pathological or not, even though she has known the person concerned for a long time, and although her [the patient's] "results of spiritual research" have become the subject of general discussion. All that Dr. Steiner described through the years as

---

21 Even today (winter 1934), so-called Classes circulate among members as letters—for instance, in Holland, where they are taken seriously.

symptomatic of pathological clairvoyance, because he wanted every member to learn to recognize it, all that he wrote and said about it in lectures and books, and the concrete examples he freely gave to all members (for example as it found expression in some members' paintings) because it boded ill for the Society—all this is to be ignored, and we should instead turn a loving, blind eye? And what every earnest reader of Dr. Steiner's books not only can do, but ought to, Frau Dr. Wegman says she neither can nor wishes to.

But there was worse to come. Fräulein Benthien had also told Frau Dr. Wegman all kinds of reincarnation stories.

> Now I have never gone into incarnation questions at all, one really cannot do this. And I cannot respond to the things people say about me, for instance asking questions such as "Were you this or that individuality?" You have to understand that this is impossible. These are deep secrets that we keep locked in our own hearts. I really cannot help it if other people say such things; after all they have a certain degree of freedom to say what they wish. I am not these people's keeper. In the end I don't have anything to do with it.

The question referred to by Frau Dr. Wegman was asked, very inappropriately, by a Berlin member at the Annual General Meeting of April 1930. The same question had previously been asked by Herr Englert at an earlier General Meeting, in order to put an end once and for all to the intolerable "reincarnation gossip" that was rife in the Society. But his question was formulated in personal terms, and was rejected by Frau Dr. Steiner, who even protected Frau Dr. Wegman from it, and dismissed the question on her behalf. The "deep secrets that we keep locked in our own hearts" had for years however been the subject of open discussion by those whose "keeper" she did not want to be, but who saw in her the leader of the Michael School. And she had a great deal to do with "these people," who wanted to lay the world at her feet in the form of World School Associations, World Conferences, and Youth Camps, and who had been meeting for years at Arlesheim as an *"Übervorstand"* to influence and determine the aims of the Society.

Those who, in Frau Dr. Wegman's own words, had spoken of what should remain "locked in one's own heart," and who had said "such things," did not however give up hope of saving the situation, and began denying everything, even claiming that they had never said or heard anything about Alexander. To rescue the meeting from this mire of deceit, a Norwegian member then stood up and, turning to Dr. Zeylmans, gave him precise chapter and verse about where, when, and how Dr. Zeylmans had spoken in Oslo about the reincarnation of Alexander and his followers, and about what this meant for the Society in terms of the real meaning of the Christmas Foundation Meeting of 1923. The Norwegian member stressed that he was speaking out only because he felt duty-bound to reveal the truth, and not because of any feelings of enmity, for he was in fact a good friend of Dr. Zeylmans and had enjoyed excellent collaboration with him in Holland, in The Hague. Herr Englert told of another instance, describing how he had heard the same things in Vienna from members who were later known everywhere as the most devoted friends of Frau Dr. Wegman. He reminded Frau Dr. Wegman that, on his return, he had immediately come to see her to learn her view about such talk, and that she had replied that it was all a pack of lies spread about by her opponents to make her supporters seem ridiculous. Her supporters clearly tried to imitate this same slant on the matter at this General Meeting, and would have succeeded if honest members had not taken it upon themselves to speak the uncomfortable truth. Let it be said in passing that it also became apparent that Frau Dr. Wegman herself had not always kept silent.

A further, extremely grave question still had to be dealt with at this General Meeting. Members of the Anthroposophical Society were among those who had suffered severe losses owing to the bankruptcy of a factory in Einsingen. Because the Anthroposophical Society itself did not have any kind of connection with this business, the fact that individual members had ploughed large sums of money into it must be attributed to the fact that investors had been given the misleading idea that support for this factory would further the cause of Anthroposophy. The first cursory investigations revealed that the name of the Goetheanum and even of Dr. Steiner

The "Memorandum"

had been outrageously misused by certain members in Germany and Holland. The names of these members made it probable that, together with Frau Dr. Wegman, they had tried to create a financial basis for their own particular ends. If this were the case then Frau Dr. Wegman would have been guilty of an incomprehensible dereliction of her duties as a *Vorstand* member. Unfortunately this turned out to be true. However, when Frau Dr. Wegman was questioned in the General Meeting about her connections with the Einsingen factory, she replied that her only tie with it consisted of having once given some recommendation or piece of advice on the matter. She had given this advice when asked by the factory owner.

I said to him, "Well, yes, there may perhaps be people in Holland who might be interested." However, I also said very clearly to him, "You must try not to ask money from anthroposophists, but from other people altogether." What happened then was that Dutch friends, such as Herr T[ymstra] came to Herr v. L[eer], who said he was willing to support this factory, taking it upon himself not to raise money from anthroposophists but from people who showed an interest but had absolutely no relationship to Anthroposophy. That was very much due to me, since I said this and got friends to raise money from people who were not anthroposophists. I was just trying to give advice—nothing but good advice. They took this up. We found very many non-anthroposophic friends to support the venture, and I did not give further thought to it. However, when I heard that things were not going well, I opposed it energetically.

❧

To avoid misunderstanding about what follows, we must expressly state here that Frau Dr. Wegman cannot be held responsible for the financial mistakes of the factory directors. The accusations against her lie in a quite different area: her behavior as member of the *Vorstand* toward both the Society as a whole and individual members.

At the General Meeting she stated that she had only ever acted in this matter as a private individual, never as a *Vorstand* member. She was also asked whether she had succeeded in making the private nature of her connection to the enterprise sufficiently clear, so that any institution that she directed independently of the Anthroposophical Society would also not be linked with the Einsingen factory, for example as recipient of expected profits. Frau Dr. Wegman replied:

> I am happy to give you an answer to that: There are no links between the Clinic and Einsingen, no financial links whatever, nor are there any spiritual links. No connections whatsoever exist between the institutes, the curative education institutes, and Einsingen. Nor are there any such links between Weleda and Einsingen. Everything is absolutely in order. There have never been any links, certainly not to the Clinic. I was always rigorous—yes, there was simply no question of it, no question of it at all! And I had no inclination whatever to involve myself financially in Einsingen. All I did was give advice, which I thought that people would implement properly. I cannot help what people actually did with it.

The General Meeting decided to set up a commission of experts to investigate the—still opaque—facts of the matter.

The report that this commission later presented[22] confirmed once more that the Anthroposophical Society had had no involvement at all in the Einsingen factory and its bankruptcy. However it was also found that others had not viewed Frau Dr. Wegman's private links with the enterprise as private, and that her name had been sufficient to give financial backers the impression that there was an anthroposophic interest in this matter. The explanations that Frau Dr. Wegman had given at the General Meeting turned out to be MISLEADING AND WHOLLY AT ODDS WITH THE FACTS discovered by the committee's thorough and painstaking investigation. Without quoting all the technical details, we can here cite the report's salient passages. These illustrate the essential point—that is, the world of

---

22 The committee consisted of six members: Herr Dr. Grosheintz (chair) from Dornach; Herr Kreutzer, an industrialist (Nuremberg); Dr. Frankl, a lawyer (Dornach); Dr. A. Im Obersteg, solicitor (Basel); Herr Knopfli, bank director (St. Gallen); and Herr Aisenpreis (for the Goetheanum building administration), Dornach.

fantasy inhabited by those members who so lightly misuse the name of the Goetheanum for their very personal ambitions for power.

In the report it says:

Frau Dr. Wegman stands by what she said at the meeting: "I was not speaking as a member of the *Vorstand* but as a private person." She thus adheres to the view that all her advisory and financial efforts for Einsingen were her own private affair. On the other hand, her involvement is expressly motivated by what she sees as Dr. Steiner's interest in Einsingen. For this reason alone, the commission cannot share Frau Dr. Wegman's view that a *Vorstand* member may take an active part as a private individual, rather than as *Vorstand* member, in a matter that was important to Dr. Steiner,[23] and also has no need even to inform the *Vorstand*.

The commission also regards such a separation of the roles of *Vorstand* member and private individual as something that can, at the very least, cause incalculable misunderstandings, since no one can outwardly implement this separation and the authority of the *Vorstand* member will always remain visible behind the private individual....

Frau Dr. Wegman stated that she would write to her Dutch friends to ask them if they could help obtain backing from financial sponsors in Holland. Herr K[irchner], at that time the Clinic's administrative director, traveled to Holland on this business, which was successful.

Once more they turned to Holland, relying on officials of the Anthroposophical Society to act as intermediaries. One of these officials (Dr. Zeylmans) had a dream that was interpreted by those involved as evidence that Dr. Steiner wished Einsingen to be supported. It should be remembered that this was January 1926. These events can only be properly assessed when seen against the background of events, views, moods and battles within the Anthroposophical Society at that time—between the end of 1925 and the beginning of 1926.

---

23 He had made particular suggestions for technical processing of the raw material. These were barely tested in the laboratory and had no real effect on the enterprise. However, they were used to mislead financial sponsors.

The name of Dr. Steiner, and of the Goetheanum, was outrageously misused.

In the end Herr K[irchner] was delegated to Einsingen. Although he formally resigned from the Clinic at the time of his departure for Einsingen, he exerted a lasting influence from there on the Clinic's financial conduct. He continued to keep the Clinic's accounts, and when it needed money, an employee was directed to turn to Herr K. in Einsingen, who sorted it out. Herr K. returned to the Clinic shortly before the [factory's] collapse, but subsequently had dealings, nevertheless, with the person who directly brought about the bankruptcy....

Weleda came into contact with Einsingen through Herr L[eer], who had had a leading position in both businesses....

The aim was to finance the following: the Waldorf School, or the School Association (this was the time of the WORLD SCHOOL ASSOCIATION), and the clinics and laboratories at Arlesheim....

Since Herr v. L. did not, after all, feel justified in managing on his own any sums of money that might be available, he asked Frau Dr. Wegman and Gr[af] K[eyserlingk] to append their names, so that these three individuals could together dispose of funds as Rudolf Steiner (!) would have wished.

In meetings held in 1926, proposed use of expected profits was discussed in extremely clear-cut terms. So much so, indeed, that in the summer of the same year an individual highly regarded in financial spheres traveled to Dornach for no other reason than to warn Herr Steffen and Frau Dr. Steiner of the great efforts being invested there in DEVELOPING THE FINANCIAL MEANS FOR A POWER BASE, but that this financial basis was, to an expert eye, a wavering and insecure one.

Nevertheless it proved impossible either for the chair of the Society, Frau Dr. Steiner, or Herr Wachsmuth to gain access to reliable information and documentation from those involved in Einsingen, or to get anyone to listen to their wishes and warnings. Herr Steffen described in detail at Christmas how he had given very definite, but vain warnings about founding the limited partnership.

It is clear from the whole report that those circles that wished to create for Frau Dr. Wegman a special leadership position within the Anthroposophical Society, at the same time also wanted to secure this through an external power base. In trying to do so, however, they did themselves the utmost damage. In the service of this aim, they misused the name of the Goetheanum and went behind the back of the Dornach *Vorstand*. All this occurred with the knowledge of individuals who otherwise claimed so vehemently to have received positions of unique responsibility from Dr. Steiner. Characteristic of such people is the fact mentioned in the report that there were even officials who turned away from real knowledge and allowed dreams to dictate their free actions. In addition, the chief financial backer was spun a story about supposed reincarnations.

The committee stressed above all that the greatest injustice had occurred through the misuse of Dr. Steiner's name. Instead of citing misunderstood and even misquoted sayings by Rudolf Steiner, it would have been better to stick to what he himself wrote in the *Mitteilungsblatt* of July 15, 1924:

In the future I will have to make the most earnest, concerted efforts to ensure that no anthroposophists' funds go to support business enterprises that have no immediate link with the Anthroposophical Society as such. This was disregarded on one occasion in the past, but it is now absolutely necessary that no further business enterprises are backed by the money of anthroposophists.

☙

Let us also briefly mention that the court cases brought by Mademoiselle Sauerwein were discussed as well, and the General Meeting passed a resolution disapproving of the conduct of the French General Secretary. When this resolution was passed unanimously, only Dr. Kolisko protested, and insulted the whole gathering by saying that all those present—apart from himself of course—were incapable of deciding anything because of the unfit state they were in. When Dr. Wachsmuth censured Dr. Kolisko's behavior on behalf of everyone, Dr. Kolisko cited the advanced hour as a reason for their unfitness. Dr. Wachsmuth remarked that it was only ten past seven in the evening; and the meeting continued to demonstrate its capacity for taking decisions for several further hours.

1931–1933

At the Annual General Meeting of March 31, 1931, the committee presented its report on the Einsmgen factory to members. As a result the Clinical-Therapeutic Institute's incorporation into the Anthroposophical Society, which took place in 1925, was also revoked.

In the meantime more and more members had found their way back to the Goetheanum, from which they had been shut out so long by maneuvers of certain of the Society's officials.

This arose not just as an outward affiliation, but also as an expression of members' wishes for Anthroposophy to be represented in the way Herr Steffen had represented it all along. Many were also badly shaken by the appalling examples that had shown what headlong calamity threatened if that small group exposed the anthroposophic movement to any further occultic nonsense, coupled with financial adventurism.

How important it was to clarify one's own relationship to Anthroposophy, and what inner struggles were involved in the process, was shown by the thunderous applause that greeted a speech by Dr. von Baravalle at the Annual General Meeting.

Dr. von Baravalle said:

> I took the floor so that the views could also be heard of someone who was formerly an independent member, that is, not a branch member of the German Society, but who then joined the group that sought direct affiliation with the Goetheanum. I would like to share some of the reasons that gave rise, in the real, truest sense of the word, to a "JOINING MOVEMENT."[1] Above all, I must counter ideas floating around that the trouble was all caused by a few people not getting on with on another—who, through all kinds of complication, began to dispute and disagree—and now, when they see an opportunity, a way out, they take it and become

---

1   In contrast to the "resignation movement" (*Austrittsbewegung*).

independent. That reminds me of the unbelievably painful type of comment about the disputes in Dornach owing merely to two women falling out with each other [see page 108]. Moreover, when one hears reports that read as smoothly as those produced by the German executive council, one can wonder where one has been all the time. Everything is presented so smoothly and calmly, so that one wonders if all the struggles one went through were just a dream. I have to say that I am very grateful that I had a connection all these years to all the people I worked with in the Waldorf School, and went through the pain of all that happened. For it was A SPIRITUAL BATTLE ON THE GRANDEST SCALE, a spiritual battle that might nearly have been enough to break someone who went through it as, say, a young man—indeed sometimes very nearly did so. The things that affected one at the time were not subjective.

This was an objective, mighty battle that demonstrated how spiritual movements may lead to absurd extremes, and clearly did so in fact for those who were involved in this time of great difficulty. All possible kinds of unhealthy spirituality came into effect, and kept up their influence to the end. I particularly want to speak because I wish to make a point to some younger members. Those who were personally connected with everything through Dr. Steiner's work, the older members, gained such a wealth of experiences in their own life through this collaboration that they have a much easier time of it now. But when younger people hear such speeches, they say to themselves no doubt: "What are these old crows up to, these individualists who don't want community," and so on and so forth. Yes, but they did not leave because they could not get along with the others—no one can say that I wasn't able to get along with the others—but they left at a point, at a moment where something most holy within us was really under threat. I have to say that the way some ideas are carelessly expressed is impossible: this talk of "community" and everything else that was said, such as that we should stick together at all costs, and the view that everyone is equally at fault—that because there is discord between us we are on the same footing. Discussion really gets us nowhere.

If this way of thinking were to take me over completely—this was my own objective experience—then from that moment on I would no longer be an anthroposophist. I was most clearly confronted with this way of thinking in my years of working together with the Kolisko phenomenon. This was a way of thinking that he repeatedly applied, to all that we worked on over the past ten years. Each time that I took some action, a decisive action that I felt to be free, that made me feel possibly justified in calling myself an anthroposophist, then each time I experienced the same thing: Dr. Kolisko literally saw red, was furious about it. I need no other confirmation, for I had it at the Waldorf School. Each time that I became freer inwardly, when I did a deed of some kind—one knows one has done this afterward—Kolisko and his way of thinking was inevitably in conflict with it. The next day, after the most awful battle, when what I had fought for was accepted, then I was told, "We all wanted that! That was our view all along!" Then one had to ask oneself whether yesterday had really happened, and what it had all been about. This experience made one slowly, little by little, an anthroposophist! And one also had to ask: What motivates the people who also experience such things but quite systematically speak out against them, who even get furious when one discusses them?

When I returned to Stuttgart and met people who had affiliated themselves directly with the Goetheanum, I had a different experience. We discussed various matters together, and I knew that something was lighting up in them and that this was a deed that spreads light, and if one helps this along one becomes a little bit better. You can think what you like, but I had the definite feeling that something in the whole air of Stuttgart, including the school, was getting brighter. One simply had the feeling that a channel was opening up, through which the life of the spirit, the joy of the spirit reappeared. One could really share in this joy that Herr Steffen expressed again today: of light dawning. The old ways of thinking have run dry, and a few years ago one was just alone. One felt bowed down. I often asked myself whether I was still sane. All "cultivated" people disputed my view. I was often close to doubting my own health and sanity. And if I had not kept going… I might perhaps have given the same lectures, spoken the same words, but I would no longer have been an anthroposophist. I felt bitter when people said, "If you want to be an anthroposophist, you have to have this or that quality." Things reached such a point that I felt I had to make a decision. One fine day I inwardly ripped up everything I had been told an "anthroposophist" ought to do or be. I told myself instead that I would go back to normal, healthy human reason. I was really very close to thinking that this might mean I was turning my back on Anthroposophy. Nevertheless, I dared to take this step and found Anthroposophy instead. Anyone who has experienced this knows that it is not empty talk, that one's humanity is at stake here, that the deepest forces are involved and drawn upon. These forces become brighter. Here at the Goetheanum, we experience them, and that is something very beautiful—this feeling of joy that a new light is dawning here through the way that Herr Steffen is building things up, how a quite different way of thinking is bringing about quite different things. It almost seems to me as if the world of spirit is coming closer toward us now. It is because of this that I have taken part in this "joining movement" and experienced a little of the joy that radiates from this whole deed, all the way to Germany.

❦

At Easter 1931, all the difficulties of the *German Society* were discussed in Dornach. Through the years a close interrelationship had evolved between the destiny of the German Society and that of the General Society, since the aims and attitudes of certain German executive council members, as has often been mentioned, contributed in a major way to the difficulties in the Dornach *Vorstand*. Dr. Stein and Dr. Kolisko were both very much at the root of the conflicts. It would have been very difficult for Frau Dr. Wegman to assert her position against the other members of the Dornach *Vorstand* if she had not been certain of continual support from well-known German members, and thus had a substantial proportion of the German members behind her during that period. For years, Dr. Unger had been virtually the only one in the German executive council who offered some resistance to these machinations, and opposed the claims of Dr. Wegman and her party. Dr. Stein and Dr. [Eugin] Kolisko were his natural opponents in the German executive council, and their negotiating skills and underhand craftiness succeeded in drawing various different council members onto their side or, when this failed, at least rendering their opposition ineffective. At the German Extraordinary General Meeting on April 6, 1927, Dr. Unger once more managed to calm the growing unease amongst German members, by making himself the guarantor of free anthroposophic work, and at the same time accepting liability for ensuring wholly neutral administration of the national Society. During 1928 this attempt was recognized to be ineffective, since Dr. Stein and Dr. Kolisko did not cease their continual, one-sided maneuverings. The fact that Dr. Stein did not recognize Dr. Steiner's will, for example, revealed how unsustainable the situation was.

After Dr. Unger's death, opposition to the German executive council naturally increased, although it tried, by coopting further members, to encourage more widespread trust. Many German members quite rightly said that this move did not diminish but simply made less apparent the influence within the German executive council of opponents of Frau Dr. Steiner and Herr Steffen. It did not take long for this executive council to fall apart. In December 1930 and January 1931, Fräulein Mücke, Herr Stegemann, and Dr. Piper withdrew, so as to register their protest at least, and to allow something new to come about. In the same months, many German groups took the difficult decision to withdraw from the national association and affiliate themselves directly with the General Anthroposophical Society in Dornach (the first was the Rudolf Steiner working group in Stuttgart, on December 7, 1930). Members of this first group wrote a letter to all German branches in which they expressed disagreement with the way leading individuals in the German executive council behaved in April 1930, at the meeting of General Secretaries and the Annual General Meeting in Dornach. But even worse was the way these people behaved toward Herr Steffen on November 28 and 29, which is at

The "Memorandum"

odds with all that we would have done in the same situation, and leaves us no alternative but to seek direct affiliation with Dornach.

Gradually, other groups came to this same realization, that negotiation would achieve nothing more and that a positive step was needed. The smaller German executive council tried one last time to stem the growing tide of departures, the "resignation movement," by means of an extraordinary General Meeting of German members on January 30 and February 1, offering the creation of a "special Society" to the groups that had left. But the clear lack of any remaining basis of trust led further German executive council members (Rector Bartsch, Dr. Poppelbaum, and Dr. Rittelmeyer) to resign as well. This just increased the speed of the "departure movement." By the time of the Easter General Meeting in 1931, seventy-six German branches had left the former German Society, and affiliated themselves directly with the General Anthroposophical Society. The Goetheanum had no other option initially but to "accept this flow of will" (as Dr. Wachsmuth expressed it). Yet it was clear that the huge amount of work involved in managing and consulting with so many German groups and individual members could not be run on a permanent basis from Dornach. One of the reasons, after all, that Rudolf Steiner had started the national Societies was to relieve the Goetheanum of this work. People therefore turned to Herr Steffen for advice about how to regulate the situation in Germany. Herr Steffen gave this advice at the Easter 1931 General Meeting, but expressly asked every member of the *Vorstand* of the General Anthroposophical Society for his or her individual agreement, and also obtained this; and in addition asked the meeting itself to voice its assent. Only with the agreement of these two bodies did he suggest six active German members, who in his opinion were well suited to carry out a new, reorganized, and UNIFIED German Society. These six members (called the "initiative group") accepted the task and started bringing the German groups and members together on the basis of principles that Herr Steffen had given as guidelines for work throughout the whole Society: overcoming everything of a sectarian character through strict methodology in scientific work, and support for artistic performances and the Goetheanum itself. In all other respects the groups should, as previously, remain quite free in their work.

A large majority of German groups and individual members recognized that these suggestions for what was needed for the whole movement were also a healthy foundation for a new German Society. They thus joined forces once more and established a new, reorganized Society together. The former German executive council resigned at the end of April 1931, dissolved what little was left of the old Society, obliging its groups and individual members to decide whether they wished to join the newly forming Society or not. (The Free Anthroposophical Society in Germany also dissolved itself in the spring of 1931, after its membership fell to very low levels.)

The "initiative group" had barely begun work when, already at the end of April 1931, a number of German working groups got together to form a separate affiliation in Germany. This took place without any regard for the fact that the initiative group had made concrete proposals for a unified national Society, and that repeated assurances had been given to the groups that did not wish to trust the initiative group that they would be able to manage contributions independently and set up a bank account in the name of someone decided by themselves and so on. The guarantee of every group's freedom to work in the way it wished was also of no help. An "Anthroposophical Working Group in Germany" was founded, without the Society's chair, Herr Steffen, being informed. He was thus confronted, as on previous occasions, with an already accomplished fact, which he was then supposed to endorse. None of these groups concerned themselves with the advice given by Herr Steffen, which was intended to overcome the disasters of the last six years. They acted as if the Society had developed smoothly since the death of Rudolf Steiner. Many members who joined this "Anthroposophical Working Group in Germany" most likely really did not know what had been going on, or thought it had been little more than personal disputes. But the leaders of this "Working Group" must have been aware of what they were doing, for some of them were the same people who had caused the difficulties of previous years. Yet they preferred to use the slogans of "neutrality" and "mutual understanding" to conceal their opposition to the Goetheanum management. It was clear to members who had followed the events of recent years that the founding of this Working Group was an attempt to hold up the necessary process of clarification, and to provide a breeding ground for all the vices that the rest of the members so urgently wished to dispel.

What made the situation completely impossible for the General Anthroposophical Society, however, was that Frau Dr. Wegman and Fräulein Dr. Vreede offered their support to this "Working Group," even though they themselves had endorsed the initiative group and its task of reestablishing a new, unified Society. THIS POSITION ADOPTED BY THE TWO *VORSTAND* MEMBERS AMOUNTED TO CONTEMPT FOR THE *VORSTAND* ITSELF AND THE SOCIETY AS REPRESENTED BY THE GENERAL MEETING, AND LEFT IT IN AN ABSURD SITUATION.

The attitude of the "Working Group" was impossible right from the start. Its representative, Herr von Grone, had expressed reservations immediately after the General Meeting, but Dr. Wachsmuth, who had seen such difficulties on the horizon, expressly urged Herr von Grone not to make any unauthorized decisions, and to await the results of negotiation. Nevertheless he went right ahead with the founding.

When this "special group" turned to the Goetheanum, asking to be recognized as the "Anthroposophical Working Group in Germany," the chair of the General Anthroposophical Society had to refuse such recognition, since by agreeing to it he would have legitimized a second German Society. This would have been in direct conflict with his efforts to create a unified Anthroposophical Society in Germany, to which he was now obliged by the consent given by both the Dornach *Vorstand* and the Society's General Assembly. It was impossible for him to turn his back on a remedy that had barely even begun to take effect. He therefore had no other option but to reject, in future, all membership applications that came from the "Anthroposophical Working Group in Germany," only signing those where a particular location was indicated, such as the "Anthroposophical Working Group in Munich," etc. HERR

STEFFEN NEVER REFUSED TO RECOGNIZE LOCAL GROUPS OF THIS KIND OR THEIR ADMINISTRATORS. But as had always applied in the past, for German members as well, there were only three types of membership: member of the Anthroposophical Society in Germany, member of a local group recognized by the Goetheanum, or, in exceptional cases, private member in Dornach. Yet Herr von Grone quite illegally took it upon himself to alter membership cards of the General Society to include the designation *"Working Group,"* without the knowledge or permission of those responsible for membership. Such deception assumed new proportions through clever juggling of the words *"Working Group"* and *"working groups."* Despite everything, the Working Group in Germany—unrecognized by the Society's chair—still gained support from the circles surrounding Mr. Dunlop in England and Dr. Zeylmans in Holland, who were also in contact with Frau Dr. Wegman.

The Working Groups were, without doubt, centers of support for Frau Dr. Wegman in various areas of Germany. Either consciously or unconsciously, they disregarded the fact that the Society had been in danger of becoming a questionable sect, as well as the fact that what was needed was to cure this ill. When it is a question of safeguarding the inner essence of Anthroposophy, we cannot cover up the mistakes and failings of individual people with supposed Christian charity. If such people were severely attacked in the disputes that occurred, we have to understand the inexorable, objective need. (In 1913, when the Anthroposophical Society had been founded, Rudolf Steiner also had to battle with sentimental and dishonest "peace mongers" who were enamored of very similar absurdities.)

The initiative group still made efforts to create some common basis by holding discussions with leading members of this Working Group. These attempts failed, however, because the offer of discussion was turned down on many occasions, or because the chief figures involved (for example Dr. Kolisko and Dr. Lehrs) did not turn up. In a discussion that took place at Herr Stocluneyer's apartment in October 1931, between about thirty

German members of some standing, Herr Rector Bartsch made an attempt at unity whose generosity could hardly have been surpassed. He asked those representatives of the Working Group who had come, "What do you wish us to do so as to meet your needs. What do you expect of us?" Dr. Kolisko replied simply, "Nothing at all."

Over the course of three years, up to Easter 1934, a more and more clear-cut separation took place among the German groups. The great majority, consisting of more than seven thousand members, worked within the German Anthroposophical Society, and thus pursued the Goetheanum's proposals for curing the Society's ills. The remaining members, less than a thousand all told (in roughly twenty five different groups) collaborated in the so-called Work Communities, ignoring the events of the past few years and emanating more and more obvious—either silent or vocal—opposition to the aims of the Goetheanum leaders. Circumstances were similar in various other countries, and thus also in the General Anthroposophical Society. Holland and England were the only countries where those supporting the Goetheanum were initially in a minority, who therefore had to emancipate themselves from the leadership of Mr. Dunlop and Dr. Zeylmans.

In England this happened already in the winter of 1929/30, but in Holland it occurred later. It must also be mentioned in relation to the Anthroposophical Society in England that the chair [Herr Steffen] ceased signing membership cards presented by Mr. Dunlop only when the latter refused to reveal the applicants' addresses. This was the sole exception to Herr Steffen's normal practice. He was thus denied knowledge of the place of residence of people he was expected to accept into the Society. A previous letter from the Dornach secretariat was cited as justification for this refusal to give addresses: having previously asked for them in vain, this letter stated that the office would make do with an indication of the group to which each new member belonged. The London executive council simply chose to ignore the fact that addresses had been asked for both in Dr. Steiner's time and later even in the *Mitteilungsblatt*. It therefore departed wholly from the stipulations laid down by Dr.

Steiner himself [see page 203]. In addition to this official refusal, Mr. Dunlop also stressed in a discussion in London that he was withholding addresses because he could not allow the possibility of Dornach sending information direct to members. It was for the same reason that the London executive council protested so vocally against the translation of the *Mitteilungsblatt* arranged by the Dornach *Vorstand* in response to urgent requests by English-speaking members. This translation was intended not only for England, however, but also for America, Australia, New Zealand, and so on, and was therefore not simply an internal matter for the English Society. At the same time this Society had been producing its own newssheet (*Anthroposophical Movement*) that was a decidedly partisan paper and had for a long time been omitting important parts of the Goetheanum's *Mitteilungsblatt* for political reasons. Instead it quite openly adopted a hostile stance toward everything that did not issue from Frau Dr. Wegman or Fräulein Dr. Vreede. It thus gave English members an extremely one-sided view of things.

At the Annual General Meeting of March 31, 1932, Herr Steffen expressly and emphatically underlined the need for a deepening of anthroposophic work, and in this connection urged all members to give thought to the right method. He referred the members to Rudolf Steiner's works, and stressed that he was not speaking of something "new," but of a methodology that Dr. Steiner had repeatedly described as indispensable. Fräulein Dr. Vreede and others immediately took offense and interpreted what Herr Steffen had said as though he wished to claim a certain method for himself and his colleagues as the only right one, turning all other, equally legitimate methods into heresy. This determined refusal to understand portrayed itself subsequently as an "all-pervasive understanding" that had the capacity to think its way into others' perspectives, at the same time noting regretfully that these others were incapable of raising themselves up to a similar "all-embracing tolerance." Confronted by this attitude on later occasions one continually had to wonder whether such lofty tolerance was in fact a means of erasing every distinction between truth and untruth, right and wrong.

Herr Steffen was in fact appealing to the need for a distinction between truth and untruth, between method and no method at all. He summed up his views at another General Meeting in the words "My method is to seek truth."

Over the course of time the Anthroposophical Society had been forced to see much done in its name that was wholly irreconcilable with its true being. The kind of over-sensitivity that viewed any attempt to draw attention to mistaken methodology as a personal attack or inquisitorial intervention, and shouted it down, was always apparent among those who avoided exposure to free and open criticism, and who wished to be left alone to continue pursuing things that had brought the Society to the brink of the abyss.

Although it was difficult to voice any criticism without being immediately stamped as partisan, nevertheless discussion and argument occasionally took place about specific scientific findings. The members of the medical section had ample opportunity to ponder questions of methodology. In the magazine *Natura,* one can still read and assess plenty of such material. All that we wish to do here is relate how Frau Dr. Wegman behaved in the face of justified criticism. At a meeting of the medical section in the spring of 1932, several articles by Dr. König were the particular subject of stem criticism by other doctors. These were textbook examples of a quite uninhibited, random "combinations" of various, unconnected things, intensifying to an exalted mysticism, all well spiced with quotes from Dr. Steiner. Dr. König himself later referred to these essays as "youthful errors." But the question under discussion at this time was whether the editors were willing to include corrections and objections made by others. Frau Dr. Wegman's reply was a decided *no.* Dr. Kolisko added that such objections would be more likely to damage the reputation of the magazine than anything else would. Frau Dr. Wegman did however admit that she did not agree with much that Dr. König had written, and said she wanted to suggest to him that he should give no more lectures, or write any more, for the time being. Yet she did not do this. On this occasion Dr. Husemann declared that under such circumstances he had no further interest in *Natura,* and could no longer take part in a venture that did not tolerate scientific criticism.

This picture is complemented by a study of the magazine itself, which played a large part in discrediting Anthroposophy within serious medical research circles. Nowadays this magazine is wholly rejected by the numerous doctors belonging to the Anthroposophical Society who refuse to have anything to do with pseudo-scientific cliques.

Such things were however not restricted to medical circles. In the September 1930 issue of the Youth magazine *Der Pfad* (the path), which appeared at that time, Dr. König published an essay, "Birth Control as a Birth Problem," in which he made the strangest comments. In January 1931, Dr. König organized a conference, together with the Hanover Christian Community, at which lectures were given exclusively on themes such as sexuality, crime, drugs, and so on. The program for this conference was announced throughout the Society. In protest to this, the Goetheanum *Mitteilungsblatt,* no. 4, January 25, 1931, printed clear and urgent warnings and prohibitions that Dr. Steiner had expressed. In characteristic response, those responsible sharply censured the criticism that had been voiced, which had cited Dr. Steiner's own words rather than their own mistake. People even dared to call Dr. Steiner's words "antiquated." At this, Frau Dr. Steiner had no other choice but to intervene and, in the *Mitteilungsblatt,* no. 7, February 15, 1931, she wrote the following.

My Reply

The September issue of *Der Pfad* magazine, which was aimed above all at young people, contained an essay by Dr. König entitled "Birth Control as a Birth Problem." After giving an interpretation of Raphael's *Sistine Madonna* and Michaelangelo's *Pietà,* which was a travesty of artistic sense, this essay closes with the following rather sensational image:

> The world of spirit is silent. It begins to speak only when an individual turns to it in all freedom. Then the unborn begin to speak and to tell of their unspeakable suffering. However,

sufferings always become deed. Let us not wait until the despair of the unborn moves them to action. Even if we are few who wish to listen to them, can we not show them the way toward Earth?

It is not only the dead but also the unborn who swell to huge numbers today. Will anyone who is inclined to the spirit prevent their entry into the earthly world?

The problem of birth control can be solved only when the truth about birth is grasped. But this means:

> Recognize the secret of birth!
> Hear, at last, the call of the unborn

The imaginative experience described may deeply move those who have such an experience. But they should first come to terms with it on their own. To present it like this, with a certain authoritative gesture, and to append a verse to it that aims to exert an effect upon the soul is not right.

In a lecture by this author, which I heard myself, he linked not only the Gospel of St. John but also lectures by Rudolf Steiner on the Fifth Gospel (which, by the way, the latter did not authorize for use by other lecturers and writers), with many embryological observations. For example, the calling of one pair of disciples was compared with the allantois, that of another with the yolk sac, and so on.

These revelations were presented in a certain solemn and celebratory mood, as if they claimed occult inspiration as their source. They thus had a suggestive effect and were accepted by many in awed reverence, though others of course rejected them indignantly.

In our Society this started something like a stream, a separate movement. That is why it is also a good idea for members to know how Rudolf Steiner felt such themes should be handled.

Above all he thought it necessary, if one wanted to work as an occult teacher, to wait until one was forty-two years old, since even thirty-five was not old enough. Only then, he felt, could one be aware of the whole responsibility that is called for in speaking of occult facts.

Truths expressed by Rudolf Steiner about the realities of the human condition—not just in response to a momentary situation—do not lose their validity, for the wisdom of experience that they contain are a thousand years ahead of our time. Thus to use the word *antiquated* in regard to them, as has already happened, is to express a still immature wisdom.

The Anthroposophical Society may reject the words of Rudolf Steiner as "antiquated," but it should, at least, first have the chance of knowing what these words mean.

When the world comes toward us with questions, the purest answer is still that given by Rudolf Steiner. If our young people are urged "not to wait until the despair of the unborn moves them to action," it must at the same time be a duty to remember the following words of Rudolf Steiner: "This is the most dangerous area that one can touch upon, for whenever thoughts are led in this direction, they are always DARKENED in a certain respect."

The lecture to which Frau Dr. Steiner referred was later described by Dr. König himself as a "sin of youth." But at the time, and on later, repeated occasions, daring to criticize or even only ask questions meant being branded as malicious and dogmatic. (Dr. Rittelmeyer however agreed that criticism of the Hanover conference was justified.)

It was all the more difficult to defend oneself against unhealthy tendencies when people like Dr. Kolisko and Dr. Zeylmans were not only leading figures in the medical section but also had great influence as Society officials. This allowed them to insist, on the one hand, that whatever came from the medical section should be sanctioned, and on the other to demand that their medical colleagues support the aims of Frau Dr. Wegman in all that concerned the Society's affairs. If one failed to do this one was kept at a distance from medical section work. Thus the sect that had formed in one part of the Society was centered on the group of official leaders of the medical section.

As time went by a growing number of members nevertheless came into conflict with these sectarian tendencies, which were so at odds with a free life of the spirit. In the medical section itself, Dr. Steiner had in 1924 gathered a close circle of colleagues around himself, to which a certain number of doctors belonged apart from Frau Dr. Wegman. The number of members of this inner circle was clearly stipulated by Dr. Steiner, and he announced their names to the assembled section members. After Dr. Steiner's death, the position of this circle within the section became quite different, in particular through the way that Frau Dr. Wegman very soon started to expand it. Several new candidates were invited to attend a gathering, without being informed of the reason. Without any sort of preparation they suddenly found themselves involved in a kind of festival, from which they were dismissed again immediately after. From then on they were part of the inner circle. They were given no freedom of choice about whether they themselves wished to be part of this circle or not, nor granted any chance to ponder the meaning of such a step beforehand.

Thus a wholly alien spirit was imposed upon what Dr. Steiner had founded. This was further demonstrated when it became apparent that this expansion was to be kept secret from the rest of the section—once more in complete contrast to the way Dr. Steiner chose his colleagues. When one of the new members of this inner circle thought it perfectly natural to inform other members of the section, this was immediately described as betrayal [later, Dr. Wegman announced that the circle was disbanded]. To this must be added a further fact related by Dr. Palmer—at that time leader of the Clinical-Therapeutic Institute in Stuttgart—at a later Annual General Meeting. Shortly before the expansion of the inner circle took place, Frau Dr. Wegman told him that such an expansion was out of the question. In other words it was out of the question for him and others.

These few examples are already enough to portray a mindset that had to employ denial and secrecy to keep those people away who did not endorse Frau Dr. Wegman's claims and ambitions, particularly in Society matters. As a result, a number of doctors were more or less excluded at an early stage from medical section work, though not excluded formally. Even those who kept on trusting for a while that the medical section could continue as Dr. Steiner intended soon had to recognize that useful cooperation was not possible. Thus more and more colleagues withdrew. What was occurring throughout the Anthroposophical Society happened here on a smaller scale.

Because of the impossibility of real discussion and exchange within the medical section, it frequently became necessary for doctors to discuss medical matters elsewhere. Those who had themselves created these conditions were the ones who took the most offense at such supposed indiscretion, expressed at General Meetings. Their indignation, however, was out of place since it was through their own actions that the medical section had itself done widespread damage to the reputation of the Anthroposophical Society. It was actually a duty to bring such things to the attention of the members.

⁂

The Annual General Meeting of 1932 produced a further example relating to method, but in a quite different sphere of work. School exercise books were used to prove to W. J. Stein that he had given lessons in the Waldorf School in Stuttgart on the spiritual hierarchies, and that he had used the grotesque comparison of military ranks in doing so. Rudolf Steiner had absolutely forbidden teaching children anthroposophic concepts—even correct ones—but this had no effect. The idea that had always been upheld—that anthroposophic teachings should not find their way into an anthroposophicly orientated pedagogy—threatened to become an empty phrase, especially since this was not an isolated instance. In spite of all this, the English *Vorstand* gave Dr. Stein a vote of confidence, and sent a declaration to this effect to the Dornach *Vorstand*, in a particularly offensive move.

This same attitude became apparent when Dr. Kolisko wrote a booklet in 1934, "First Lessons in Chemistry," which was scientifically inadequate and wholly at odds with anthroposophic pedagogy. Dr. von Baravalle dealt with both these aspects in a detailed criticism of the booklet, which he presented to the college of teachers of the Waldorf school, as well as to the General Meeting later on. It is true that Dr. Kolisko soon withdrew the booklet from bookshops, but he continued to allow it to be used internally as study material in schools. The representatives of the Rudolf Steiner Schools Fellowship in Germany protested against this in no uncertain terms on April 22, 1934, and this was announced in the *Mitteilungsblatt*.

These kinds of difficulties continued to recur, which had first been caused by Fräulein Dr. Vreede's attitude toward questions of methodology and leadership of the Society in 1930, which had prevented any lectures being given in celebration of the seventh anniversary of the Christmas Foundation Meeting. In 1933, the tenth anniversary, Fräulein Dr. Vreede once more intervened. The idea had been to let Rudolf Steiner and his work stand on its own, both through artistic performances and through readings of his most sublime lectures. This corresponded to a general and real need. It would also have avoided any unhappiness about lectures from one side or another. But Fräulein Dr. Vreede informed Herr Steffen in a letter that she and a few others—among whom were Dr. Zeylmans and Mr. Kaufmann—would give a series of lectures at Christmas under the general theme of "Ancient and Modern Mysteries." Shortly after this she demanded that this program be printed in the *Mitteilungsblatt*. Both the letter and the program then appeared in the *Mitteilungsblatt* of November 26, 1933, and this alternative conference did indeed take place in a small room at the Goetheanum. These lectures, however, had an audience of only about forty, whereas the main conference was attended by more than a thousand people.

1934

All the difficulties that for so long, and for the same repeated reasons, had led to hopeless disputes found an initial conclusion through the important decision taken at the Annual General Meeting of March 27 and 28, 1934. By a vote of 774 to 94, with twenty-three abstaining, a motion was passed that decisions made by Herr Steffen, Frau Dr. Steiner, and Dr. Wachsmuth would be binding for the Society. This decision came in answer to a question that Herr Steffen posed to the General Meeting in the following statement:

At the General Meeting, the chair of the General Anthroposophical Society felt it necessary, in view of all that had happened and as a consequence of Mr. Kaufmann's unjustified accusations, to resign his position. He handed this role to Frau Dr. Steiner, and left the meeting. But Frau Marie Steiner declared that she would only remain in the *Vorstand* if Herr Steffen continued as chair, and she too left the hall.

At this, Herr Dr. Wachsmuth was obliged by the General Meeting to convey to Frau Dr. Steiner and Herr Steffen its overwhelming majority decision that the Society should be newly constituted through these three people, Frau Marie Steiner, Herr Steffen, and Herr Dr. Wachsmuth.

The Society's constitution was laid down at the Christmas Foundation Meeting.

Those who are thus charged with this task, who are deeply concerned with Rudolf Steiner's work, therefore lay before the General Meeting the following question that naturally arises for them: "Is it the will of the Anthroposophical Society to entrust continued guidance of our work, in the spirit of the Christmas Foundation Meeting, to these three individuals; and to regard decisions that they make as binding for the Society?"

A report of this General Meeting appeared in the *Mitteilungsblatt*, no. 16, April 22, 1934. In what follows, we would like to stress a few points about which not all members are yet sufficiently clear.

Sometime before the General Meeting the so-called Statement of Intent was handed in to the Dornach *Vorstand*, with prior notice of the three speakers who were to represent it at the meeting. These were Dr. Kolisko, Dr. Zeylmans, and Mr. Kaufmann. During the long discussions to which this Statement of Intent gave rise, it could be shown that its main content was composed of flagrant lies and intentional distortions of the facts. The Statement follows:

STATEMENT OF INTENT

For about the last eight years, the undersigned groups and members have had to witness increasing differences of aim within the Anthroposophical Society. This has given rise to a deepening division within the organism of the Society.

In addition, it has now come to our attention that a motion for altering the statutes has been submitted to this year's Annual General Meeting, which would most radically alter the basic constitution of the Anthroposophical Society. In response, we must state that we are unable to recognize such an alteration, which would empower the chair to reallocate roles within the *Vorstand*, to change the right of signature, or to exercise sole right of signing membership cards.

We regard this motion as an attempt, via a change to the "Statutes"—which were, after all, drawn up to satisfy state authorities—to alter the Society's very constitution as given by Rudolf Steiner in the "Principles" and accepted by the Foundation Meeting at the 1923 Christmas conference. Doing this would legalize the situation that has arisen in the Society over the past few years.

But leaving aside these proposals for altering the statutes, the situation in the Society previously described obliges us to present the following statement of intent to the *Vorstand* and members:

We adhere to the General Anthroposophical Society's constitution as created at the 1923 Christmas Conference.

We cannot recognize as binding for the whole Society decisions that, are issued by only three of the *Vorstand* members, as has become customary in recent times.

The same applies to majority decisions in the General Meetings, through which, in the past eight years, most important motions have been passed without prior consultation, whether in the *Vorstand* or with officials and leading members of the Society.

The situation has arisen that two members of the *Vorstand* are left without any means of responsible participation in leading the Society and, likewise, that a large number of leading members in various countries are denied the possibility of playing a part in the Society's development or of undertaking anthroposophic work at the Goetheanum itself. Since three members of the *Vorstand* started managing everything on their own, much valuable work by existing groups has been undermined and rejected. Groups in other countries have been reorganized from Dornach, and the attempt has been made to restructure the whole Society as this part of the *Vorstand* would wish.

We do not dispute the idea that alterations to the Society's constitution might become necessary if circumstances require it, but such changes can proceed only when the whole organism of the Society takes responsibility for them.

In contrast to the interventions mentioned, we support the principle of autonomy of groups as one of the most important foundations of the life of the Anthroposophical Society. A particularly important aspect of this is that groups can freely choose those with whom they collaborate.

We absolutely reject the idea that only those members are true to the Goetheanum who agree with a leadership dictated by the three members of the *Vorstand* currently holding the reins, and are therefore ready and willing to go along with this.

The Goetheanum is spiritually effective wherever anthroposophic work is undertaken. We know that we are putting our best energies into such work, and we have—each according to ability—been trying to play our part in the most varied areas of endeavor. We also wish to undertake such activity at the Goetheanum in Dornach, since it exists for all members.

We regard it as our task to allow those people connected with us access to the whole spiritual life at the Goetheanum.

The history of the Society clearly shows that there are those who wish to be active within it who, though they seek the same Anthroposophy, cultivate it in a different way. Rudolf Steiner always acknowledged this fact and took it into account in the "Principles" and in appointing the founding *Vorstand*. We are therefore convinced that the Society can fulfill its task only when the present tendency toward centralization that has seized hold of Society administration is countered by an element of plurality. We find this necessity expressed in words by Rudolf Steiner: *"One achieves unity in the area of Spiritual Science through individualizing and differentiating, not by centralization."* These words, spoken by Rudolf Steiner in 1923, express an essential principle of anthroposophic community per se, beyond the immediate circumstances that provoked them. Such living diversity is preferable to a formal unity and is an effective means of bringing people together. For a large proportion of members, such differentiation is the breath of life. This means that a structure and division that takes account of this should be formed within the Anthroposophical Society. Moreover, we are also convinced that large numbers of contemporary people will be able to flourish within the Society only when this principle is adhered to.

On such foundations, as free, independent groups and members, we will continue our work within the General Anthroposophical Society. This is also the best way to meet the demands of our times. More than ever before, the world today demands from us direct insights of the spirit, the will to social collaboration, and an open heart for human needs.

※

The very first sentence is characteristic of the authors' attitude: "For about the last eight years the undersigned groups and members have had to witness increasing differences of aim within the Anthroposophical Society." It is strange to talk of "having had to witness" after they themselves spent years striving with all their might to impose their will on the Society. Then the odd reference to "eight" years, rather than nine—no doubt necessary so as to overlook 1925, a year that it is essential to consider to really judge all that happened.

Then we are told that the alteration to the statutes "would empower the chair to reallocate roles within the *Vorstand* [and] change the right of signature." When Dr. Kolisko was asked to explain this distortion of the words of the statute alterations, he could reply only that he "saw" in them what was expressed in the Statement of Intent.

The motion for altering the statutes, which in compliance with regulations has been available for four weeks, runs as follows:

Dornach, February 19, 1934
To the *Vorstand* of the General Anthroposophical Society
To the attention of the chair, Herr Albert Steffen, Dornach

The undersigned hereby submit an application to the next General Meeting, to word articles 6 and 13 of the official statutes as follows:

§6 Membership will be acquired on written application, through admission by the *Vorstand*, and on signing of the membership card by the chair.

§13 The *Vorstand* publicly represents the association. Legal signatories on behalf of the association are: the chair alone, and either the secretary or treasurer together with the chair. The chair can, by his sole signature, invest *Vorstand* members with general authority, or authority in specific spheres of work.

Signed:
Paul Buhler
Dr. E.O. Eckstein
Dr. Otto Fränkl
Ehrenfried Pfeiffer
Paul Eugen Schiller
Günther Schubert
Dr. Richard Schubert

Thus Dr. Kolisko, Dr. Zeylmans, and Mr. Kaufmann—responsible officials of the Society—had for weeks been misleading members of German groups and of the Dutch and British national Societies by intentionally distorting an important piece of text.

It was nonsense to talk of a "radical alteration to the constitution." Nor was it possible to speak of any infringement of the "Principles." As regards the important point of the signing of membership cards, Dr. Steiner had himself made the following arrangement:

Concerning the administration of the Anthroposophical Society.

The *Vorstand* wishes to present the following for implementation of the statutes: One becomes a member at the moment that the chair of the Anthroposophical Society signs the membership card presented by branch officials....

Branch officials are asked to maintain an ongoing name and address list of members belonging to their group, and to send a copy of this to the secretariat in Dornach....[2]

Members will be in general informed of things through the *Mitteilungsblatt*. In special cases, branch officials will receive news with a request to pass it on to individual members.[3]

The *Vorstand* of the Anthroposophical Society
(*Newssheet*, January 20, 1924).

Then it is said that the proposed changes "would legalize the situation that has arisen in the Society over the past few years."

This claim, that the situation of recent years has been an illegal one, is not only absurd, but could not in any way be substantiated by Dr. Kolisko, who spoke on behalf of the authors of the Statement of Intent.

Then come the sentences that dismiss majority decisions by the *Vorstand* and the General Meeting.

Two things must be noted here. First, how can Society decisions be made if not through the legal bodies of the General Meeting and the *Vorstand*? In addition, how could one expect such decisions to be reached unanimously? The whole claim becomes particularly grotesque when one remembers that the German initiative group was actually based on a unanimous decision by the *Vorstand*, but that the two *Vorstand* members Frau Dr. Wegman and Fräulein Dr. Vreede then used every means to prevent it being realized.

---

2 This is the passage mentioned previously in connection with Mr. Dunlop's refusal to supply the addresses of new members [see page 189].

3 Mr. Dunlop carried this out only when he believed it did not hinder his partisan interests.

Second, as far as decisions made in the past are concerned, this claim has no basis in reality, especially if it refers again to the "eight" years. The only real sense of the claim is as an attempt to render all further leadership of the Society impossible. Under the guise of complaints about procedure, things are presented in the hope of creating a certain impression among unsuspecting members. The real reasons why consultation became impossible in the *Vorstand*, and with Society officials, have already been sufficiently dealt with in this memorandum. So too has the fact that, in spite of everything, all *Vorstand* members were always asked their view on important matters, such as Goetheanum conferences and restructuring of the German Society.

The statement "National Societies have been reorganized from Dornach, and the attempt has been made to restructure the whole Society as this part of the *Vorstand* would wish" was revealed as a complete lie when Dr. Kolisko explained what was meant by them. As an example he cited the restructuring of the German Society, describing this action as an intervention by Herr Steffen. We have already described what actually happened, which derived from the fact that over 7,000 of the more than 8,000 members in Germany disassociated themselves from Dr. Kolisko and his followers.

It is then stated, "We do not dispute that alterations to the Society's constitution might become necessary if circumstances require it, but such changes can proceed only when the whole organism of the Society takes responsibility for them." This tangle of words gains meaning only when one tests such an "insight" against the effects that those propounding it have been producing in the Society for years. In fact, people have been trying to make changes without taking any account of the General Meeting and the *Vorstand*. The faithful followers of Alexander have been assuming overall responsibility for the "organism of the Society," and through the founding of unsanctioned enterprises claiming for themselves the distinction of some *"Übervorstand."*

The demand that all five *Vorstand* members should be recognized to have equal rights, after all that has happened, is the expression of the perspective that has caused the greatest difficulties in recent years. "Appointments" [by Dr. Steiner] and "higher perspectives" are supposed to carry us beyond the uncomfortable facts and make every lie palatable.

The "Statement of Intent" was a natural offspring of the "Declaration" of 1926. Both were issued by the same circles and had the same aim: to use agitation as a means of awakening in uninformed and naïve members a mood that could be made use of to further the power-strivings of a small clique. Cleverly concealed, distorted, or freely invented facts were meant to turn attention away from the real state of affairs, and deprive members of every real means of making their own judgments. Members were not to be informed but misled; they should have no opportunity of finding things out for themselves, but should "declare" and "state as their intent" what was prescribed to them by Dr. Kolisko, Dr. Zeylmans, Mr. Kaufmann, and a few others.

Some colleagues at the Goetheanum, and the German initiative group, directed the following questions to those who represented the "Statement of Intent":

> How can you claim that a proposal exists to alter radically the constitution of the Anthroposophical Society?
> How can you claim that a proposal exists that would empower the chair to reallocate jobs in the *Vorstand*, and alter the right of signature?
> What do you think gives you the right to mislead members in Germany, England, and Holland through such false allegations?
> How can you say that the state of affairs in the Society in recent years has been illegal? Give some examples.
> Please give examples of any worthwhile work that has been undermined or rejected.
> Who has ever prevented groups from freely choosing those who work for them?
> Who in Dornach has reorganized groups in other countries?

When it transpired that no answers to these questions were forthcoming, but that they were simply glossed over, those who had asked them replied themselves in the form of the following motion, at the same time citing reasons for it:

Motion

The General Meeting of March 27, 1934, rejects the so-called Statement of Intent by Messrs. Kolisko, Zeylmans, Dunlop, and Kaufmann as a declaration whose aim, through lies, distortion of the historical facts, and slander, is to create a predicament in which all work in the Anthroposophical Society is paralyzed. The General Meeting asks those members who unwittingly supported this document, to make their own inquiries into the actual facts.

Grounds

We have ascertained that nowhere in the motion to alter the statutes is there any mention of an "alteration empowering the chair to reallocate jobs within the *Vorstand*" or to "alter the right of signature." This is a false representation.

We have ascertained that there is no infringement of the Principles or the Christmas Foundation, as given in the text of the Principles and in the *Mitteilungsblatt,* no. 2, 1924. On the contrary, we note that the authors of the so-called Statement of Intent are still unaware after ten years of Rudolf Steiner's remarks about this. Once more the Statement of Intent gives a false representation.

We have ascertained that the actual motion was submitted four weeks ago, in compliance with regulations, and is accessible to everyone. Yet in England, Holland, and Germany people speak of a motion that simply does not exist. We call this a distortion of the facts.

The sentence about "reorganizing groups from Dornach" is a slander that has not the slightest basis in fact, and for which no concrete example could be produced. This "anonymous" accusation was hurled at Herr Steffen during discussions. It appears that people desire a *Vorstand* whose chair they can continually insult in the worst way.

Herr Steffen's large-scale undertakings were the best examples of valuable work undermined or rejected. Fräulein Dr. Vreede not only undermined this work but also made it impossible, thus depriving the Society of it.

We consider the demand that the five *Vorstand* members should work together as an untruthful one, given that it is proposed by members who, since Rudolf Steiner's death, have done everything they could to create the conditions that make such a demand impossible to fulfill. To compel its fulfillment would be tantamount to paralyzing all work in the Society, especially if decisions taken by the General Meeting or by a majority in the *Vorstand* cannot be recognized.

This motion and grounds was handed in by the following Goetheanum colleagues:

>Dr. Roman Boos
>Paul Bühler
>Dr. E. O. Eckstein
>Curt Englert-Faye
>Dr. Otto Frankl
>Wilhelm Lewerenz
>Ehrenfried Pfeiffer
>Paul Eugen Schiller
>Dr. W. Schomstein
>Guenther Schubert
>Dr. Richard Schubert
>Jan Stuten

and by the members of the German initiative group:

>Dr. Hermann Poppelbaum
>Dr. Hans Blichenbacher
>Ernst Stegemann
>Martin Munch
>Dr. Hermann v. Baravalle

If there had been any last chance of reconciliation, this was lost when Frau Dr. Wegman and Fräulein Dr. Vreede gave public support to the content of the "Statement of Intent." Fräulein Dr. Vreede's behavior was once more characterized by her attempts to disrupt the meeting with untrue assertions. She claimed, for instance, that the last part of her letter about the 1933 Christmas conference had been left out. She had to be shown the relevant issue of the *Mitteilungsblatt* before she gave up this attempt to mislead. She also claimed that she had been dropped as a lecturer, but then reluctantly had to retract this when unable to cite any proof. On the contrary, although she herself had for years been systematically preventing the chair, Herr Steffen, from organizing conferences or other events, no one stopped her and others from holding an "alternative conference" at Christmas 1933. Her behavior was such that, in the end, the meeting no longer wished to listen to her.

Dr. Zeylmans employed similar tactics, trying to cast a false light on Herr Steffen in the General Meeting by saying that he had disturbed the peaceful work of an unsuspecting group in Bandung (Java) by mentioning the Society troubles in a letter to it. Only after the General Meeting did it turn out that Dr. Zeylinans had himself informed this group of events a long time previously, and in his own way. Surely the chair of the Society has the right to express views about all the affairs of this Society! Added to which there is an enormous difference between the way Herr Steffen speaks to the members in such cases, and the highly dubious reports of the Dutch General Secretary, which for years now have succeeded in alienating Dutch members from the Goetheanum.

Frau Dr. Wegman gave her support to the "Statement of Intent" in a letter to Herr Steffen, which was read out to the General Meeting on her behalf. This letter runs as follows:

Arlesheim, March 24, 1934
Dear Herr Steffen

Once more an Annual General Meeting approaches, once more the emotions of members will be whipped up to a frenzy, once more these emotions will be used to attack decent people, whom Rudolf Steiner valued and loved, to undermine their standing and systematically destroy them. Moreover, you as chair of the Anthroposophical Society allow this

The "Memorandum"

to happen. You think it is good for people to admonish one another. Yet you do not consider what is being demolished in the process.

Now a group of seven people submits a motion. With this motion they wish to supply you, Herr Steffen, with rights that far exceed those of chair. I see nothing good in this. It is a still greater deviation from Dr. Steiner's principles, and a step in the direction of making the Goetheanum accessible only to a certain group of people, while others are excluded. This has been more or less the case for many years already. As a member of the *Vorstand* I cannot agree to the legalization of this state of affairs, which is being implemented by three *Vorstand* members.

I support the Statement of Intent by the group composed of the Working Group and the Dutch and English national Societies, because they are right to defend themselves against one-sided leadership of the Goetheanum.

As far as my work at the Goetheanum is concerned, which is specifically related to the art of healing, I hereby inform the *Vorstand* and the members that I have no intention of validating changes that could be undertaken in the section. I will continue to devote myself to the task given to the section by Rudolf Steiner, together with all those who wish to work with me and feel the will to heal awakened in themselves. Under the protection of the spirit of Rudolf Steiner we will, I am sure, have the possibility of devoting ourselves to this holy calling, far from all the disputes and disunity that are now raging in the Society. With this will to heal we now consciously remove ourselves from all disputes, and also intentionally remain at the Goetheanum, the place that Rudolf Steiner created for all of us, not only for a privileged group of people. And we want to try, together with those who have a sense for what this work means, in harmony and mindful of Christian love, to deepen the work that Rudolf Steiner so richly endowed us with, to continue it and to let it spread, untroubled by the chaos and confusion within the Anthroposophical Society.

Signed Dr. J. [sic] Wegman

P.S. I had wanted to read this myself at the General Meeting, but have been in bed with a fever for two weeks, and so have asked that it be read for me.

The mere fact that the Anthroposophical Society had to include this letter among its documents is deeply shameful in itself. The letter can be seen only as a self-portrait—and an unmasking at the same time that destroys one's final illusions. This is the same Frau Dr. Wegman who throughout the whole winter of 1926/7 did nothing to prevent the passions of tempestuous "Declarers," allowing every malicious claim about Frau Dr. Steiner and Herr Steffen, and in grave instances being guilty herself of the same thing. She actually dares to speak of being slighted as a *Vorstand* member, and to make the chair responsible for criticism of the part she has played—she, who in the meeting of November 29, 1930, described as impossible Herr Steffen's adoption of responsibility for both the past and the future, and rejected this. She affiliates herself with the absurdities of the "Statement of Intent," though it was her own behavior that made *Vorstand* meetings impossible, and misled members' meetings. It was she who, in February 1926, deceived the Society with promises and assurances, in the hope of gaining time, and gradually consolidating her own sole dominion. And it was she who treated the *Vorstand* in such a strange way in the spring of 1930, by giving false information that led to wrong assumptions, upon which the *Vorstand*'s decision about School matters was based. She subsequently made things worse by taking it upon herself to alter the words of the *Vorstand*'s letter. Aside from the untrue assertion she made on November 29, 1930—that she had not heard anything in the *Vorstand* in 1928 about Herr Steffen assuming responsibility—she made statements in the meeting of December 1930 that contained a whole series of demonstrable untruths.

It is an odd thing to speak of the "will to heal" yet at the same time to turn away from the wounds that one has oneself inflicted; and to believe that this enables one to "consciously remove [oneself] from all disputes." Moreover, those who claim to be "in harmony with Christian love" and wish to cite Rudolf Steiner on their own behalf should examine carefully whether they have the right to do so. If the Goetheanum is there "for everyone," then all must ensure that this name and the name of Dr. Steiner are not misused in the way that Frau Dr. Wegman has misused it—not only in the Einsingen affair, but every time that, as a *Vorstand* member and leader of the School, she placed herself in opposition to the truth.

It suffices to mention briefly that Mr. Kaufmann's unjustified accusations against Herr Steffen were the last straw that made changes to the leadership of the Society inevitable. Mr. Kaufmann, however, was doing no more than repeating Frau Dr. Wegman's letter when, once more appealing to Christian love, he claimed that Herr Steffen bore responsibility for things he had actually been prevented from taking responsibility for by opponents of those who numbered Mr. Kaufmann among their ranks—a responsibility he had once been ready to make great personal sacrifices to assume.

※

The self-exclusion of the *"Übervorstand"* and of two *Vorstand* members initiated by the "Statement of Intent" culminated during the summer of 1934 in the so-called Association of Free Anthroposophical Groups, founded in complete contravention of the Society's constitution. Such clear enmity to the official leadership of the Society showed that no further reconciliation could be contemplated with those responsible for this association's founding. Apart from the fact that it cannot be recognized by the *Vorstand*, the founders claim the right to accept people into this association who are not recognized members of the Anthroposophical Society, but whom the founders regard as anthroposophists—with all the rights normally accorded only to those accepted as members in the proper way. Fräulein Dr. Vreede actually took part in the founding, and has since managed these groups' correspondence, as was announced by Mr. Kaufmann in a circular letter. Frau Dr. Wegman also recognizes and supports this unlawful organization. By so doing, Frau Dr. Wegman and Fräulein Dr. Vreede have in reality shut themselves out of the *Vorstand* of the Anthroposophical Society.

Final Remarks

Having read this account of the past ten years, those who feel weighed down by the many unpleasant events that had to be included here will most quickly realize the toll it took on those who, in writing it, had to spend months reliving all those occurrences that were painful enough when first experienced. This is one of the reasons that publication of the memorandum was delayed until now instead of in the fall as planned. There is, however, another more important reason. It was extraordinarily difficult to decide whether such an account should be published at all or not. Truly, the decision to publish it was not made lightly or gladly.

The first basis for this memorandum appeared last summer when Herr Dr. Poppelbaum felt compelled to make some reply to attacks and propaganda, and wrote an account that he later had reproduced and circulated as an interim report on the history of the last ten years. A need then became clear for further considerations, having more to do with matters of principle, to be included, and it became obvious that a more detailed report would be needed. Above all, it was necessary to consider the fact that the difficult circumstances in the Society had for years been caused partly by members receiving insufficient information. As some Society officials intended, certain circles had obtained only limited information, slanted in a particular way.

This was compounded by the fact that others left much unspoken because they still hoped there would be a possibility of improving the situation without "airing too much dirty linen" in public, and that people would come to their senses. Although such expectations were partially fulfilled, this kind of reticence lost its validity over time since it could no longer lead to further improvement. On the contrary, it allowed attacks based on distortions of the truth to take their toll unhindered. The "Statement of Intent" and subsequent circular letters can only be opposed by describing the actual facts—although even these have little effect when people prefer to base their judgments on what they choose to "see."

Readers who have little or no awareness of what went on will probably be horrified by some of the reports in this memorandum. By contrast, others who experienced all this themselves will be astonished at the reticent and charitable mode of expression used in many instances. There will of course be very divergent and very personal judgments about it.

Apart from such questions of taste, which are linked only indirectly with the core of the matter, one might think it justified to ask whether actions based on reticence and charity were always the right approach, or whether this in fact helped sustain unhealthy situations for longer than was perhaps necessary. It may appear so in the abstract and with hindsight. But how far removed such a judgment is from the actual course of events can be understood if one considers that, to start, with something like a third or even a half of all members supported the claims and efforts of Frau Dr. Wegman, and that by the end this had been reduced to a minority composed of a bare tenth of members. This demonstrates the healthy consequences of a process that could only take its course through free judgment about life's realities. It was only in this way that belief in authority and dalliance with esotericism could be rejected, which was really what this was all about. Nothing good would have come of it if, for instance, the German Society had been reorganized through commands from above. Instead, thousands of members were able to free themselves from that small but powerful ruling group. It is remarkable enough that the rigid, dogmatic ones were those who got so indignant about this process, and who then misused their remaining authority to spread the most nonsensical and malicious rumors about Herr Steffen's behavior in these matters. Either one can understand Herr Steffen or not. What is not possible is to convince people who bear ill will.

Nevertheless, untrue assertions are not ineffective, especially when spread about so intentionally and energetically as they are through the open letters of Mr. Kaufmann and Dr. Lehrs. Herr von Grone circulates these texts and approves them, "trusting in the community-building strength" of their content. However, all that they are doing is repeating the demonstrably untrue points contained in the "Statement of Intent" and trying to prevent the events of recent years being seen in a true light. Uninformed and unsuspecting members can easily be confused and, without realizing it, be led down a road they would never otherwise have taken. To say that the past is over and done with is a simple and above all comfortable claim. It is a much less comfortable truth, though equally simple, to see that past causes lead to present results—uncomfortable at least for those who wish to keep silent about the past, and for those who know nothing about it but would need to find out what actually happened in order to make a reasoned judgment about its present consequences. Taking the easy, comfortable option, though, is one of the gravest dangers, since it is so easy to appeal to this sort of human weakness.

It was their awareness of this danger that led the authors of this memorandum to bring some important aspects, at least, to the attention of wider circles. They also felt this was their duty, for otherwise they could have been blamed for keeping quiet about things whose disastrous consequences they were able to foresee.

If people generally concerned themselves more with the history of the Anthroposophical Society they would soon see how nonsensical is the widespread view that life in the Society can and must unfold in a harmonious fashion. This was how it used to be, they think, and it was only after Dr. Steiner's death that all those dreadful meetings took place, because certain people like making a lot of fuss. Everyone should just let things be, and behave in a "human" way with one another!

All one needs to do, however, to be disabused of this idea is to read the wealth of reports published as official accounts of meetings of former years. There one finds that Dr. Steiner, who himself chaired the meetings, continually and energetically opposed any sentimental "peace-mongering" and apparent tolerance. Even when decisions had been taken to break off debate on unpleasant themes, he insisted that everything should be hammered out to the end, until all had been fully clarified. Such themes were sometimes even less edifying than those of the last few years. Anyone who can remember back to the 1923 delegates meeting (first in Stuttgart and then in Dornach) will know how little time Dr. Steiner had for "tolerance" and "behaving humanly" if this meant covering up uncomfortable facts and lies.

The immediate situation we now find ourselves in cannot be better characterized than by quoting the words that Dr. Steiner himself once spoke at the end of his lectures on "World-being and 'I'-being":

> People take sides with those who are wrong and write letters asking the victims of the attack to do something to preserve the friendship, to straighten things out again—after all, one must show love. When somebody commits an unkind deed against another, people do not write to the one who did the deed. Instead, they write to the ones who suffered it, that they should show some kindness and that it would be very unloving not to do something to set things right again. It never occurs to them to ask this of the one who is wrong. Such peculiar things happen in our circle.[4]

Did the Anthroposophical Society not arise in 1913 out of a conflict of huge proportions? And what were people battling against at the time? Against the nonsense that was peddled about reincarnations, "special appointments," missions, and false esotericism—in short, against lust for power.

In rejecting similar tendencies in 1934, decisions have become necessary that, in addition to the negative aspect they contain, will lead to the positive outcome that, through leadership of the Society by the three presently active members of the *Vorstand*, members will be able to feel assured of continued healthy development and earnest endeavor.

---

4   Rudolf Steiner, *Toward Imagination*, p. 168; Berlin, July 18, 1916.

APPENDIX 3

ADDRESS TO THE GENERAL MEETING IN DORNACH BY COUNT POLZER-HODITZ

April 14, 1935

If at this moment I actively enter the conflict and the events taking place in the society, it is because the experiences and observations of many years not only give me the right, but also the responsibility to do so. I am aware that I now confront a majority that, for some years past, especially here at Dornach, has formed its judgment in a particular direction—one that has found expression in the present "Memorandum." I am well aware of the difficulties I take on myself if, at this moment, I confront the said judgment with my own, which obliges me to say "No" to what a majority of the Society in Dornach now intends to do. Nevertheless, I trust in the inherent power of the facts that move me—facts that have come to my knowledge for years, which I have always sought to confront without sympathy or antipathy, always remaining candid and sincere in relation to both conflicting parties.

On a quite actively neutral basis, therefore, I wish to say something that I feel obliged to say at this moment and in this present situation. First and foremost, I must reject what is so frequently maintained—that one must decide for one side or the other. I therefore decline to be labeled as on one side or another. I refute the frivolous expression, "judgment according to one's taste" (*Geschmacksurteil*), which occurs in the "Memorandum," and I refute it equally if it is suggested that "ill will" prevents me or others from letting ourselves be convinced by many of the things adduced by the authors of the "Memorandum." Speaking for myself, I say there is no "ill will" in my present stand. It is *my* method also to look for the truth.

In the "Memorandum," a voluminous book is placed before us to influence us and prepare our wills. This being so, those who reject the "Memorandum" are necessarily obliged to speak at greater length than is customary at General Meetings.

Though my attitude in general is neutral, this cannot prevent me from giving help and support where it appears to me a matter of necessity and plain human justice, and where I believe that I am acting as Rudolf Steiner would desire.

In my judgment, the individuals whom Rudolf Steiner appointed to the *Vorstand* [executive board] and to the leadership of the Sections, each in their several ways, are to this day in their right place where Rudolf Steiner placed them. That all of them, beside their virtues, have their faults and have committed faults cannot alter this, my view. That mistakes *have* been made, both on the one side and on the other, is evident from the events of these ten years. The fact that these persons have not succeeded in finding their way together to a common task, moreover, shows me that, since the death of Rudolf Steiner, the esoteric strength of the *Vorstand* as a whole was, on the one hand, insufficient to overcome disturbing influences that came in from without, while, on the other hand, there was no one individual in the *Vorstand* able to bridge the gulf.

From the death of Rudolf Steiner, few wise conclusions were drawn that might have given rise to unity in knowledge. Instead, impossible pretensions arose (notably regarding the leadership of the School of Spiritual Science), first on the one side and then, rather less strongly emphasized perhaps, on the other. Out of good sense, a new, more free and large-minded basis might have been found for the life of the Society, taking into account the absence of a universal spiritual leader. It did not happen so. But, if the needs arising from Rudolf Steiner's death were not fulfilled from good sense and intelligence, they seek fulfilment in violent catastrophes. Such catastrophes may even destroy the basis of the Society that was possible only under Rudolf Steiner; they cannot destroy the being of Anthroposophy itself. Whatever happens does not relieve any one of the *Vorstand* members of the responsibility to stand by his or her post.

Very soon after Rudolf Steiner's passing, I recognized from things I immediately witnessed that a *genuine will to understand and work with Dr. Wegman was not present*. In real earnest, neither Frau Dr. Steiner nor Herr Steffen considered such cooperation possible. On one occasion—the year 1925 had not yet passed—when I asked Herr Steffen to accept the post of First President, he said to me, "I *could* work with Frau Dr. Steiner, but never really with Dr. Wegman." I saw, therefore, that from the very beginning there was no sincere will to understanding; rather, there was a decided will to put Dr. Wegman on one side, and this very soon showed itself in the attitude and conduct of many people in Dornach. This feeling—not openly expressed, yet determining the attitude of those concerned—*could only* give rise to all the conflicts and misunderstandings that in the course of time ensued. Beginning within the *Vorstand* and in Dornach, they very soon extended from there to the periphery and did harm to our work in all directions.

The reasons for these difficulties of understanding are indeed many and profound; they can by no means be attributed to Dr. Wegman and Dr. Vreede alone. But the Society, which had been dedicated to the service of the esoteric life, increasingly lost its esoteric character through this conflict. It became increasingly a purely external Society, in spite of repeated emphasis on the "esoteric" life, whereof a new and quite dogmatic concept was formulated.

The "Memorandum" emphasizes, and rightly so, that one must go back into the past to understand these divisions. I therefore, too, will go back into the past, but a little further still, not only to the death of Rudolf Steiner. In effect, the grudge and hostility against Dr. Wegman date back even before Dr. Steiner's death. Even before the Christmas Foundation Meeting, this opposition existed, though it did not show itself so openly. I experienced it personally and observed many things in this connection, for at that time I was in Dornach, often for long periods of time, and Rudolf

Steiner spoke with me about all those who, soon after, came into the *Vorstand,* and about many others, too. There may be some present here today who heard Rudolf Steiner speak even at that time of the intrigues against Dr. Wegman and against her work as a Doctor, and who heard him say that this might yet be the destruction of the Society. At that time, Dr. Steiner again and again put her forward and emphasized the importance of her cooperation. Moreover (I will not mention any names), I observed that those especially whom Rudolf Steiner during the last years very definitely rejected got up again after his death and pushed aside—or tried to do so—those whom he had preferred on one or another area of work.

Rejecting the motions, as I do, I am obliged to go into the deeper causes of the difficulties and to deal with esoteric matters. The "Memorandum" does so, too, quite openly, though a little crudely. I, too, therefore am justified in speaking openly today. Indeed, I find it most necessary to do so, seeing that many things come to expression in the "Memorandum" in a confused and misleading manner. In esoteric matters, I may say, I was privileged to hear and learn many things from Rudolf Steiner, and for this reason have always felt consistent and secure in my actions in these matters since his death.

First, as to the concept at which I arrived during these years concerning the leadership of the School of Spiritual Science—for me, Rudolf Steiner to this day is the one and only leader of the School, if indeed it still retains its esoteric character. The Section for general Anthroposophy can surely not be occupied or claimed by anyone out of an earnest and true sense of responsibility. Yet, the possibility for the leaders of the different Sections to find their way together in an esoteric spirit does not, therefore, appear to me as an illusionary hope, even today, provided no single one of them lays claim to the leadership by virtue of any kind of "succession," of which in this case there can be no question. The failure to realize this after Rudolf Steiner's death was always regarded by me as a mistake, and I said so at the time.

As to the Class Lessons, a regulation of these matters after Rudolf Steiner's death seems possible to me only in this way: Whoever is willing to take the responsibility in the face of the spiritual world and Rudolf Steiner, and is sustained in this by the will of a number of others, should communicate the fact to the leaders of the Sections and discuss the matter with them. In this way, I believe the continuity with Rudolf Steiner, which is the real condition, would be observed.

On a much later occasion—when the question arose of giving Herr Arenson permission—I communicated this, my attitude, to Herr Steffen. Such an assumption of responsibility, however, must always be a solemn action, involving spiritual destinies. That the privilege should be assigned in recognition of diligent "achievement" or of much learning, this would be quite unacceptable to me. We would thereby rapidly find ourselves on mere external and authoritative lines.

Now I must say something of how I understand the position of Dr. Wegman as a coworker[1] of Rudolf Steiner in the esoteric Class. Rudolf Steiner clearly designated her as such. I consider it wrong merely to identify the coworker in the esoteric Class with the Recorder in the *Vorstand*. Such an identification, I must say, seems to me in this case not only wrong but also hurtful. There was no lack of such offenses! I think I know how Rudolf Steiner understood the word *coworker*. The appointment of his coworker, or assistant,[2] for the founding and conduct of an institution of the Mysteries (as in this instance of the School of Michael) could rest only upon a deep relationship of destiny, which Rudolf Steiner recognized in full consciousness, to which he desired to do justice, and that he clearly emphasized. I have not the slightest doubt that this was so. Dr. Steiner, by this action, told Dr. Wegman that she stands in the midst of a great destiny. Not only Frau Dr. Steiner—Frau Dr. Wegman, too, stands beside Rudolf Steiner in a great destiny, which must be born with all its burdens and sufferings.

However, the coworker and assistant is never the successor who takes the leader's place; as a woman, she cannot be so. This, too, was revealed

---

1   The German word *Mitarbeiterin* used here indicates a female, the masculine of the word being *Mitarbeiter*.

2   The German word used here, *Gehilfin*, indicates a female helper.

by the facts. Humanly, however, it is understandable that Dr. Wegman, after Dr. Steiner's death, misinterpreted her task. I cannot find any justification in this for condemning judgments and persecutions or for the talk of a failure, by which all previous arrangements are wiped out. Dr. Wegman's mistake was made to be the pretext, and the intrigues that, until then, had been concealed were now turned into a regular moral execution—even moral dismemberment.

I may remark here that I have never spoken to Dr. Wegman about her incarnations, and that no one ever said anything to me directly about the Alexander matter—one heard people speaking openly enough, especially in the circle of her opponents.[3] I myself once had a conversation with Rudolf Steiner about the circumstances and conditions under which it was allowable to discuss personal matters concerning incarnations. It was in Berlin in 1917.

The initiative leading to the esoteric School of Michael came, as Rudolf Steiner said, from Dr. Wegman. With the reception of this initiative, the necessary esoteric union of destiny that the conditions of the Mysteries in modern times require was created between him and her. Before the war, Frau Dr. Steiner was Dr. Steiner's coworker in all esoteric ritual arrangements. The one thing was as necessary as the other, as indeed *all* things in Rudolf Steiner's life were necessary.

When Dr. Steiner returned from England in 1924, he gave various indications of his intention eventually to give the esoteric Class a form of ritual. Thus, it arose from the form of the ritual that was coming into being in the Mystery of Michael—which in the admission of new members

---

[3] "...some speakers [at the Society's 1934 Annual Meeting in the Goetheanum in Dornach] asserted in rabble-rousing mode that Wegman, with "seductive tones of a supposedly occult or Christian nature" and her "mystical guruship" had sought to bring the Goetheanum under her dictatorial power after 1925, and to transform it into a "kind of military camp of Alexander the Great." Together with groups of people operating with unconscious motives and in dependency upon her, she was said...to represent the real danger to the Anthroposophical Society and to be the "carcinoma" working to destroy it..." Peter Selg, *Spiritual Resistance: Ita Wegman, 1933–1935*, pp. 75–76.

that took place in September 1924—he spoke of "taking the hand" and about the promise that should be given to Dr. Wegman, as well as to him. This was clear evidence of the fact that the union of destiny previously mentioned was of real significance for the Michael Mystery. The "Memorandum" says that Frau Dr. Steiner had not only a symbolic but also a real degree (which, of course, was known to me, as well). Indeed, this should almost go without saying; it could not be otherwise for a coworker of Rudolf Steiner within the life of the Mysteries. The united establishment of a beginning within the Mysteries requires the reality of such degree, and Rudolf Steiner showed this by his deed, both in the case of Frau Dr. Steiner and in the case of Frau Dr. Wegman.

Now I must also turn against the talk of the "old" and "new" esotericism. In the Mysteries, the experience of death was always represented, though in various ways—death, entombment, resurrection, interaction with divine beings. So it was, from the most primitive forms at the beginning to the wonderful form that was given to us in the Class. Rudolf Steiner never had anything to do with an esoteric life divided into old and new. On the contrary, from the very beginning, before the war and after, he devoted his forces to the now-returning Mysteries, such as they must be in the present and in the future.

By bringing to human beings the wisdom of Anthroposophy—wisdom equally significant for the masculine and the feminine spirit—he founded these Mysteries in spiritual consciousness and gave them the necessary form and stamp for the present time. In the ceremonial presentation of Anthroposophy, this made it necessary to express the duality of man and woman; hence, too, Dr. Steiner's coworker was so by virtue of her feminine sex. During the Class Lessons, after all, we attend not only the reading of an instructive lecture, but we are also present in a "sacred action" that can unite us with the stream of the Mysteries throughout all time. If we take leave of *this* consciousness and do not call it to life again and again, we depart from what Rudolf Steiner brought as a heavenly institution to Earth.

I know that mistakes were made. They were made on both sides. Everyone is subject to them. However, they give me no grounds to deny recognition to what can never be purged and that will certainly continue in any case, quite apart from the purely external "achievements," whose significance, in my judgment, is not so very different in degree in one Section from what it is in another, and the tendentious criticism of which I must emphatically reject. The unheard-of moral calumnies, continued over many years and directed, above all, in public meetings against Dr. Wegman, I must refute—they are, in fact, directed against the will of Rudolf Steiner.

Having experienced and witnessed many things that took place even before the Christmas Foundation Meeting, and feeling them to be still at work, it sometimes almost seems to one as though a hidden and, for the most part probably unconscious, resentment against the last years of Rudolf Steiner's own life were making itself felt, while choosing Dr. Wegman as its foremost victim. Such resentment against Dr. Steiner showed itself, for that matter, on former occasions, too. One may recall the time when certain people showed it in Dornach by suddenly and ostentatiously putting on mourning garments.

I am by no means unaware that Frau Dr. Steiner, who worked so long with Dr. Steiner, is spiritually the more advanced one. Nonetheless, she lacked the sincere and friendly will to understanding. What I mean here has nothing whatever to do with external "achievements," an expression that, in any case, is self-righteous and unsuited to express the inner matters of the soul, or inner achievements in effect. These are the ones that matter in the esoteric life, unless only the head is to be engaged in it. Perpetual criticism and quibbling over insignificant details of methods might lead only to one's stopping *short* at the methods, *being afraid of their results and, in a plaintive and pedantic way, fighting shy of the real paths of life and destiny.*

I will mention one other fact to illustrate how many things took place in this area. At the opening of the Rudolf Steiner Hall in London, I often got together with Dr. Unger. On that occasion, he asked me to help in bringing about a resumption of the Mystery institutions that Rudolf Steiner had newly formed before the war. He discussed the matter with me in some detail. He considered it an absolute necessity for the Society. I had to give an evasive answer, since Frau Dr. Steiner had said to me in a conversation not long before that there were great difficulties blocking this, especially in Dornach.

From all that I have said, I must reject the motions of the community of workers [*Arbeitsgemeinschaft*] at the Goetheanum. I cannot possibly assign to one portion of the *Vorstand*, which is now falling apart, the right to throw all of the blame on the other portion, or on the strength of such thought forms (long become catchwords) as "Method," "false method," "forming judgment," "real achievements," and so on—to declare arrogantly: *We alone have the real right and capacity to carry on Rudolf Steiner's Work. We are the ones who have the true method; the others have the wrong method. Those who do not go with us are against us. You must decide whether you will go with us or go to rack and ruin with the others.* It resounds constantly in one's ears.

It is impossible to divide in this way with authority into black and white and thus—"with lock and key," as Dr. Vreede puts it—to take the Goetheanum away from the alleged black ones. By doing so, you would increasingly shut out the real spirit of the Mysteries from the second Goetheanum building; it would withdraw from there—and, I may add, *not* to America.[4] The *Vorstand* would then bear, more and more gravely, the responsibility for so many grievous hurts in soul and body to old and true anthroposophists, brought about as a direct result of the *Vorstand* conflict. Nor would it be only *that* portion of the *Vorstand* on whom the "Memorandum" lays the entire burden.

Ever since Dr. Boos violently interfered with the Class Lesson on January 1, 1927, and nearly pushed Dr. Wegman from the platform, I knew that if this was not made good again in a united spirit, on the foundation of the esoteric Class itself by the entire *Vorstand,* the General Anthroposophical

---

4   In his introductory speech, Albert Steffen had lauded the "heroic" voyage of Guenther Wachsmuth, Ehrenfried Pfeiffer, and Herman Baravalle to the US in 1933 for a lecture tour.

Society would fall into decay, would become intellectually superficial, and that in spite of the growing attendance at conferences, it would increasingly lose its true and original character.

The recently published "Memorandum" was meant to form judgments and give direction to decisions of this General Meeting. This was the reason for which it was written. However, being a provocative pamphlet—as it declares in its introduction, it does not claim to be impartial—its effect is destructive; it begets fanaticism and prepares wills along preconceived lines. This is revealed especially in the introduction and conclusion of the "Memorandum." The best that one can say for it is that it is a *"fable convenue."* It shows how systematically one has ignored, since Dr. Steiner's death, what he so often emphasized in his last years especially—the need to study history, not only on the basis of conventional sources and documents, but also to cultivate the kind of history that can be read in the spirit based on repeated earthly lives. Despite all dangers and mistakes, through the midst of which every one of us will have to pass, and that no one among us is competent authoritatively to condemn, this latter history will nonetheless have to be written.

Let us consider what has happened for the past ten years of the Society's history. It began with a battle of letters. The letters became increasingly voluminous. They grew into pamphlets, and now into books. If this were to continue in the same outer, self-justifying spirit on both sides, we would presently have libraries and archives full. This would prove only that Rudolf Steiner was not understood, that the Society had lost its way, and that the middle was left void, while people made one another ill with such literature. Do you really think we are on the right path by accumulating such controversial writings? Do you think *this* is the way for us to go on into the next century, filling *such* archives? Do you really think this printed matter will be of such importance at the turn of the century? Do you think that, with such hostile pamphlets and hostile votes, you will make peace and quiet for your real work? That is precisely the illusion!

The vote that was taken at the Foundation Meeting was one only in semblance. In reality, it was a unanimous manifestation of our will.

Rudolf Steiner, however, had told us beforehand what would be done with the Sections, by whom they would be led, and what individuals would constitute the *Vorstand*. Today, it seems, you ask for a vote of confidence in advance and do not tell us beforehand most important matters that will then be done.

Perhaps, after all, the important thing today will be that some of us must swallow the "little book" that is mentioned in the Fourth Seal of the Apocalypse. But if we spend our forces in conflict—which will not be ended by any number of expulsions—this very thing is again and again prevented.

The first Goetheanum was built as a place of the Mysteries. It was taken from us because we spoke in it in purely intellectual spirit. No one was there who could protect it. Rudolf Steiner was not allowed to protect it, because he had given it to humanity as a touchstone of their maturity. Thereafter, he laid the Foundation Stone in human hearts. *The foundation stones that rest in strong hearts of human beings are no longer bound to one place and to a single building;* they must become the foundation stones for the Mystery centers of the future in many places. Those who will plant the seeds of these can be called to do so only from the spiritual world directly and by their destiny. However, to this end, *esoteric courage,* not narrow protectionism, is needed.

The second Goetheanum building is erected for public work, for the outer work of the "little book." But the continuance of the Mysteries will come from the "little book" that works from within. Therefore, the most important need of the anthroposophic movement and Society is confidence in human beings, not resentment—*confidence, moreover, that should first be given, not claimed first by Dornach*. Confidence will answer, if confidence is given, and if Rudolf Steiner is allowed to speak through the five leaders of the Sections. It will not answer if in almost every *Newssheet* we are given moral sermons without regard to context and situation, and if, between the lines, pretensions of leadership are expressed, such as must wound many souls deeply connected with Rudolf Steiner. Rudolf Steiner himself will not speak if Dr. Wegman and Dr. Vreede are shut out.

Rudolf Steiner alone can unite all anthroposophists of past, present, and future. Changes of statutes will not do so, nor will anathemas against independent action at a time when destinies impinge on one another, and mutual understanding is, in any case, difficult.

The motions before us and the "Memorandum" are evidence of weakness, finding refuge in violent measures. But if unity *cannot* be accomplished, the only remaining possibility is that the Sections of the Goetheanum should be made open to all and that the General Anthroposophical Society should constitute itself on an entirely free basis, with the formation of autonomous groups and without central authority for the admission of members. After ten years of conflict in the *Vorstand* and in the Society, Anthroposophy can never be served by the expulsion of so large a section of membership, among whom are many old members, whom Rudolf Steiner greatly valued.

The confidence that was given freely and as a matter of course to the spiritually universal leader and teacher should today, now that we are lacking a leader, be given to the living power of Anthroposophy itself and to the human beings who have been taken hold of by it, as well as to those who will be so in the future. This should find expression in statutes, confidently allowing the formation of groups, entrusting the reception of new members in a proper form to the leaders of the groups—and not to those alone who are prepared to give assent to everything or to subscribe to all manner of conditions.[5]

---

5 Ludwig, Count Polzer-Hoditz gave this transcription to Dr. Ita Wegman. The original translation of the transcript was by George Kaufmann (later named George Adams); the translation has been slightly revised.

Appendix 4:

The Executive Board's Letter to Adolf Hitler

English Translation and Original German

Anthroposophical Society Secretariat
Dornach, by Basel, Switzerland
November 17, 1935

To the Führer and Reich Chancellor
Mr. Adolf Hitler!

Your Excellency!

The undersigned members of the executive board of the Anthroposophical Society, with its seat in Dornach, near Basel (Switzerland) find themselves compelled to trouble Your Excellency with the urgent request for your kindhearted help in the following matter.

As we have heard, the Anthroposophical Society within the borders of the German Reich has been dissolved by order of the Prussian Secret Police. The reasons stated by the responsible authority are mentioned in the enclosed copy. We hereby lodge a protest against the act of dissolution and especially against the previously mentioned reasons, for they are not born out by the facts.

The Anthroposophical Society, constituted and founded by Dr. Rudolf Steiner in 1923, has neither stood in relationship to nor in contact with Freemason, Pacifist or Jewish circles. Furthermore, the Aryan

-2-

№ 9165 19.NOV.1935

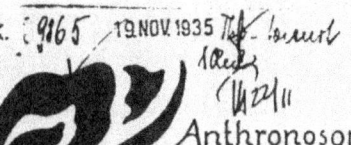

Anthroposophische Gesellschaft.

Sekretariat: Dornach 4 Basel (Schweiz). Telephon: Dornach 133. Postcheck V 5827.

Dornach, den 17. November 1935.

An den Führer und Reichskanzler
Herrn Adolf Hitler   B e r l i n .

Ew. Excellenz!

    Die unterzeichneten Mitglieder des Vorstandes der Allgemeinen Anthroposophischen Gesellschaft mit Sitz in Dornach bei Basel (Schweiz) sehen sich gezwungen, Ew. Excellenz mit der dringenden Bitte um gütige Hilfe in folgender Angelegenheit zu bemühen.

    Wie wir erfahren, ist in diesen Tagen durch eine Verfügung der Geheimen Preussischen Staatspolizei die Anthroposophische Gesellschaft im Gebiete des Deutschen Reiches aufgeloest worden. Die hierfür seitens der betreffenden Instanz angegebenen Gründe gehen aus beiliegender Abschrift hervor. Wir müssen gegen diesen Aufloesungsakt und besonders die dafür gegebenen Begründungen Protest einlegen, da diese den Tatsachen in keiner Weise entsprechen.

    Die Allgemeine Anthroposophische Gesellschaft, die im Jahre 1923 von Dr. Rudolf Steiner konstituiert und begründet wurde, hat zu irgend welchen freimaurerischen, jüdischen, pazifistischen Kreisen irgend welche Beziehungen oder auch nur Berührungspunkte nicht gehabt. Die arische Abstammung Rudolf Steiners ist überdies vom Rassepolitischen Amt in Berlin ausdrücklich bestätigt worden. Auch die Bezeichnung der Gesellschaft als "international eingestellt" ist in dem in der Aufloesungsbegründung gebrauchten Sinne durchaus unzutreffend, da die Beziehungen unter den Mitgliedern der einzelnen Länder

heredity of Rudolf Steiner has been decisively confirmed by the Race-Political Authority in Berlin. Also, the description of the Society as "internationally attuned" in the sense implied in the reasons for dissolution is completely unfounded. The contacts between members of different countries are limited solely to the exchange of thoughts concerning scientific and artistic issues, as is typical for any scientific and artistic association in Germany or in other countries.

Numerous personalities of all civilized countries will willingly confirm that especially the lecturers and artists of the Anthroposophical Society have awakened interest in German intellectual life in foreign countries. For instance, even many English-speaking personalities have learned the German language in order to become familiar with the original sources.

Furthermore, the pedagogy applied in Waldorf schools and other schools in Germany, based on the guidelines of Rudolf Steiner, has found wide recognition in non-German countries. The recent New York Congress has shown the special interest with which large American teacher associations are following the development of these schools.

Due to the above-characterized measures against the Anthroposophical Society, the following, absolutely incomprehensible situation arises for widespread foreign circles that are friendly to Germany: a society that is viewed as a valuable and active representative of German intellectual life is suddenly dissolved for reasons that do not correspond with the actual facts.

A most decisive form of protest must be lodged against the assertion made in the letter from the Prussian Secret Police, which characterizes the Anthroposophical Society in Germany as "subversive."

The above-mentioned facts, as well as a closer examination of the situation, will clearly show that such an assertion is an absolutely unjustified discrimination against a society that stands up for German culture and civilization in a most valuable way.

The Anthroposophical Society, represented by groups of members in all civilized countries of this earth (with the exception of Soviet Russia), feels especially responsible for the German cultural and intellectual life

sich lediglich auf den Gedankenaustausch in wissenschaftlichen und künstlerischen Fragen beschränken, wie ihn jede gute wissenschaftliche und künstlerische Vereinigung in Deutschland und im Ausland pflegt.

Zahlreiche Persoenlichkeiten aller Kulturländer werden gern bestätigen, dass gerade die Vortragenden und Künstler der Anthroposophischen Gesellschaft weite Kreise des Auslandes für das deutsche Geistesleben interessiert haben, ja dass sogar viele z.B. Englisch sprechende Persoenlichkeiten, um die Quellen im Original kennen zu lernen, die deutsche Sprache erlernt haben.

Ausserdem hat die Pädagogik, wie sie an der Waldorfschule und anderen Schulen in Deutschland nach den Richtlinien Rudolf Steiners gepflegt wird, in vielen ausserdeutschen Ländern groesste Anerkennung gefunden und vorbildlich gewirkt. Mit besonderem Interesse verfolgen z.B. ,wie sich erst kürzlich wiederum auf dem New-Yorker Kongress gezeigt hat, grosse amerikanische Lehrer-Verbände gerade die Entwicklung dieser Schulen.

Durch die oben charakterisierten Massnahmen gegen die Anthroposophische Gesellschaft entsteht nun bei weiten, Deutschland freundlich gesinnten Kreisen des Auslandes die folgende voellig unverständliche Situation: dass eine Gesellschaft, die als wertvolle und aktive Vertreterin deutschen Geisteslebens angesehen ist, ploetzlich in Deutschland selbst aufgeloest wird und zwar mit einer Begründung, die den Tatsachen nicht entspricht.

Auf das allerentschiedenste muss aber Verwahrung dagegen eingelegt werden,dass in dem Schreiben der Geheimen Preussischen Staatspolizei aus diesen nicht zutreffenden Motivierungen auch noch die Behauptung abgeleitet wird, dass die Anthroposophische Gesellschaft in Deutschland "staatsfeindlich" sei. Wie aus dem Obigen und aus näheren Nachprüfungen ohne

and is thus watching with deep concern over their German friends. Therefore, we kindly request Your Excellency to prevail upon the responsible authorities to abolish the discriminating term *subversive* and to annul the dissolution of the Anthroposophical Society. We have the honor to express to Your Excellency the assurance of our most profound respect.

The Executive Board of the General Anthroposophical Society
Albert Steffen
Marie Steiner, nee von Sivers
Dr. Guenther Wachsmuth

Abschrift

Geheime preussische Staatspolizei   Berlin, 1.November 1935

-3-

weiteres hervorgehen wird, stellt eine solche Bezeichnung eine völlig ungerechtfertigte Diskriminierung einer in wertvollster Weise für das Deutschtum eintretenden Gesellschaft dar.

Die Allgemeine Anthroposophische Gesellschaft, die in allen Kulturstaaten der Erde (mit Ausnahme von Sowjet-Russland) durch Mitgliedergruppen vertreten ist, fühlt sich dem deutschen Geistesleben besonders verpflichtet und schaut deshalb in grosser Besorgnis auf das Schicksal ihrer deutschen Freunde. Wir bitten daher Ew.Excellenz, bei den zuständigen Instanzen die Aufhebung der diskriminierenden Bezeichnung als "staatsfeindlich" und die Rückgängigmachung der Aufloesung gütigst veranlassen zu wollen.

Wir haben die Ehre, Ew.Excellenz die Versicherung unserer ausgezeichnetesten Hochachtung auszusprechen.

Der Vorstand
der Allgemeinen Anthroposophischen Gesellschaft

Albert Steffen

Marie Steiner, geb. v. Sivers

Dr. Guenther Wachsmuth

1 Beilage.

Bibliography

Bekh, Wolfgang Johannes. *Bayrische Hellseher: Vom Mühlhiasl bis zum Irlmaier* (11th ed.). Munich: Ludwig Verlag, 1998.

Bock, Emil. *The Life and Times of Rudolf Steiner: Volume 1: People and Places*. Edinburgh: Floris Books, 2008.

———. *The Life and Times of Rudolf Steiner: Volume 2: Origin and Growth of His Insight*. Edinburgh: Floris Books, 2009.

Emmichoven, J. E. Zeylmans van. *Who Was Ita Wegman? Volume III, 1924-1935: Struggles and Conflicts*. Chestnut Ridge, NY: Mercury Press, 2005.

Goethe, Johann Wolfgang von. *Biographische Einzelschriften. Gedenkausgabe der Werke, Briefe und Gespräche*, vol. 12. Zürich: Artemis Verlag, 1949.

Grosse, Rudolf. *Die Weihnachtstagung als Zeitenwende: und die Grundsteinlegung des Ersten Goetheanum*. Dornach, Switzerland: Verlag am Goetheanum, 2013.

Hemleben, Johannes. *Rudolf Steiner. In Selbstzeugnissen und Bilddokumenten*. Reinbek, Germany: Rowohlt Verlag, 1992.

Heyer, Karl. *Wer ist der deutsche Volksgeist?* (2nd ed.). Basel: Perseus Verlag, 2013.

Krueger, Bruno. *Leben und Schicksal: Vom Weg eines Wahrheitssuchers*. Unna, Germany: WEGE Verlag, 1993.

Lindenberg, Christoph. *Rudolf Steiner: A Biography*. Great Barrington, MA: SteinerBooks, 2012.

Lissau, Rudi. *Rudolf Steiner: His Life, Work, Inner Path, and Social Initiatives*. Stroud, UK: Hawthorn Press, 2005.

Meffert, Ekkehard. *Die Zisterzienser und Bernhard von Clairvaux: Ihre spirituellen Impulse und die Verchristlichung der Erde*. Stuttgart: Engel, 2010.

Meyer, Thomas H. *D. N. Dunlop: A Man of Our Time*. London: Temple Lodge, 1996.

———. *Ludwig Polzer-Hoditz, a European: A Biography*. London: Temple Lodge, 2014.

———. *Wegmarken: Im Leben Rudolf Steiners und in der Entwicklung der Anthroposophie*. Basel: Perseus Verlag, 2012.

Meyer, Thomas, and Andreas Bracher. *Helmuth von Moltke 1848-1916: Dokumente zu seinem Leben und Wirken* (2 vols.). Basel: Perseus Verlag, 2005, 2007.

Poturzyn, K. v. (ed.). *Wir erlebten Rudolf Steiner: Erinnerungen seiner Schüler*. Stuttgart: Verlag Freies Geistesleben, 1957.

Prokofieff, Sergei O. *May Human Beings Hear It! The Mystery of the Christmas Conference*. London: Temple Lodge, 2004.

Selg, Peter. *Rudolf Steiner's Intentions for the Anthroposophical Society: The Executive Council, the School for Spiritual Science, and the Sections*. Great Barrington, MA: SteinerBooks, 2011.

———. *Rudolf Steiner, Life and Work* (7 vols.). Great Barrington, MA: SteinerBooks, 2014– (in progress).

———. *Spiritual Resistance: Ita Wegman, 1933–1935*. Great Barrington, MA: SteinerBooks, 2014.

Selg, Peter, and Sergei O. Prokofieff. *Crisis in the Anthroposophical Society: And Pathways to the Future*. London: Temple Lodge, 2013.

Shepherd, A. P. *Rudolf Steiner: Scientist of the Invisible*. Rochester, VT: Inner Traditions, 1954.

Steiner, Rudolf. *Architecture as a Synthesis of the Arts*. London: Rudolf Steiner Press, 1999.

———. *Aus schicksaltragender Zeit* ("Out of Destiny-Burdened Times"). Basel: Rudolf Steiner Verlag, 1959.

———. *Autobiography: Chapters in the Course of My Life, 1861–1907*. Great Barrington, MA: SteinerBooks, 2000.

———. *The Christmas Conference for the Founding of the General Anthroposophical Society*. Hudson, NY: Anthroposophic Press, 1990.

———. *The Destinies of Individuals and of Nations*. Hudson, NY: Anthroposophic Press, 1990.

———. *Esoteric Lessons 1910–1912: From the Esoteric School*, vol. 2. Great Barrington, MA: SteinerBooks, 2012.

———. *The Foundation Stone / The Life, Nature & Cultivation of Anthroposophy*. London: Rudolf Steiner Press, 1997.

———. *"Freemasonry" and Ritual Work: The Misraim Service*. Great Barrington, MA: SteinerBooks, 2007.

———. *The Karma of Untruthfulness: Secret Societies, the Media, and Preparations for the Great War* (2 vols.). London: Rudolf Steiner Press, 2005.

———. *Secret Brotherhoods: And the Mystery of the Double*. London: Rudolf Steiner Press, 2004.

———. *Der Meditationsweg der Michaelschule*. Basel: Perseus Verlag, 2011.

———. *Vorträge und Kurse* über *christlich-religiöses Wirken, Bd.2 Spirituelles Erkennen–Religiöses Empfinden–Kultisches Handeln* ("Lectures and Courses on Christian Religious Work, Vol. 2: Spiritual Knowledge—Religious Feeling—Cultic Activity"). Basel: Rudolf Steiner Verlag, 1993.

Unger, Carl. *Schriften, 3 Bde., Bd.2, Versuch einer positiv-apologetischen Erarbeitung anthroposophischer Geisteswissenschaft*. Stuttgart: Freies Geistesleben, 1966.